Early Childhood Education Series

Leslie R. Williams, Editor **Millie Almy, Senior Advisor**

Bambini:
The Italian Approach to Infant/Toddler Care
LELLA GANDINI & CAROLYN POPE EDWARDS, Eds.

Educating and Caring for Very Young Children: The Infant/Toddler Curriculum
DORIS BERGEN, REBECCA REID, & LOUIS TORELLI

Young Investigators:
The Project Approach in the Early Years
JUDY HARRIS HELM & LILIAN G. KATZ

Serious Players in the Primary Classroom: Empowering Children Through Active Learning Experiences, 2nd Edition
SELMA WASSERMANN

Telling a Different Story:
Teaching and Literacy in an Urban Preschool
CATHERINE WILSON

Young Children Reinvent Arithmetic: Implications of Piaget's Theory, 2nd Edition
CONSTANCE KAMII

Supervision in Early Childhood Education: A Developmental Perspective, 2nd Edition
JOSEPH J. CARUSO & M. TEMPLE FAWCETT

The Early Childhood Curriculum: A Review of Current Research, 3rd Edition
CAROL SEEFELDT, Ed.

Leadership in Early Childhood: The Pathway to Professionalism, 2nd Edition
JILLIAN RODD

Inside a Head Start Center: Developing Policies from Practice
DEBORAH CEGLOWSKI

Uncommon Caring: Learning from Men Who Teach Young Children
JAMES R. KING

Teaching and Learning in a Diverse World: Multicultural Education for Young Children, 2nd Edition
PATRICIA G. RAMSEY

Windows on Learning:
Documenting Young Children's Work
JUDY HARRIS HELM, SALLEE BENEKE, & KATHY STEINHEIMER

Bringing Reggio Emilia Home:
An Innovative Approach to Early Childhood Education
LOUISE BOYD CADWELL

Major Trends and Issues in Early Childhood Education: Challenges Controversies, and Insights
JOAN P. ISENBERG & MARY RENCK JALONGO, Eds.

Master Players: Learning from Children at Play
GRETCHEN REYNOLDS & ELIZABETH JONES

Understanding Young Children's Behavior: A Guide for Early Childhood Professionals
JILLIAN RODD

Understanding Quantitative and Qualitative Research in Early Childhood Education
WILLIAM L. GOODWIN & LAURA D. GOODWIN

Diversity in the Classroom:
New Approaches to the Education of Young Children, 2nd Edition
FRANCES E. KENDALL

Developmentally Appropriate Practice in "Real Life"
CAROL ANNE WIEN

Quality in Family Child Care and Relative Care
SUSAN KONTOS, CAROLLEE HOWES, MARYBETH SHINN, & ELLEN GALINSKY

Using the Supportive Play Model: Individualized Intervention in Early Childhood Practice
MARGARET K. SHERIDAN, GILBERT M. FOLEY, & SARA H. RADLINSKI

The Full-Day Kindergarten:
A Dynamic Themes Curriculum, 2nd Edition
DORIS PRONIN FROMBERG

Assessment Methods for Infants and Toddlers: Transdisciplinary Team Approaches
DORIS BERGEN
The Emotional Development of Young Children: Building an Emotion-Centered Curriculum
MARION C. HYSON
Moral Classrooms, Moral Children: Creating a Constructivist Atmosphere in Early Education
RHETA DeVRIES & BETTY ZAN
Diversity and Developmentally Appropriate Practices
BRUCE L. MALLORY & REBECCA S. NEW, Eds.
Understanding Assessment and Evaluation in Early Childhood Education
DOMINIC F. GULLO
Changing Teaching, Changing Schools: Bringing Early Childhood Practice into Public Education–Case Studies from the Kindergarten
FRANCES O'CONNELL RUST
Physical Knowledge in Preschool Education: Implications of Piaget's Theory
CONSTANCE KAMII & RHETA DeVRIES
Caring for Other People's Children: A Complete Guide to Family Day Care
FRANCES KEMPER ALSTON
Family Day Care: Current Research for Informed Public Policy
DONALD L. PETERS & ALAN R. PENCE, Eds.
Reconceptualizing the Early Childhood Curriculum: Beginning the Dialogue
SHIRLEY A. KESSLER & BETH BLUE SWADENER, Eds.
Ways of Assessing Children and Curriculum: Stories of Early Childhood Practice
CELIA GENISHI, Ed.
The Play's the Thing: Teachers' Roles in Children's Play
ELIZABETH JONES & GRETCHEN REYNOLDS
Scenes from Day Care
ELIZABETH BALLIETT PLATT
Raised in East Urban
CAROLINE ZINSSER
Play and the Social Context of Development in Early Care and Education
BARBARA SCALES, MILLIE ALMY, AGELIKI NICOLOPOULOU, & SUSAN ERVIN-TRIPP, Eds.
The Whole Language Kindergarten
SHIRLEY RAINES & ROBERT CANADY
Experimenting with the World: John Dewey and the Early Childhood Classroom
HARRIET K. CUFFARO
New Perspectives in Early Childhood Teacher Education: Bringing Practitioners into the Debate
STACIE G. GOFFIN & DAVID E. DAY, Eds.
Young Children Continue to Reinvent Arithmetic—2nd Grade
CONSTANCE KAMII
The Good Preschool Teacher
WILLIAM AYERS
A Child's Play Life: An Ethnographic Study
DIANA KELLY-BYRNE
The War Play Dilemma
NANCY CARLSSON-PAIGE & DIANE E. LEVIN
The Piaget Handbook for Teachers and Parents
ROSEMARY PETERSON & VICTORIA FELTON-COLLINS
Promoting Social and Moral Development in Young Children
CAROLYN POPE EDWARDS
Today's Kindergarten
BERNARD SPODEK, Ed.
Visions of Childhood
JOHN CLEVERLEY & D. C. PHILLIPS
Starting Sc hool
NANCY BALABAN
Ideas Influencing Early Childhood Education
EVELYN WEBER
The Joy of Movement in Early Childhood
SANDRA R. CURTIS

Bambini

The Italian Approach to Infant/Toddler Care

Lella Gandini
Carolyn Pope Edwards
EDITORS

Teachers College, Columbia University
New York and London

Published by Teachers College Press, 1234 Amsterdam Avenue, New York, NY 10027

Library of Congress Cataloging-in-Publication Data

Bambini : The Italian approach to infant/toddler care / Lella Gandini, Carolyn Pope Edwards, editors
p. cm.—(Early childhood education series)
In English.
Includes bibliographical references and index.
ISBN 0-8077-4009-8 (cloth)—ISBN 0-8077-4008-X (pbk.)
1. Early childhood education—Italy—Case studies. 2. Child care—Italy—Case studies. I. Title: The Italian approach to infant/toddler care. II. Gandini, Lella. III. Edwards, Carolyn P. IV. Early childhood education series (Teachers College Press)
LB1139.3.I8 B26 2000
645'.1'0945—dc21 00-044117

ISBN 0-8077-4008-X (paper)
ISBN 0-8077-4009-8 (cloth)

Printed on acid-free paper

Manufactured in the United States of America
08 07 8 7 6 5 4

CONTENTS

Foreword

Robert N. Emde, M.D.

A well-known positive stereotype exists about Italian culture that is captured in a saying among North American travelers: If you want to have an especially warm reception in Italy, bring along a young child. Italians love children! One cannot help but think of this background when reading about the infant/toddler programs described in *Bambini.* This is a book about a special culture, one that immerses the infant and young child in a network of relationships with shared meaning that overlaps considerably with scientific knowledge about development and with what we generally regard as the best practices for care. It is a special culture that also challenges those of us in North America who would like to emulate much of it. Let me forecast some of the features of the culture as revealed in this book and then point out the connections for American readers.

VALUES

A culture is built upon values. Three sets of values stand out in the descriptions in this book of programs from four Italian cities—those regarding relationships, children, and teachers and staff.

Values Regarding Relationships

All programs place a high value on a network of relationships. This includes valuing a structure that has continuity of staff and a connectedness for children who are in a community of relationships that, in turn, are trusting and emotionally supportive. In other words, such relationships involve teachers, other staff, parents, and members of the wider community from which all are drawn. There is a shared meaning across these relationships that produces an atmosphere of attention to multiple points of view, including conflict and experiences in discussing conflict, repairing it, and reaching new points of view. There is an atmosphere of respect in which everyone is involved in continuous learning and reflection. Relationships are not taken for granted or considered static. Instead, the programs devote time to observation, critical discussion, and reflection about the different relationships that are developing.

Values Regarding Children

Another feature of the special culture has to do with an intensive focus on the child. There is simultaneous support, both for the relationship embeddedness of the child (for example, facilitating development of what is mutual and shared), as well as the individuality of the child (facilitating development of what is creative and unique in each child). Each child is valued as a child, not just for what adults want the child to become. As might be expected from the emphasis on building and maintaining relationships, the child is especially valued as sensitive and responsive to others. The child is involved in activities in which meaning is negotiated with others in working on projects and in choosing what is documented for display and discussion. The child learns cooperation and has opportunities to experience interpersonal conflict, as well as its management, negotiation, and possible resolution. The child is valued as active and participatory, as an apprentice, rather than as a target for learning. The children in the Italian programs are involved in repeated experiences of negotiated learning that are relationship-based within a network of relationships with adults and other children. Children learn procedures for interactive learning or a "style" for learning in which they are eager to ask questions and solve problems with others. Everyone expects to learn together.

Values Regarding Teachers and Staff

Perhaps most striking of all to the outsider is the set of values regarding teachers and staff. Central to all programs is the valuing of substantial amounts of time for discussion, supervision, and reflection. Teachers and other staff spend a major part of their time each week in collaborating with others in mutual supervision, as well as in critical discussions based on their experiences and observations. Supervision is valued as helpful and important wherein all participants are learning and developing together. This seems in stark contrast to child care settings and programs in the United States wherein all too often there is little time allotted for such activities and where supervision tends to be perceived as a system for accountability and monitoring, rather than being helpful. In *The Hundred Languages of Children* (Edwards, Gandini, & Forman, 1998), we have read about this supportive system of pedagogy in the preschools of Reggio Emilia. But in this book it is elaborated in other programs for the ages of 0–3, wherein attention is also given to aspects of emotional development, as well as to cognitive development. Consider these comments from the infant-toddler center in Parma (Chapter 7).

> This type of professional development has helped define a new sense of professional identity among teachers. That identity is marked by communication with and listening to children, families, and colleagues. Our model of professional development encourages teachers to practice "reading" attitudes and emotions, paying attention to them, and understanding them. It has made teachers more aware of how delicate it is to intervene in the close relationship between children and parents.

CONNECTIONS

The chapters in this book offer opportunities for connections with work in North America. I will mention two areas of connections that will engage readers. The first concerns connecting with recent research, and the second with some current programs in the United States.

Connecting with Research in Early Development

Happily, early developmental research over the past three decades supports many of the practices described in this book. Researchers have documented the extent to which the human, soon after birth, is biologically prepared by evolution for the activation of a set of "basic motives" or "fundamental developmental processes" (Emde, 1988). The human infant is active and social from the start, predisposed to look at the contours of the human face and listen to the human voice, and primed for social interactions in many other ways. Evolution has also predisposed adult caregivers and older children to interact with babies in special ways in order to fit with their social inclinations. This is indicated by the well-known, high-pitched voice, exaggerated slow speech, and mock surprise expressions that accompany "motherese" and other features of "intuitive parenting," as described by the Papouseks (1979). The human infant is also an emotional being, motivated for monitoring and expressing experience according to what is pleasurable and unpleasurable. The infant's biologically prepared emotional signals are used to communicate states of eagerness, needs, and pleasure. Sometime after 6 months, the infant begins a life-long process of seeking emotional signals from significant others in situations of uncertainty in order to guide behavior—a phenomenon we refer to as "social referencing." Another basic motive also deserves emphasis. The human infant is, from the start, information-seeking—a motive that Jean Piaget (1936) referred to as "cognitive assimilation"—and one I prefer to think of as a basic tendency to seek out the new in order to make it familiar or to "get it right" about the world (see also Nelson, 1986).

Is this surprising? That there is such a degree of cognitive and socio-emotional readiness in infants has indeed been surprising to researchers. But there is a crucial proviso. These basic motives and growing competencies do not thrive without a caregiving environment that consistently helps the infant regulate both behavioral and physiological functioning. The infant requires a primary caregiver who is consistently and emotionally available (Sameroff & Emde, 1989; Sameroff & Fiese, 2000; Sroufe, 1995). What we also know from clinical work and research is that primary caregivers need emotional support from others—a fact that becomes increasingly important as the infant becomes more challenging as a toddler and as mothers as well as fathers become immersed in the demands of work, career, and complex contemporary life.

Readers will discover that the match of the above with the approach of the Italian programs is clear. To quote from the Pistoia group:

> We take it as our starting point to base our work on the principle of establishing meaningful relationships in the centers for young children. . . . This careful attention to relationship is consistent with the latest research in child development. We have moved from theories focused narrowly on individual development to ones addressing children in context.

And then there is a connecting with what we know about the roots of moral development. Recent research has also documented how moral development begins much earlier than we have typically thought. Morality senses are built up through repeated interactions with emotionally available caregivers. What we can describe as moral motives emerge from the more basic motives discussed above. Let me provide some examples. The socially motivated infant through repeated face-to-face interactions with mothers during feeding and play, learns turn-taking procedures by 4–5 months of age (Stern, 1985). Thus, turn-taking and the rudiments of reciprocity, or the "Golden Rule," present in all moral systems in some form, have roots quite early.

So also does the moral sense of standards for the way the world should be. The basic motive of cognitive assimilation, of "getting it right about the world," when exercised with caregivers and through repeated experiences leads to a mental map of standards about the way the world should be. This is evidenced by a dramatic acquisition in emotional development that occurs toward the end of the child's second year. The toddler, on occasion, may become distressed when a familiar object is broken, dirty, or seen as not the same—a phenomenon conceptualized as the emergence of distress when internalized standards are violated (Kagan, 1981; Kochanska, Casey, & Fukamoto, 1995). As is true for a sense of turn-taking and reciprocity, all systems of morality also rely on an individual's internalizing standards or ideals with an emotional response of discomfort giving pause when there is the perception of a violation.

Still another early moral sense has been documented by researchers that also involves an emotional response. The toddler, during the second year, begins to evidence distress when confronted by the expressed pain of a another person, often a caregiver. The toddler also begins to engage in prosocial behavior such as caring, soothing, helping, or sharing. In other words, the development of empathy has its origins early (Zahn-Waxler, Radke-Yarrow, Wagner, & Chapman, 1992). Although research is ongoing, what evidence we have suggests that the development of empathy and prosocial inclinations also require experiences with emotionally available caregivers who model such inclinations.

Again, readers will discover a match of the above with the experiences provided by the approaches of the Italian programs described in this book. The consistent network of caregiving relationship experiences seems well-suited to provide opportunities for these aspects of early moral development. The same is also true with respect to a final aspect of early moral development that deserves comment.

During the second and third years with the acquisition of speech and of narrative capacities, the young child, by engaging in playful dialogues, develops imaginative capacities in which alternatives for action can be represented and expressed. Envisioning alternatives for action and multiple perspectives is a central part of the Italian experience, and it is considered by most to be an important moral sensibility. (For research bolstering the early roots of morality, see Emde & Easterbrooks, 1985; Emde, Biringen, Clyman, & Oppenheim, 1991; and Emde, Kubicek, & Oppenheim, 1997.)

Connecting with American Programs

Two current programs in North America are noteworthy in terms of our thinking about making connections with the Italian culture and practices described in this book. Early Head Start programs in the United States are new, publicly funded, and designed to serve children living in economic disadvantage. Montessori programs are more long-standing, are largely privately funded, and serve children from families who can pay. Both programs are broadening their horizons and can learn from the experiences of the Italian infant/toddler centers.

Early Head Start began with its first funded programs in 1995. It developed from the recognition that more could be achieved with many disadvantaged children, living in conditions of poverty and stressful environments, if they received help earlier than the Head Start programs available for 3–5-year-olds. Concomitant with this recognition was an increasing appreciation that the Head Start programs in the United States had important goals not only for fostering learning but for fostering socio-emotional competence (Zigler & Muenchow, 1992; Zigler & Styfco, 1993). Both were important for school readiness. The national committee that met to formulate the guidelines for Early Head Start also took into account that the earliest years were different from the preschool years with respect to the centrality of caregiving relationships. The Early Head Start guidelines put a stress on a continuity of positive relationships and the importance of the development of turn-taking, emotional regulation, the emotions of pride and pleasure in mastery, early imaginative capacities, negotiation, and the sharing of positive emotions (U.S. Department of Health and Human Services, 1994). This conceptual statement about what is important shows strong connection with the philosophy of the Italian programs. Other features of Early Head Start are also consistent with the philosophy and practices described in this book. Early Head Start programs must be community-based and demonstrate plans for family involvement and staff development.

Since Early Head Start programs are new and vary enormously in different communities, a subgroup of programs have been linked as a "national laboratory" in order to assess outcomes with both qualitative and quantitative measures; in other words, research is underway to discover what works under what circumstances and for whom. Clearly, Americans involved in this work can learn a great deal from the Italians. Moreover, it is likely that the Italian programs can learn from research results in the United States, for one sees in this book that concerns with documentation and with investigations of process have, thus far, eschewed consideration of "outcomes" and more quantitative approaches. Thus, there is much room for cross talk among us for which this book contributes greatly.

The same can be said for another large group of programs in North America, the Montessori programs that have important roots in Italian culture, but have developed separately from the experiences described in this book. Originally started by Maria Montessori in Rome at the beginning of the last century on behalf of poor children, Montessori programs have taken forms in America that have similarities to the philosophy and practices of the Italian programs. Like these programs, Montessori programs give prime emphasis to understanding the child's individuality and building on child initiatives. Montessori programs also give emphasis to a structured, consistent environment and curriculum to provide repeated experiences involving mastery and success. Such programs value building strengths for conduct that include respect for others and attending to and completing tasks (Chattin-McNichols, 1992; Loeffler, 1992).

Currently Montessori programs are broadening their views to include involvement in the public sector, communities, and more diverse populations including the disadvantaged ("Montessori," 2000). Like Early Head Start, Montessori is becoming interested in expanding its knowledge base about what works under what circumstances in today's world. Again, this book should stimulate an active dialogue with Montessori educators. In future exchanges, it is hoped that the Italian programs can also learn from Montessori programs in North America, particularly as the latter become more involved in documentation and research.

BRIDGING TO STYLE

As the editors indicate in the Introduction, this book is intended as a forum for discussion. And as they point out, English-speaking readers will notice that the Italian authors exhibit a difference in style—a flowing, exuberant, and sometimes indirect manner of narrative and discourse. Among the rewards of this style are fresh and even poetic images. I think especially of the many images that portray the growth of one's autonomy *with* connectedness. Let me end with a beautiful statement from the program in Pistoia (Chapter 8):

> From everything that has been said, it can be seen how important it is to help children build their individual identities and, at the same time, to find a sense of belonging. To be and to belong: these become one in defining growth. Thus, it is not by chance that in the repertoire of traditional tales, there are several about children lost in the woods who learn to find their own path back home. Indeed, to grow means to free one's self from the fears of being lost and being alone. We must help children form active relationships with the places of their lives. Then, they can set out on their own adventures and find a path of growth, strengthened by the sense of security that comes from an identity that is recognized by others and in which they recognize themselves.

REFERENCES

Chattin-McNichols, J. (1992). *The Montessori controversy.* Albany, NY: Delmar.

Edwards, C., Gandini, L., & Forman, G. (Eds.). (1998). *The hundred languages of children: The Reggio Emilia approach—advanced reflections* (2nd ed.). Stamford, CT: Ablex.

Emde, R. N. (1988). Development terminable and interminable: I. Innate and motivational factors from infancy. *International Journal of Psycho-Analysis, 69*, 23–42.

Emde, R. N., & Easterbrooks, M. A. (1985). Assessing emotional availability in early development. In W. K. Frankenburg, R. N. Emde, & J. W. Sullivan (Eds.), *Early identification of children at risk: An international perspective* (pp. 79–101). New York: Plenum.

Emde, R. N., Biringen, Z., Clyman, R. B., & Oppenheim, D. (1991). The moral self of infancy: Affective core and procedural knowledge. *Developmental Review, 11*, 251–270.

Emde, R. N., Kubicek, L., & Oppenheim, D. (1997). Imaginative reality observed during early language development. *International Journal of Psycho-Analysis, 78*(1), 115–133.

Kagan, J. (1981). *The second year: The emergence of self-awareness.* Cambridge, MA: Harvard University Press.

Kochanska, G., Casey, R. J., & Fukamoto, A. (1995). Toddlers' sensitivity to standard violations. *Child Development, 66*, 643–656.

Loeffler, M. L. (Ed.). (1992). *Montessori in contemporary American culture.* Portsmouth, NH: Heinemann.

Montessori in the public sector; organizing initiatives (2000, April). Presentation by the North American Montessori Teachers Association Conference, Denver, CO.

Nelson, K. (1986). *Event knowledge: Structure and function in development.* Hillsdale, NJ: Lawrence Erlbaum Associates.

Papousek, H., & Papousek, M. (1979). Early ontogeny of human social interaction: Its biological roots and social dimensions. In K. Foppa, W. Lepenies, & D. Ploog (Eds.), *Human ethology: Claims and limits of a new discipline* (pp. 456–489). New York: Cambridge University Press.

Piaget, J. (1936). *The origins of intelligence in children.* New York: International Universities Press.

Sameroff, A. J., & Emde, R. N. (Eds.) (1989). *Relationship disturbances in early childhood: A developmental approach.* New York: Basic Books.

Sameroff, A. J., & Fiese, B. H. (2000). Models of development and developmental risk. In C. H. Zeanah (Ed.), *Handbook of infant mental health* (2nd ed.). New York and London: Guilford.

Sroufe, L. A. (1995). *Emotional development; The organization of emotional life in the early years.* Cambridge, UK, and New York: Cambridge University Press.

Stern, D. (1985). *The interpersonal world of the infant.* New York: Basic Books.

Zahn-Waxler, C., Radke-Yarrow, M., Wagner, E., & Chapman, M. (1992). Development of concern for others. *Developmental Psychology, 28,* 126–136.

Zigler, E., & Muenchow, S. (1992). *Head Start.* New York: Basic Books.

Zigler, E., & Styfco, S. J. (Eds.). (1993). *Head Start and beyond: A national plan for extended childhood intervention.* New Haven, CT, and London: Yale University Press.

U. S. Department of Health and Human Services. (1994, September). *The Statement of the Advisory Committee on Services for Families with Infants and Toddlers.* Washington, DC: Author.

ACKNOWLEDGMENTS

This book represents the culmination of efforts by many people whose help, support, and intelligence have carried the project from its beginning. We are grateful to the colleagues who contributed chapters and from whom we have learned so much. With regard to translating and editing the chapters, we have numerous people to thank. Above all, Amy Ruth Baker, who spent a year in Pistoia, Italy, as part of the requirements for her master's degree in education at Smith College, worked skillfully and with dedication to help translate several chapters from Italian and also to edit others. Karen Haigh, Pat Hearon, Judy Kaminski, Susan Kertzer, Alison Rogers, and Linda Willis each read one or more chapters and made useful editorial suggestions. We also thank several students at the University of Nebraska—Nicole Miller, Linda Willis, Elisha Huck, and Fuming Zheng—who joined in reflecting on and (in the case of Nicole) translating and transcribing several videotapes from Pistoia. Susan Liddicoat, editor at Teachers College Press, was the kind of supportive and critical editor that all writers hope for.

Furthermore, many institutions with which we have been associated have been instrumental in assisting us. In our work over the last several years, we have been partially supported by grants and/or institutional resources of the American Academy in Rome, University of Nebraska Institute for Agricultural and Natural Resources, University of Kentucky, and University of Massachusetts at Amherst. The editors of *Innovations in Early Education: The International Reggio Exchange* also played a key role in bringing the interviews with Carlina Rinaldi and Cristina Bondavalli to the American public and then joined with Reggio Children in giving permission for the material to be republished. Ferruccio Cremaschi, director of the publishing company Edizioni Junior, supported the project from its very beginning; he gave permission to reprint material included in his publications and has undertaken a modified Italian version of this volume.

Many of the chapters and probably most of the ideas within them have been shared with audiences at conferences and professional development meetings in Italy and the United States. The enthusiastic, attentive, and critical response of educators in both countries has deepened our questioning, sharpened our thinking, and given us spirit to prepare this volume. We dedicate this book to the educators who work with the youngest children, and we hope that it will help increase the awareness of the crucial and lasting importance of the delicate work they do.

INTRODUCTION

Lella Gandini and Carolyn Pope Edwards

For the past three decades, certain Italian regions and localities have been sites of extraordinary efforts by educators and public officials, working together with parents and other citizens, to build high-quality public systems of care and education to serve families with young children. While Reggio Emilia in the Emilia Romagna Region has achieved the highest level of international recognition, other cities of northern and central Italy have witnessed parallel efforts and related success stories. For example, Bologna, Milan, Modena, Parma, Trento, San Miniato, and Pistoia are among the significant sites of innovative experiments in their own right, with important lessons to share. Indeed, the narratives unfolding in disparate parts of Italy in the sphere of comprehensive family-centered early education have taken on great interest to those outside the country, as educators and policy makers throughout Europe (and increasingly, the world) seek to share and learn from one another's records of experience.

This book describes Italian experiences in providing early care and education by focusing on four cities—Milan, Parma, Reggio Emilia, and Pistoia—with outstanding city-run systems designed to serve the youngest children (under age 3) and their families. Milan is Italy's second largest city, with a population of 1.3 million, and is famous as the industrial and commercial powerhouse of northern Italy in the Lombardy Region. Parma, population 170,000, and Reggio Emilia, population 136,000, are both found in the prosperous agricultural region of Emilia Romagna just south of Lombardy. Pistoia, the smallest of the four with 86,000 inhabitants, is located near Florence in Tuscany in central Italy and has two internationally known economic resources: the manufacture of railroad cars and buses as well as the cultivation of trees.

 ISBN 0-8077-4008-X (paper), ISBN 0-8077-4009-8 (cloth).

The four cities were chosen for their diversity along various dimensions. They are diverse in size (particularly the contrast between Milan and the three smaller cities), region, history, cultural traditions, and problems faced (e.g., immigration, unemployment, funding for social programs). They are also diverse in the solutions they have found, for their systems illustrate a broad range of experiments and innovations in the arena of infant-toddler care and education.

The infant-toddler services to be described have their own particular history separate from that of preschools, although (as we shall see) the two sets of stories are interwoven in many ways and involve many of the same key actors. The infant-toddler services were created under their own legislative mandates placing them in part under different systems of funding and oversight from those applicable to the next older age group of preprimary children, aged 3–6 years. Moreover, these Italian programs for the youngest children are not well known to North Americans. The preprimary programs (called *scuole dell'infanzia*, or "infancy schools") are described in several books and articles reporting on preschool services in international perspective (e.g., Corsaro & Emiliani, 1992; New, 1993; Pistillo, 1989). Our earlier books (Edwards, Gandini, & Forman, 1993, 1998) also highlight the work of the preprimary schools in the famous city-run system of Reggio Emilia, which has now hosted hundreds of visitors from throughout the world and influenced early childhood educational debate and discussion in a far-reaching way.

In comparison with this flourishing interest in Italian preschool services for children aged 3–6 years, attention to the services for children under age 3 is just beginning to grow. Perhaps this is because in the United States, programs of care and education for the youngest children have been so much less credible to the general public. Across the nation, infant-toddler services have suffered from severe problems of access, availability, and affordability, although there may be signs that this may at last be changing (see Lally, Chapter 1, this volume).

Thus, the time for Italians to tell us more about their work is opportune for several reasons. One is the renewed emphasis on the quality of relationship and care in light of the new findings in brain development research that show how warm, responsive, consistent care and its continuity foster many aspects of successful social, emotional, and cognitive development in young children. A second reason is the increasing need for infant-toddler care on the part of working families, as a global economy transforms working opportunities and conditions, and as welfare support diminishes. And a third reason, among still others that one could cite, is the establishment in 1995 of the Early Head Start initiative serving infants from birth to 3 years, and the resulting need to develop this large, expanding federal program in the best possible way. All of these reasons provide a good rationale to study the experiences of our colleagues in Italy.

The Italian achievements in early childhood education stand out with great distinction. They have aroused admiration and enthusiasm in

North America at least partly because their underlying philosophy and pedagogy display so many elements originally developed in the United States, both of progressive educational philosophy from previous decades and of the latest professional thinking about the early years. Progressive educational theory coming from both sides of the Atlantic Ocean now emphasizes the same key themes. An integrated theoretical and research basis is seen as necessary for applied work, and practice is seen as essential in nourishing research. Early care, education, and intervention are understood to be complementary. Strong rapport and caring relationships provide the foundation of trust necessary at the base of the service triangle, with implications for professional roles, system organization, and curriculum (Greenspan & Weider, 1997). Open and ongoing negotiation among all stakeholders (including advocates and the public as well as families and professionals) is critical to defining and reaching for high-quality programming for young children.

The infant-toddler programs of those Italian cities that have made the most consistent investments of financial and human resources are praised for their family-centered philosophy; combined mission of care, education, and intervention; and innovative approaches to design of space and environments (Kamerman & Kahn, 1994). Different cities, as we shall see, have specialized in providing different kinds and combinations of services. Some cities continue to focus effort and funding on the earliest established, full-day programs, called *asili nido.* (The first term translates as "asylum" or "safe haven," and the second as "nest," referring to the historical roots of this institution in the charity asylum or crèche.) Other cities provide not only these services but others as well, intended to serve demonstrated or expressed needs that are particular to their citizens. Through continual dialogue and exchange, the administrative, political, and educational leaders in each city have shared and built upon the successes and experiences of others, and have given each other reciprocal support in solving problems. Some of the very educational leaders who have been most influential in bridging theory to practice, offering new possible theoretical interpretations through their practice, formulating policy, designing programmatic and curriculum innovations, and setting the terms of public and professional debate, have contributed chapters to this book.

TRACES OF THE HISTORICAL CONTEXT

What are the roots of the ideas and initiatives that have favored the recent developments of care and education for infants and toddlers in Italy? What are the precedents of civic commitment and public investment to guarantee the well-being of the youngest children and their families? One of the issues to consider here is how new ideas stem from old ones; a second, related issue is how energies emerge periodically to give new impetus to work on recurrent or deeply ingrained human or social problems.

The concern connected with the survival and healthy growth of young infants has led to the production of medical and advice treatises in the Mediterranean world dating back at least as far as the second century A.D. (Gandini, 1984). In fact, there has been a continuous thread of writings revealing the felt need to intervene and instruct about care of the youngest children. Another constant, prior to the twentieth century, was high infant mortality, which was once met with general resignation but is now regarded with dismay.

If we look only closer to our times, the first decades of the nineteenth century mark the beginning of public awareness and concern in the Italian peninsula for infants who were orphaned, abandoned, poor, or otherwise socially precarious. From about 1815 onward, public outcry and debate were heard, and actions to help the "deserving" working poor and the most destitute were taken by private capitalists and religious institutions, supported by medical authorities, and later also by public funding.

The first initiatives were based on a private, custodial, and charitable approach to providing shelter for poor and abandoned infants, such as in foundling homes (a centuries-old institution in Italy and elsewhere in Europe), crèches, charity asylums, and *scuolette* or "little schools," which first appeared in Milan. In many Italian cities and towns, the vestiges of these charitable institutions still exist. One notable example is the Hospital of the Innocents in Florence, which dates back several centuries and yet just recently has been made by the Italian Parliament the national center for documentation and analysis of infancy and adolescence (Centro Nazionale, 1998).

As a reaction to the appalling quality of some of those institutions, a priest, Ferrante Aporti, with the help of private benefactors, opened a well-organized charity asylum at Cremona in 1831. His intent was to alleviate the conditions of infants and young children, without making a clear distinction by age, and offer them social and moral upbringing.

This initial effort, therefore, was both religious and educational, but as Aporti's approach attracted the favor of committed Liberals, the effort became politicized and nationalistic. They were engaged in the mission of creating a unified state and encouraging the education, moralization, and improvement of the living conditions of the masses, perceived as menacing (Catarsi & Genovesi, 1985). They saw these institutions as a means of preventing children from becoming destitute and made into potential criminals.

The initiative of Aporti was so successful that it became a movement, and by 1844 there were 144 such institutions in the various Italian states, concentrated mostly in Piedmont, Lombardy, Emilia Romagna, and Tuscany, but also in Campania and Sicily. During this period of growth, the organization and funding of these institutions by the bourgeois patrons also took on the aim of investment in a productive workforce for the industrial economy then developing.

A similar aim was tied to the possibilities for women to participate in the new industrial textile labor force, in particular in the silk factories that were developing in the north of the country. Not only did women go to work in textile mills, but even those who had infants and young children to care for, since mill owners needed women workers badly enough to accommodate their offspring as well. Nurseries for young infants of working mothers were set up at certain mills such as the one in Pienorolo, Piedmont, where cradles were rocked by the mill's hydraulic engine (Della Peruta, 1980). Public factories such as the tobacco industry also established nurseries for working mothers; furthermore, these institutions became more frequent and better organized in the early decades of the twentieth century, and large industries such as Fiat and Olivetti developed their nurseries next to their plants.

The fortune of the Aportian asylum had declined in the middle of the nineteenth century for various reasons. One was the disastrous result of the revolutionary events of 1848–1849, which changed the focus of unification efforts in Italy from popular participation to diplomatic solution. Another reason was the result of the reactionary campaign of the Church against these institutions, through the authority of the Inquisition, which had started already in 1837 and slowly took effect (Catarsi & Genovesi, 1985).

Another type of institution involved the use of public finances to provide investment in solutions that covered wider strata of population, namely municipal nurseries. These initiatives were promoted by public administrations of the small, separate states that shared the Italian peninsula prior to national unification in 1860. After the unification of the Italian state, these institutions continued to evolve, but with difficulties. The paradoxical tendency of the central administration of the new lay state was to entrust to the Church the management of the care and education of young children, evidently a matter considered of scarce importance. Thus, "these institutions, which were born secular at a time when clerics held power, became clerical at just the time when the country was governed by a secular, liberal class" (Catarsi & Genovesi, 1985, p. 39).

Not until the early twentieth century did the public sector intervention begin to take on the characteristics of a national movement, as the result of ideas and groundwork laid over many years by different groups and liberally minded individuals (Rizzini, 1980). At the beginning of the twentieth century, Maria Montessori began her work of bringing education to children of a deprived area of Rome, based upon respect for the minds of children and appreciation of their potential for autonomy and learning. In 1907, she started her experiment in a housing development by creating a place for children *(Casa dei Bambini),* whom she defined as the "forgotten citizens." She worked with them and demonstrated how, once they were supported, they could learn and flourish.

The ONMI Centers and the Medical-Hygienic Model

The character of efforts to aid needy infants took a dramatic change, however, with the coming to power of the Fascist Party in 1922. The Fascist

Regime, with its procreative ideology extolling motherhood and population increase (Ipsen, 1996), took upon itself the merits of earlier liberal ideas, especially the call for national reforms; in 1925 it passed a national law for the "Protection and Assistance of Infancy." This law created a new government structure, the National Organization for Maternity and Infancy (ONMI), to organize a system of centers to assist and instruct indigent mothers and take custody of infants under the auspices of the Ministry of the Interior.

From the beginning, ONMI was hierarchical and top-down in organization, with strong guidelines, role definitions and qualifications, and a deficit model that contrasted "deprived, ignorant families with knowledgeable, clean, organized providers" (Rizzini, 1980, pp. 130–131). The goals of ONMI included reducing infant mortality (still at a high level, 12.7 percent, in the years 1921–1925), by teaching new and expectant mothers about prenatal care, good hygiene, proper feeding practices and schedules, and the like. The ONMI child care centers accepted infants in reasonably good health and adopted a custodial, medical-hygienic model of care. Such attention to order, health, cleanliness, regularity of schedules, and avoidance of "spoiling" infants, which characterized the ONMI approach, was in fact a general trend in many western countries of the 1930s. The ratio of children to adult caregivers was maintained at about 20 to 1, and much furniture and equipment (such as potty-chairs and playpens; see Figure 1.1) were used to keep children safe and controlled.

The ONMI organization remained largely in place for about 50 years with only minor legislative, organizational, and ideological changes, even throughout the social upheavals of the 1960s and early 1970s. In 1971, however, major national legislation to institute a new kind of infant-toddler center was finally passed, drawing on the strong support of labor unions and the women's movement. Although ONMI centers continued to coexist alongside the first new infant-toddler centers, in December 1975 the last 604 of them were officially transferred to city administrations, finally ending the ONMI era.

Asili Nido: A New Plan for the Care and Education of Infants and Toddlers

Italian Law 1044, authorizing an entirely different system of public infant-toddler care, was approved by the national government in Rome on December 6, 1971. This followed by only three years the major national law of 1968 that recognized parents' rights to a free preschool education for their children, aged 3–6 years of age. The new law, instituting public social services for children under 3 years of age, had two stated goals: first, providing adequate assistance to families in need; and second, facilitating and supporting women's entry into the workplace. In fact, 1971 also marked the passage of a national maternity law providing workingwomen the right to maternity leave for two months prior and three months after childbirth, with full pay (see Mantovani, Chapter 2, this volume).

FIGURE I.1. At the ONMI Centers the care of infants, including toileting, was scheduled at fixed times during the day for the whole group. This photograph shows 18–24-month infants in Rovereto, Trento, in the 1930s.

Law 1044 provided that the *asili nido* were to be administered according to an advanced model of democratic decentralization. Three levels of government were involved, with funding from the national government, planning from the 20 regions into which Italy is divided, and management by the municipalities with wide social participation. In a few years the national funding proved to be inadequate, so many municipalities supplemented those funds with contributions from their city budgets. Overseeing the distribution of funds and development of the system was the Ministry of Health (rather than the Ministry of Education, as was the case for the preprimary schools), a leftover trace of the view prevailing under ONMI that infant care is mostly a matter of health and hygiene.

Regional Laws

Specific concerns for supporting the well-being of both families and children were included in Law 1044, particularly in the articles laying out how the regional governments were to regulate issues of facilities, organization, and administration. The law required the following: respect for the needs of families; management based on family participation and representation of social institutions; adequate, qualified staff to guarantee attention to children's health, as well as psychological and pedagogical growth; and technical characteristics of space and organization sufficient to guarantee the harmonious development of children.

This national law did not dictate implementation in detail. Instead it left room for regional governments to pass laws of their own regulating *asili nido* in their respective areas. Because of this responsibility given to regional governments, it is instructive to explore how Law 1044 was supplemented and instituted at the regional level (Lucchini, 1980). In Emilia Romagna and Tuscany, for example, the regional laws governing establishment and management of the *asilo nido* included advanced and forward-thinking statements about the rights and needs of young children. Emilia Romagna is known throughout Italy as a perennial leader in social programs and reforms. Indeed, 80 *asili nido* had been opened in various municipalities throughout the region even before the passage of Law 1044.

The first versions of these regional laws aroused such political opposition that they were not approved by the national government in Rome, and less controversial versions had then to be put forward. But the spirit of the first versions remained strong, as revealed in the work that followed to establish, organize, and manage the infant-toddler centers.

In an interview dealing with the beginning of the experience with infant-toddler centers in Reggio Emilia, Loris Malaguzzi (1998) said:

> We had many fears, and they were reasonable ones. The fears, however, helped us; we worked cautiously with the young teachers and with the parents themselves. Parents and teachers learned to handle with great care the children's transition from a focused attachment on parents and

> home to a shared attachment that included the adults and environment of the infant-toddler center. (pp. 61–62)

Many cities with committed leaders and educators led the way in creating intentionally educational environments for the youngest children. These programs would simultaneously provide pedagogical structure and family participation. The experiences of these cities became invitations for reflection and were resources to others in sharing ideas and strategies (Bondioli & Mantovani, 1987).

In several of these leading cities, the administrators and educators not only talked among themselves but also met with researchers in psychology and child development. A fruitful long-term collaboration between researchers and educators was begun. The educators wanted to learn more about infant development, while at the same time the researchers realized that the *asilo nido* was a unique natural setting for studying children and adults living together outside the home. In the words of Bondioli and Mantovani (1987), "The exchange that has above all else characterized the relationship between *nido* and research in Italy has contributed to legitimizing and disseminating new images of the youngest children and their needs" (p. 26).

QUESTIONS ADDRESSED IN THIS BOOK

Yet, even as the name of Italy becomes associated with interesting and important examples of quality infant-toddler programs and services, more and deeper questions begin to be asked, such as the following:

- What are the goals of the best known of these Italian programs, and how well have the goals been implemented?
- How do these programs serve the multifaceted needs of families, children, teacher-caregivers, and the public in a coherent and integrated way?
- From the point of view of respected Italian educational leaders, how have recent forces and trends in society, culture, and politics come together to make the Italian nation and its municipalities such vital sources of creative experimentation and innovation in the domain of early care and education?
- How does the quality of the services offered differ between the different regions and localities of Italy?
- Since the differences among the systems discussed in this volume are not primarily in terms of quality-level achieved, how can they instead be understood as particular, localized visions driving the many innovations?
- What exactly are the lessons of the Italian experiences for other countries?

What special strategies and ways of thinking about the problems are most important and potentially valuable to others?

What theories underly these most important principles and practices?

How can the principles and practices be described and explained so as to help them travel well to other nations, cultural contexts, political and economic situations, and historical moments, specifically to North America?

Some of these and other questions are addressed in the chapters that follow, which are organized into four parts. Each part consists of three or four related chapters and ends with a short closing piece. These passages come out of the history of Italian early childhood education and represent segments of influential philosophy or political speeches.

The eminent American psychologist, Robert Emde, has set the stage in the foreword by highlighting key themes of the book. He stresses the importance of an integrated research base for applied work, the complementarity of early care and early intervention, and the importance of trusting relationships among all partners as the foundation for professional work with children.

Part I presents three chapters necessary for understanding the Italian experiences and their contrast with those of the United States. Chapter 1 is an appraisal of where the United States stands today with respect to progress in improving infant-toddler care and education. Chapters 2 and 3 then take the reader inside the Italian situation to analyze the major historical, philosophical, and political roots of the Italian progress in early care and education.

Part II presents chapters that represent the programmatic visions and experiences of leading educators who have helped create the programs in Reggio Emilia, Milan, Parma, and Pistoia. The authors of Chapters 4 to 8 do not describe all aspects of their respective systems, but instead select themes or issues that have particularly engaged the innovative energies of each city.

Part III moves beyond discussion about particular programs and systems to consideration of some strategies or practices found within them. The authors of Chapters 9 to 12 describe key ways of working that stand out as noteworthy for educators outside as well as inside Italy. These strategies include the *inserimento,* or "period of transition" for the new child and family; *documentation,* a tool for reflection; *diario,* or "diary" or "memory book"; and *inclusion,* the fundamental approach to all relationships between people in the programs.

Finally, in Part IV, researchers from both Italy and the United States add their voices and reflections to help interpret the significance of the Italian innovations and their meaning for Americans. Chapters 13 to 15 discuss studies planned and conducted cooperatively by researchers in partnership with practitioners, a model particularly suited to Italian ways of thinking and working together. In Chapter 16 we summarize the book's major lessons and discuss how best to define and discuss "quality," or what is good in education and care for very young children and their families.

A final note to readers as they launch into this book concerns the writing style. Because most of this book was written originally in Italian, it will acquaint readers with modes of explaining, describing, and persuading, as well as particular choices and uses of words, that are familiar in Italy. To English-speaking audiences, especially to Americans, Italian expressive styles and word usages may seem poetic, holistic, and indirect, even after translation. They may contrast with a common North American preference for writing that emphasizes linear, logical, direct organization and economy in expression. The differences in discourse styles and word choices between the two intellectual traditions required effort in translation in order to communicate effectively without losing the quality of each author's expressive language. As we seek to dialogue across cultural boundaries, we have to involve many levels of listening and seeking to understand. The discourse and style differences between Italians and North Americans remind us of our particular historical, linguistic, and cultural traditions and are part of what we can appreciate and learn from one another.

REFERENCES

Bondioli, A., & Mantovani, S. (1987). Introduction. In A. Bondioli & S. Mantovani (Eds.), *Manuale critico dell'asilo nido* [Critical handbook about infant-toddler centers] (pp. 7–39). Milan: Franco Angeli.

Catarsi, E., & Genovesi, G. (1985). *L'Infanzia a scuola. Educazione infantile in Italia dalle sale di custodia alla materna statale* [Infancy in school: Early childhood education in Italy from custodial asylum to state preschool]. Bergamo, Italy: Juvenilia.

Centro Nazionale di Documentazione ed Analisi sull'Infanzia e l'Adolescenza [National Center for Documentation on Infancy and Adolescence]. (1998). *Infanzia e adolescenza: Diritti e opportunitá* [Childhood and adolescence: Rights and opportunities]. Florence, Italy: Istituto degli Innocenti di Firenze.

Corsaro, W. A., & Emiliani, F. (1992). Child care, early education, and children's peer culture in Italy. In M. E. Lamb, K. J. Sternberg, C. P. Hwang, & A. G. Broberg (Eds.), *Child care in context* (pp. 81–115). Hillsdale, NJ: Erlbaum.

Della Peruta, F. (1980). Alle origini dell'assistenza alla prima infanzia in Italia [At the origins of early childhood assistance in Italy]. In L. Sala La Guardia & E. Lucchini (Eds.), *Asili nido in Italia* (pp. 13–38). Milan: Marzorati.

Edwards, C. P., Gandini, L., & Forman, G. (Eds.). (1993). *The hundred languages of children: The Reggio Emilia approach to early childhood education.* Norwood, NJ: Ablex.

Edwards, C. P., Gandini, L., & Forman, G. (Eds.). (1998). *The hundred languages of children: The Reggio Emilia approach—advanced reflections* (2nd ed.). Stamford, CT: Ablex.

Gandini, L. (1984). Brutto in fascia bello in piazza [Ugly in the cradle handsome in the square]. In L. Gandini (Ed.), *Dimmi come lo vesti: Ricerca sull'abbigliamento infantile* [Tell me how you dress your child: A study of children's clothing] (pp. 33–88). Milan: Emme Edizioni.

Greenspan, S. I., & Weider, S. (1997). An integrated developmental approach to interventions for young children with severe difficulties in relating and communicating. *Zero to Three, 17*(5), 5–18.

Ipsen, C. (1996). *Dictating demography: The problem of population in Fascist Italy.* New York: Cambridge University Press.

Kamerman, S. B., & Kahn, A. J. (1994). *A welcome for every child: Care, education and family support for infants and toddlers in Europe.* Washington, DC: Zero to Three, National Center for Clinical Infant Programs.

Lucchini, E. (1980). Nasce l'asilo nido di tipo nuovo: Dalla 1044 alle prime leggi di attuazione regionale [The new type of infant-toddler center is born: From law 1044 to the first regional laws]. In L. Sala La Guardia & E. Lucchini (Eds.), *Asili nido in Italia* (pp. 191–286). Milan: Marzorati.

Malaguzzi, L. (1998). History, ideas, and philosophy. In C. P. Edwards, L. Gandini, & G. Forman (Eds.), *The hundred languages of children: The Reggio Emilia approach—advanced reflections* (2nd ed., pp. 49–97). Stamford, CT: Ablex.

New, R. (1993). Italy. In M. Cochran (Ed.), *International handbook of child care policies and programs* (pp. 291–311). Westport, CT: Greenwood Press.

Pistillo, F. (1989). Preprimary education and care in Italy. In P. Olmstead & D. Weikart (Eds.), *How nations serve young children: Profiles of child care and education in 14 countries* (pp. 151–202). Ypsilanti, MI: High Scope Press.

Rizzini, M. (1980). Asilo nido e sviluppo sociale: Dal primo "presepe" all'ONMI [Infant-toddler centers and societal development: From the first creche to the ONMI]. In L. Sala La Guardia & E. Lucchini (Eds.), *Asili nido in Italia* (pp. 39–138). Milan: Marzorati.

PART I

CONTEXTS OF CAREGIVING: HISTORY, CULTURE, FAMILY, AND POLITICS

Part I provides the reader with background information and an interpretive framework for making sense of the Italian experiences in early care and education. J. Ronald Lally, in Chapter 1, opens this section of the book by telling two contrasting stories about the field of infant-toddler care and education in the United States today. One is the good news of forward progress; the other is the bad news of stalled progress. He argues that both stories tell part of the truth, and then goes on to explain why Italy, in contrast to the United States, has had different and fewer obstacles to success. Americans, he concludes, are not only eager but also ready to learn valuable lessons from the Italian experiences about providing high quality care and education for infants, toddlers, and their families.

In Chapter 2, Susanna Mantovani, a noted program innovator and intellectual leader from the University of Milan, describes the central themes and philosophical assumptions, along with changing parental values and needs, that have come together to create and transform Italian infant-toddler programs and services over the past three decades.

Chapter 3, by renowned policy expert Patrizia Ghedini from the regional administration of Emilia Romagna, describes the social forces and political conditions that have come together in recent years to transform the Italian welfare state. She presents the new reform strategies and legislation that devolve greater autonomy and responsibility onto local government and provide greater collaboration between public and private spheres. This discussion provides a bridge for understanding and exchange with people involved in policy initiatives in favor of young children in the United States.

Chapter 1

Infant Care in the United States and How the Italian Experience Can Help

J. Ronald Lally

There are two stories to be told about the care of children under 3 years old in the United States. The first is a story of progress. As we move into the next century, we in the United States find both state and federal governments pledging increased funding for infants and developing regulations to insure quality for larger and larger portions of the citizen population using infant care. Government is moving to regulate components of care that set the stage for quality. The Head Start performance standards (Administration on Children, Youth and Families, 1996) that guide all Head Start and Early Head Start funded care, for example, now have these specific requirements:

1. Group size for children 0 to 36 months of age should be no larger than eight with a caregiver to child ratio of 1 : 4.
2. Each child should be assigned to primary caregivers and no child should be left unassigned.
3. Children should stay with the same caregivers for as much of their first 36 months as possible.

Head Start also requires programs to consider the establishment and development of secure and trusting relationships between infants and caregiv-

---

ers as the starting point of quality infant care and as the base for healthy development. Before these guidelines were established, no such federal performance standards existed for infants.

We also see states such as California, Florida, Kansas, Nebraska, North Carolina, and Vermont developing comprehensive strategies to strengthen their infant and toddler care workforce (Fenichel, Lurie-Hurvitz, & Griffin, 1999). Some of these strategies include:

1. Providing free training and technical assistance to providers
2. Making available increased compensation, bonuses, and other inducements to keep experienced practitioners in the field
3. Expanding the number of model sites where people can observe best practice
4. Increasing the number of subsidized child care slots available

In addition, many child care agencies are currently creating structures for more and better training for infant-toddler caregivers, and many caregivers are flocking to the training that exists. Because of recent media attention to the importance of the early years, more of the general public want greater assurances of the quality of care that their children are receiving. Parents want to know what quality care looks like and how they can play a bigger role in assuring that their children get the care they need. As we move into the twenty-first century, the United States is on the brink of providing quality care to its infants and toddlers.

But as this book is written, quality care is not yet available to the vast majority of the nation's children. According to research done in the mid-1990s (Helburn et al., 1995; Galinsky, Howes, Kontos, & Shinn, 1994), about 10 percent of infant and toddler care could be judged as "quality care" and 40 percent was judged as actually harmful. The good news is that we know how to provide quality care, that good practice is becoming required practice, that more people are learning how to provide good care, and that more families are demanding it. Thus, the United States is poised to provide quality care and has taken preliminary steps to do so. The bad news is that we have not yet and may not ever take the final step.

The reason this last step may not be taken is uniquely "American" and stems from cultural mores deeply embedded in the fiber of life in the United States. There is strong resistance to providing child care for infants and toddlers outside their homes in the United States. This is the second story that needs to be told—a story of ambivalence and conflicted goals. It starts with a lack of agreement in the United States about the answers to four questions:

1. Should very young children be cared for outside their homes?
2. Which children should be cared for outside their homes?
3. Who should pay for the care?
4. Who should control it?

The obstacles to quality care for infants and toddlers in the United States are produced by strong, and sometimes conflicting, ideologies. One is the deep belief in the sanctity of the family. Another is a belief in individual freedom and responsibility. Still another is capitalism. Powerful voices speaking from well-established philosophical and political bases call for differing outcomes. Many say that the early development of the infant is too precious to be put in the hands of those outside the immediate family, particularly the state. Others call for cheap, loosely regulated, and unsupervised care to be made available for poor families to get mothers to leave the welfare roles and go to work. Still others fight any attempts to ensure better wages for caregivers, to reduce the number of children providers can care for, or to enforce training requirements because of the belief that those decisions should be part of parent-provider negotiations and regulated by the supply and demand of the marketplace. All share a reluctance to accept the new realities of work life, home life, and child rearing that face families at the turn of the twenty first century.

Yet this resistance was not always present. During World War II when the needs of the individual were asked to take a back seat to the common good—all citizens working together to win the war—the United States had some of the most forward-looking services for infants, toddlers, and their families in the world. The Kaiser Corporation, for example, developed child care services for women in their employ that included highly trained staff, good ratios, specially designed environments, and even hot meals prepared for women to pick up and take home with them after their working shift ended. But after the war when the men came home, these services disappeared. In their place came old and strong "American" attitudes: The care of young children was the responsibility of the family, and the women's place was in the home. If the women left the home to work as did, for example, many African American women to work in other people's homes, child rearing was still seen as the exclusive responsibility of the family. As we distanced ourselves from World War II, our memory of the services provided to workingwomen faded. On the one hand, child rearing came to be seen as a most important activity to be done by mothers to guide the child in the values and beliefs of the family. On the other hand, it was seen as a service that anyone should be able to perform and one that should require no special training or pay. These "American" attitudes still drive much of the thinking about early care today.

Although many do not know it, the battle for quality infant and toddler care is not new to the United States. It is one that has persisted for over thirty years. During the late 1960s there were a number of leaders in the country both conceptualizing and conducting quality infant and toddler programs. Led by the pioneering work of Bettye Caldwell, Julius Richmond, and Alice Honig at the Syracuse University Children's Center, quality infant care and other services for infants became a serious topic of study for educational and developmental psychologists. In 1969 a group of about fifty academics, interested in the care of infants outside the home, was called together under the auspices of Charles Gershenson, Director of the Children's Bureau of the U.S. Department of Health, Education, and Welfare. The group met biannually for five years seeking out and studying relevant child care research and pilot programs, and wrestling with the topic of developing appropriate services for infants, toddlers, and their families. The work of this group, given the name Upstart by Irving Lazar, was responsible for bringing the topic to the desks of policy makers as a serious issue for social planning. Members of the group, with other leading early childhood educators, even developed a series of booklets sponsored by the Department of Health, Education, and Welfare, recommending best practice for the federally supported child care that was anticipated.

This work in the United States was happening during the late 1960s and the early 1970s when the leaders of most other industrialized nations recognized that their family demographics were quickly changing and decided to adjust social policy. It became evident to them that some support and subsidy must be provided by the state to help either parents or providers with the care of the young so that children would not suffer the consequences of inadequate care. Formal supports for families were put in place to make up for the erosion of the informal supports formerly provided by family and neighborhood. This conclusion was reached by almost all industrialized nations in the 1970s, but rejected by the United States as too socialistic. Notions of exclusive family responsibility for child care still lingered in the United States, even though by the end of the 1970s a majority of women had been drawn into the workforce, members of extended families had moved away from each other, and many neighborhoods had turned from places of support into places to sleep. At this point it is instructive to compare the history of the United States in regard to the care of very young children with that of Italy.

In both the United States and Italy, 1971 was a pivotal year. In that year the policies toward the care of the children of the two nations proceeded down very different paths. As mentioned by Gandini and Edwards in their introduction to this volume, in 1971 two national laws were passed in Italy. The first helped families in need and facilitated and supported women's entry into the workplace. The second provided five months of full paid perinatal leave for working women (see also Mantovani, Chapter 2, this volume). In the United States, a bill sponsored by Senator Walter Mondale, and Congressman John Brademas passed through both Houses of Congress and was sent to the President to be signed into law. Called the Comprehensive Child Care Act, it would have provided provisions similar to the Italian law. It was vetoed by President Richard Nixon and dismissed by him as an attempt to "Sovietize" our youth. The United States has never again been as close to having a policy that took into consideration the changing climate for women, work, and family life by attempting to provide families with comprehensive support and quality child care.

This book contains the distillation of 30 years of professional thought about how to provide high-quality infant services in a country that wanted them. Readers will reap the benefit of years of sophisticated discussion about how to provide best practice, but should keep in mind that this richness was in great part made possible by an Italian cultural commitment to Italian children and Italian families. As a society, Italians saw how work and family life had changed, and they decided that their society, as a whole, must take action on behalf of children to provide support for families. Because of this, Italian infant and toddler programs operate in a different context than do programs in the United States.

The distinctions in context between Italian care and care in the United States are many. One key difference is paid parental leave. Simply put, more families in the United States are desperate for care for very young infants. In Italy, infants rarely enter care before 6 months of age. In the United States, there is a clamor for care as early as 6 or 7 weeks. This is often a direct result of people fearing the loss of a job or income if they stay longer at home with their infants.

A second clear distinction is the way that the care of the young is conceptualized. In Italy, it is seen as an appropriate activity, socially and intellectually enriching, to be carried out for the benefit of all the children of a community. In the United States, it is usually seen as a service to help families do something with their children while parents are engaged in something else or as a service for children in poverty or with special needs.

A third difference is the notion of infant and toddler care as a profession. In Italy, caregivers are expected to keep careful records on and to discuss with peers and supervisors the children they serve, in order to formulate the best way to provide care to each child. In the United States, only a small percentage of caregivers are treated as professionals. Instead, they are usually seen as glorified baby-sitters with little need for study, contemplation, supervision, or a living wage.

Finally, the major distinction between the countries is that most care in the United States is not even partially subsidized. Care arrangements are most often first seen as business arrangements between parents who need someone to keep their child while they do something else and caregivers who try to provide that care at a reasonable cost to the parents. Economics often weighs most heavily on decisions made about curriculum and program quality. In Italian cities such as Reggio Emilia, it is infant development, not child handling, that is center stage in planning. Infants and toddlers start care in September and leave care the end of June. The program is conceptualized as an educational experience similar to a school year. However, to help families that need it, during the month of July, a summer program is available for infants and toddlers and for preschoolers. During August, most Italian workers, who have more benefits than workers in the United States, take their month vacation with their children. In July, teachers rearrange the environment, plan for next year, and take vacation during the remaining four to six weeks. They will return around August 20 to have meetings, one by one, with the new entering families and to prepare for the September opening.

Both parents and teachers believe that children are being enrolled for the positive benefits they will get from the early child care experience. Much more than care taking is anticipated. It is expected that the child will be intellectually and socially enriched. In the two countries, the systems and the expectations of the systems are quite different. These significant differences, therefore, make blanket adoption of the Italian approach difficult in the United States.

There is, however, much that can be learned and adapted from the Italian experience. Although practice is currently quite different in the two countries, there is beginning to be a concurrence of theory. Most infant care theoreticians in the United States agree with the Italian philosophy that children's motivation toward mastery, self-regulation, and social commerce and their reliance on relationships with trusted caregivers for support and guidance must be seen as central to program planning.

From all we know about how infants learn best, we in both Italy and the United States have concluded that infants must have a hand in the selection of what they learn. For those who would like to implement this idea, there is great help in this book. The approach endorsed and explained includes the infant as an active partner in the process of "curriculum" selection. It also calls for infant curricula to be flowing and flexible. The book illustrates how infant curricula can be well planned, yet remain dynamic enough to move and flow with changing infant interests. It shows how caregivers need to anticipate developmental stages but also need to allow for individual variations in learning style and be broad enough in approach to respond to all developmental domains simultaneously.

In my own work (Lally et al., 1995; Lally, 1997, 1998, 2000), I have put forward the notion of the need for a responsive curriculum for infants and toddlers. I advocate a curriculum in which a good portion of lesson planning has to do with preparing caregivers and environments so that lessons can be learned by infants through exploration and discovery, rather than through direct instruction. In a responsive curriculum, often the most critical curriculum work is not the planning of lessons but the planning of settings that allow learning to take place. Much of my approach explores ways to help caregivers get "in tune" with each infant they serve, and learn from the infant what he or she needs, thinks, and feels. Yet even in-tune caregivers need to be willing to plan and replan how to form a relationship with the individual child and best meet each one's needs and relate to each one's unique thoughts and feelings.

The portions of this book that explore the role and power of documentation give great assistance to those needing help with this planning and replanning part of the work. The authors show how documentation can help caregivers maximize the child's sense of security in care and his or her connection with caregivers and peers, and optimize connections with the child's family (see especially, Gandini and Goldhaber, Chapter

10, this volume). Also clearly illustrated is the importance of attention to environments, materials, group size, and management policies in promoting safe and interesting places to learn.

This book comes to the shores of the United States at a perfect time. Alarmingly, much of the popular advice about how adults should react to infants and toddlers in view of recent brain research findings is leading child care providers to focus on adult-selected and adult-driven activities. In a rush to make sure that windows of opportunity do not close before children under 3 are given the experiences they need, there have already been anxious calls for various types of early stimulation. Many of these suggestions are amazingly shortsighted, and some are even detrimental to development.

Because of the worry that critical periods will be missed, there is a proliferation of rigid learning games and educational materials emphasizing adult-directed lessons and activities. Curriculum activities are being mapped onto developmental domains and specific lessons developed in each area with the hope of insuring various forms of infant mastery. Rote learning sessions, exposure to audio- and videotapes in many languages, and hologram mobiles are only a few of the stimulants our next generation of infants have in store for them.

We hope that the "Italian Way" and the message of this book will help reverse this new trend. In Italy, caregivers study the children in their care and keep detailed records of their interests and skills so that they can facilitate the child's learning. They are trained to search for how to use the children's natural interests and curiosity to lead them to the appropriate next steps they should take. They routinely include family members in both conversations and decisions about their child's development. These are lessons that we in the United States should take to heart because they are the basis for good care.

But we in the United States also need to learn a harder lesson. The United States as a society must provide quality child care support for its families with infants and toddlers. The simple facts of life are that U.S. parents cannot afford to pay, and providers cannot stay competitive and charge, the costs necessary for the provision of quality infant and toddler care. In the United States we have not accepted the fact that quality care for infants and toddlers cannot be left to the forces of a free market economy. Good care for infants and toddlers is not a money-making proposition. It must be subsidized. In the 1950s and early 1960s these costs were absorbed by a family and neighborhood system with people at home who took care of children. From the 1970s to the present, U.S. infants and toddlers have paid the cost by receiving inadequate care. Often the children have absorbed the costs by being endangered, afraid, and bored. Many times they have been in groups that were too large and whose composition changed too frequently. Too many times they have experienced little hope of establishing intimate and secure connections with their caregivers and peers.

This book shows *how* good care can be provided, and *that* good care can be provided to infants and toddlers. Let us take its messages to heart.

REFERENCES

Administration on Children, Youth and Families. (1996). Head Start Program performance standards. *Federal Register, 61,* 215.

Helburn, S. W., et al. (1995). *Cost, quality, and child outcomes in child care centers, executive summary* (2nd ed.). Denver: University of Colorado at Denver, Economics Department.

Fenichel, E., Lurie-Hurvitz, E., & Griffin, A. (1999). Seizing the moment to build momentum for quality infant/toddler child care. *Zero to Three, 19*(6), 3–17.

Galinsky, E., Howes, C., Kontos, S., & Shinn, M. (1994). *The study of children in family child care and relative care.* New York: Families and Work Institute.

Lally, J. R. (1997). Brain development in infancy. *Bridges* (California Department of Education), *3*(1), 4–6.

Lally, J. R. (1998, May/June). Brain research, infant learning, and child care curriculum. *Child Care Information Exchange,* pp. 46–48.

Lally, J. R. (2000, March). Infants have their own curriculum: A responsive approach to curriculum planning for infants and toddlers. *Head Start Bulletin, 67,* 6–7.

Lally, J. R., Griffin, A., Fenichel, E., Segal, M., Szanton, E., & Weissbourd, B. (1995). *Caring for infants and toddlers in groups: Developmentally appropriate practice.* Washington, DC: Zero to Three, National Center for Infants, Toddlers, and Families.

Chapter 2

Infant-Toddler Centers in Italy Today: Tradition and Innovation

Susanna Mantovani

Infant-toddler centers, organized by local authorities to serve children aged 6 months to 3 years, are found throughout Italy, but with an uneven distribution. The percentage of children served by city-run services is 9 percent overall, but reaches highs of between 20 percent and 30 percent in certain large north-central cities (like Milan, Florence, Genoa, Turin, and Bologna) as well as some of medium size (like Reggio Emilia, Parma, Modena, and Pistoia). Besides these programs, a growing number of centers have been organized by cooperatives or the private sector (profit or nonprofit) to meet families' ever increasing needs. Demands for early childhood care began to grow across different families and social groups in the middle 1980s, marking a clear difference from the two preceding decades.

HISTORY OF THE CONTEMPORARY INFANT-TODDLER SYSTEM

In the early 1970s, Italians, like citizens of many other European countries (e.g., Sweden, Denmark, Norway, and France), began to experience increases in women's employment and demanded reform of welfare policies. They obtained from their governments substantial public investments in child care, considered primarily as a service for working women.

 ISBN 0-8077-4008-X (paper), ISBN 0-8077-4009-8 (cloth).

The Italian public held negative or at least ambivalent attitudes towards infant care, based in part on fears of potential damage to children or to the mother–child relationship. Mothers who used infant care experienced guilty feelings, or were induced to do so. One especially notable series of actions in 1971 revealed just how torn the public was toward the care of infants outside the home. At that time, under pressure from labor unions and the women's movement, the Italian Parliament passed a law providing publicly supported child care for infants and toddlers up to 3 years of age. To counteract this mandate, however, opposing political forces succeeded in obtaining quick approval of another law guaranteeing women's rights to five months of maternity leave with full pay. This law also included a provision for working mothers to remain at home with their young infants for three extra months at half-pay and, beyond that still, six additional months without pay.

The collision of these perspectives resulted in infant care outside the home being considered a right of working families, but one posing inherent risks to children—something to apply for when really in need. Because infant care was considered primarily a service to families rather than an educational program for children, it was first placed (as in other European countries) under the authority of health and social welfare departments.

Gradually, however, an educational concept for early childhood services began to be developed. Eventually, in the 1980s, public administrators in most parts of Italy moved infant-toddler services out of health and social welfare departments into their departments of education to create continuity with preschool services and to recognize a strong, specific pedagogical focus.

Clinical and educational psychologists also voiced the concern on the part of the public about the child's separation from his or her mother. These professionals responded by beginning to develop ways to support close connections between families and infant care centers, for example, through drawing out and ritualizing the transition process at the time of the child's first entry into the program. They considered the daily routines of feeding, sleeping, and diapering to be crucial relational opportunities and gave them special attention. They elaborated on the child's emotional and social needs and evolved a very particular set of practices that came to typify the Italian scene in infant-toddler centers. The overall approach to intervention was based on several theoretical sources, including writings of the psychoanalysts, such as Anna Freud and Margaret Mahler; the attachment work of John Bowlby and colleagues; and the notable early intervention breakthroughs of the educational psychologists, Irène Lézine in France, and Emmy Pikler in Loczy, Hungary (Appell & David, 1970; Gerber, 1979; Lèzine 1981; Mantovani, 1975).

This concern and attention by psychologists came to merge with and reinforce the growing pedagogical attention to the early years. Furthermore, the new infant-toddler system began to merge with the older, better-established preschool system. This system is almost universal nowadays in Italy. Recent national data indicate 94 percent coverage for children 3 to 6 years of age. Furthermore, the data point to a general agreement that attending preschool is the normal and good thing to do for children older than 3 years of age (Becchi, 1999).

Both of these synthetic trends contributed, in my view, to the development of a well-balanced model. This model takes into account educational theory, social-emotional issues of children, parental needs, and the development of what is called a "culture of childhood." The model, born of experience in the infant-toddler centers, contributed indeed to the growing public demand for professional and friendly care for children and their parents.

In 1979 the National Group of Work and Study on Infant-Toddler Centers was founded by a very mixed group of professionals, including researchers, educators, and administrators and coordinators of early childhood services in various cities. The association had as its first president, and inspirational leader, Loris Malaguzzi, until his death in 1994. The Group has organized a national conference every 2 years, published several books, sponsored and participated in research studies and training initiatives, and spawned nine regional affiliates.

Members speak out and become active when political and cultural issues about early childhood arise, and they consult regularly on government committees such as a National Observatory on Childhood, a committee that creates the national action plan on childhood policies every 2 years. At present the Group is active in advocating for a major new national law concerning early childhood services (see Ghedini, Chapter 3, this volume). It serves as a reference point for those establishing child care cooperatives and for other nonprofit organizations seeking to extend early childhood services, especially in southern Italy.

CHANGING ATTITUDES TOWARD INFANT GROUP CARE AND EDUCATION

A fundamental modification in the national attitude regarding the important educational potential of infant-toddler centers emerged along with these cultural and political initiatives, in tandem with other significant changes in Italian life. Among these changes were the evolution of family patterns, the increase in the number of women employed outside the home, and the favorable public recognition and response to the variety of innovative services available to children. The infant-toddler centers, initially viewed by Italians as emergency services, are now considered to be much more than that. Now they are viewed as daily-life contexts with the potential to facilitate the growth and development of all children. Thus, in recent years, many parents, including those of middle- and upper-middle-class background (who possess the economic resources to afford any kind of child care), tend to prefer the infant-toddler center because it gives them the possibility to share the tasks of care and education during the first years of life. The increasing demand is documented by research studies and national data collected by the National Institute for Statistics (ISTAT). In just the same way that preschool programs are the preferred option by families for children aged 3–6 years old, infant-toddler centers are now considered, if available, the best solution for care for children under the age of 3. Musatti (1992), among others, has shown that increasing demand for infant-toddler care stems from a combination of parental needs and desires. To get a good place for their child, families are prepared to accept daily schedules not fully compatible with their jobs and other inconveniences such as time required for initial transition (see Bove, Chapter 9, this volume) and the need to find private help when their child is sick. Parents even accept relatively high fees, compared to the free preschool care upcoming once their child is past the age of 3. Full-time fees in the municipal infant-toddler services are based on a sliding scale relative to family income and can reach as high as the equivalent of $500 (U.S.) per month, or even twice that amount in a private center.

Today the question for parents is no longer whether it is good for their child to be in care out of the home, but how to get a place in a good center. Convinced that the center is the best solution once their child is 12 months old, thousands of families in the big cities find themselves on waiting lists. There is even growing confidence in child care for children under one year of age. Parents consider infant-toddler centers to be good, safe, stimulating environments for their babies, as well as emotional and educational supports for parents. Many cities, such as Modena, are developing special programs designed to welcome babies as young as a few months old and their mothers.

Parents increasingly seem inclined to think that sharing responsibilities with a well-trained team of professionals, rather than with baby sitters or grandparents, is the best choice for their child and for themselves. They consider several aspects of infant-toddler care to be critical. With regard to staff, professional training is considered essential. Parents also seek opportunities for early socialization experiences among children, in settings that encourage both significant relationships and autonomy. For themselves, they search for an openness from teachers to parents and meaningful contacts with other parents. Furthermore, they look for access to support and counseling services when needed. After these primary concerns, parents consider educational aspects, such as the opportunity for their children to experience early cognitive stimulation that the caregivers embed in a variety of constructive and creative social activities.

To support the quality of these centers, many local authorities have organized an extensive system of professional development and in-service preparation of teachers. This in-service system compensates for the poor quality of Italian preservice training received by most caregivers.

Italian Views About Measurement and Outcomes

In considering how Italian practices in care and education of young children are seen in North America, it is important to remember that early childhood educational practices in Italy were born out of classic European pedagogy. Pestalozzi, Rousseau, Froebel, and Montessori, if correctly interpreted, saw childhood as a period of life important in and for itself. In Italy, as throughout much of Europe, early childhood has not been viewed as a prologue to "real life" that will take place only in later years. As a result, Italian parents, caregivers, and researchers tend to be scarcely interested in, even at times annoyed by, pressures toward evaluating child outcomes. The great, unending North American emphasis on educational evaluation runs contrary to the prevailing attitudes within Italian educational philosophy. We reject the exclusive promotion of particular educational practices or programs intended to measure, evaluate, and accelerate aspects of development in order to increase children's school performance in later years. Instead, in Italy, we consider infant-toddler centers and preschools to be supportive and nurturing education and life contexts, not places to "develop competence" in children. We demonstrate this conviction through sustaining strong relationships with families, full-time scheduling, serious attention to transition and daily routines, and generous time devoted to children's free and symbolic play.

Italian families, along with the policy makers who respond to parental values, are not influenced by arguments that early childhood services should be evaluated in terms of measurable outcomes. Rather, parents voice their demands for services focused specifically on children rather than organized around the needs of working mothers. In fact, mothers not employed outside the home also request at least part-time educational and socialization opportunities for their children under the age of 3, having grown to expect and utilize the universal access to the full-time preschool services for children aged 3 to 6.

The Italian educational community also is concerned with continuously improving the quality of services provided. We are experimenting with evaluating the learning environment using the Early Childhood Environmental Rating Scale (Harms, Clifford, & Cryer, 1998) and the Infant-Toddler Environmental Rating Scale (Harms, Cryer, & Clifford, 1990) as staff development tools. These seem to be more culturally compatible techniques of evaluation because they include self-analysis and reflection.

Within Italian educational circles, there is also an increasing use of qualitative instruments of evaluation that allow for the description and examination of the setting and are not used in assessment of children. Other important qualitative instruments describe aspects of service delivery, such as availability, access, satisfaction of caregiv[illegible]
the balance between education and care. The Europea[illegible]
conceptualized this approach for early childhood care[illegible]
guer, Mestres, & Penn, 1992).

The Role of the Caregiver-Educator

A key factor lying behind all of these changes in pare[illegible]
creasing confidence in infant care has been, in my opin[illegible]

role of the caregiver-educator. Today, parents consider caregivers the best possible consultants and sources of support on educational matters (Bondioli & Mantovani, 1987). Parents view them as competent and reassuring professionals with positive experience in raising normal children in everyday contexts, that is, professionals of everyday life.

In the 1970s, when services for young children were first being developed, caregivers received basic training either as health nurses or as preschool teachers (with nonspecific preparation in early childhood socialization and education). They attended 3 or 4 years of vocational school and graduated at age 17 or 18 with a certificate; no further education was required. Because this preservice preparation was inadequate, massive amounts of in-service professional development became necessary. Such training is generally center-based and included as part of caregivers' contracted work schedule. Today, an impending new national law will require 3 years of college-level preservice education and provide preparation commensurate with contemporary views about education and social-emotional development of young children.

At first, in-service training was based on recognizing and understanding child development. In the early years when services were being orga-

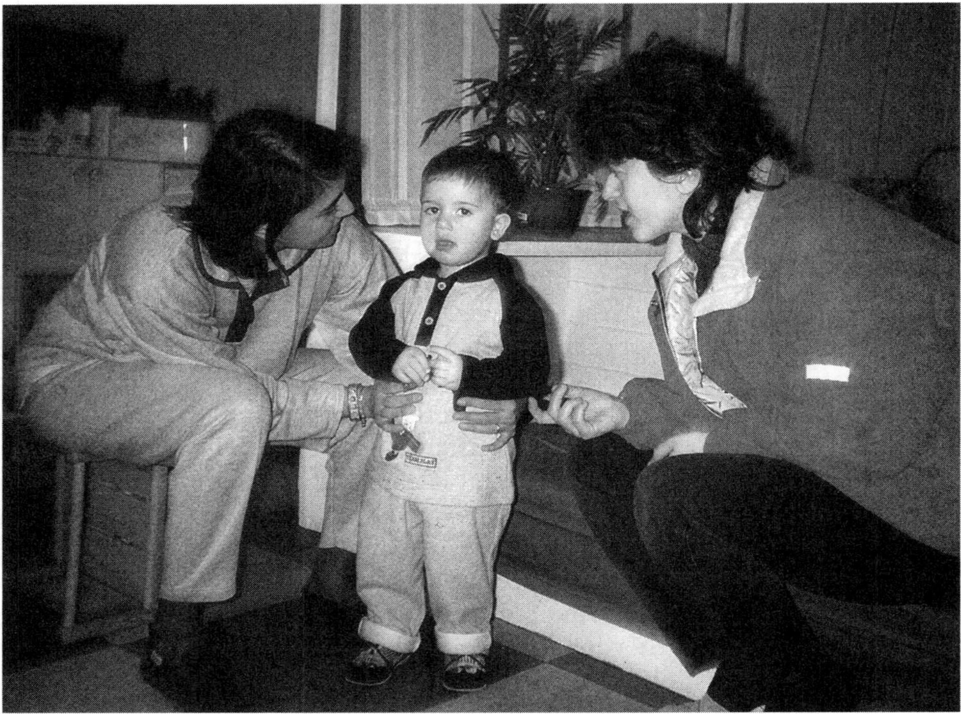

FIGURE 2.1. Separation and reunion are delicate moments in the day of a very young child. Parent and teacher by being close to the child together can render that transition serene. (Infant-toddler Center Console Flaminio, Milan)

nized, administrators wanted to help caregivers become better interpreters of the signals of children so they could provide appropriate, safe, and stimulating environments and interact with children effectively. Because pedagogical theory concerning children under 3 was so scanty, most of the training involved development of observational skills. Caregivers gathered descriptive observations to discuss with their teams, and these served as a basis for considering children's social-emotional needs and for developing curriculum activities. They also devoted time and effort during group work to improving their teamwork, organization, conflict resolution, and communication skills with families. Thus, in the early 1970s, in-service professional development was based on group supervision, discussion, and planning, rather than specific training in curriculum and learning activities, which came only later after caregivers became more confident of their competency in relational areas and teamwork.

In the early years, educators saw the child's separation from the mother mainly from the child's point of view and thought about whether that separation could harm the child. In-service professional development, therefore, was aimed at preparing a caregiver *for the child*. Caregivers were expected to become sensitive and stable figures, able to offer occasions for play and to mediate each child's integration into the group, and competent in making the environment warm, protective, safe, and stimulating.

Further, caregivers planned for gradual transition from the home to the center for each child, as was done in other countries like France and Sweden at that time. They followed what was known about mother-child separation and the importance of substitute figures. They asked mothers to be present when the infants first entered a center, but they did not clearly know how to organize the mothers' presence. Caregivers asked mothers to leave for short periods of time while the infants played, but asked them to come back before the time to feed the child. Only when the children were adjusted did the caregivers also take over the routine of eating and sleeping.

We in the educational community asked ourselves: What should be the role of the caregiver toward the child? Should the caregiver become a kind of substitute mother, or something different? Slowly, through what I see as an important evolution, we came to accept the emotional responsibility of the caregiver to form a strong relationship with the child. We conceived the idea of a *primary caregiver* for each child. Such a significant figure was expected to be emotionally engaged with the child, though in a way different from the mother's, and to form an individualized relationship aimed at opening the child up to the group. This conceptualization of the role of caregiver as mediator of socialization turned out to be a fruitful one. Researchers carried out many studies on the period of transition and adjustment (*inserimento*) (Mantovani & Musatti, 1983).

However, it was not easy for caregivers, whether new or experienced, to assume such a delicate and complex role. It required a fine balance, avoiding, on the one hand, the extreme of no emotional engagement, and on the other hand, the opposite extreme of coming onto the child as a mother (or even someone better than the child's own mother). We became aware that it was impossible to be a caregiver, even a significant primary caregiver, without knowing the family relationships well and taking them into account. A young child is so embedded in family relationships that we cannot establish a good and balanced relationship with that child alone. We developed practices to get to know the parents, especially the child's relationship to his or her mother. These practices became important tools taught as part of professional development. Caregivers learned to do interviews with mothers prior to attendance as well as close observations of the mother-child relationship during the period of transition.

Thus, the early focus of caregiver attention on the child alone gradually widened to include the mother and family. We recognized that mothers often had strong feelings of ambivalence about turning over part of their child's care and education to other women, even ones they saw as competent. In turn, caregivers had their own ambivalence toward mothers and toward their own role within the relationships. Caregivers watched the conflicts within mothers, who seemed simultaneously upset and relieved when their children cried at their departures and when they found out that their child had eaten and rested well at the center. Sometimes mothers seemed unable to leave *until* their children had burst into tears at their going, at which moment they would either prolong their stay or else run out without even saying good-bye.

All this ambivalence placed emotional stress on caregivers; at times, the mothers' behavior aroused harsh judgments by caregivers that were only partially eased by group discussion. Caregivers wondered why mothers, during initial interviews, did not give a faithful picture of their children and their habits, autonomy, and competence. Caregivers asked whether it was even useful to inquire during interviews about such matters, when the child's competence was easily observed in the center context. What was the purpose of meeting with mothers and talking with them?

The answers to these questions became clear with time. It became evident that the personal contact between mother and caregiver was the first step to building mutual trust, the first part of a long process not to be taken for granted. It became evident how important it was for the caregiver to learn to share responsibilities with the parent without losing her own specific role, and to help mothers feel important, understood, and supported. Mothers would then become more serene in the sharing and more able to communicate feelings of trust also to the children. The problem was not really with the children, for children could always adjust. To put it in the words of Riri, a very expert caregiver with whom I have had the privilege to work, "For moms it is more difficult; with grandmothers sometimes it seems impossible!"

When the well-being of the child was defined as the common and mutual goal, then it became clear that caregivers, supported by teamwork, had to take responsibility for the mother's process in finding her role in the center. They had to be aware of her emotions and doubts, to become not her surrogate but instead her competent, trusted, professional partner. As partners, the caregivers would need to be warm, patient, and understanding of the mother's occasional difficulties in leaving the presence of her child. At the same time, the caregivers could help the mother to see how the effort was worthwhile because it would offer the child a new, rich environment.

It was perhaps the first big step that transformed caregivers in the eyes of parents from competent rivals (at best, as children's teachers) into possible and desirable consultants. However, this shift was not easy for caregivers to accept, because they often felt unprepared for such a role.

During this time of change and reflection, the new practices for individual transition and adjustment seemed somehow rigid, emotionally overloaded, and at times a burden on caregivers. However, as the work developed, another new idea grew alongside the increasing understanding of the potentialities of the center context. This was the idea of doing group transitions into the center, so that a small group of parents and children could go through the period of transition together. The parents could thereby provide one another support and make the well-established rituals of transition less dramatic. This new practice is still under debate, but, in my opinion, it can be a clear improvement over individual transition when it comes about as a team choice and is directed by expert caregivers.

To summarize, the caregiver's role has evolved from exclusive attention on the child to attention and responsibility *for the child and parents together*. I would contend that this new view is a distinctive feature of the Italian experience in infant-toddler caregiving and can only be understood by keeping two features in mind. The first feature is the *high degree of continuity* characterizing the entire Italian educational system and specifically early childhood education. Caregivers, apart from infrequent job turnover or periods away from the job due to circumstances such as maternity leave, stay with the same group of children for up to three years. The second feature is the *high degree of family participation and involvement*. This participation, present since the origins of municipal infant-toddler services, creates the organizational possibility and conceptual basis for developing a genuine partnership with parents.

Continuity of Care

Whereas in the United States there is a problem with turnover of caregivers, the Italian system of infant-toddler care has benefited from continuity of caregivers. In Italy there is high unemployment, but caregivers, working in a public infant-toddler center, have full benefits and paid vacation time, ultimately earning a salary similar to that of a preschool teacher.

Continuity allows the caregiver to make an investment in relationships with both child and family. It provides time for people to get to know one another, talk, and observe their relationships as they develop over time. Continuity makes it possible to overcome the intense emotions aroused by transition into the center and to have a long period of good work based on reciprocal knowledge and mutual trust with the children and families. The engagement and its fruitful results provide the payoff for the effort required in organizing such a system of 3-year cycles for caregivers and children. The continuity makes it possible for caregivers to witness child development, change, decreasing dependency, growing autonomy, and intellectual and social achievements. The practice marks the educational development of infant-toddler centers (though it has always been the standard in preschools serving children aged 3 to 5).

Family Participation

Family participation is high in many of the municipal education systems that include services for infants, toddlers, and their families. The organizing principle behind this is called *gestione sociale*, or "community-based management" (as defined in Spaggiari, 1998), the practice of sharing responsibilities for running the institution between caregivers, parents, and representatives of the community. Community-based management originated as a political principle and aimed to guarantee democratic control of public services by their users, serving alongside representatives of other community institutions on elected boards.

FIGURE 2.2. Providing a small group of young children with carefully chosen recycled material, in a pleasant and cozy space, offers them a play of discovery that is a rich source of tactile, visual, cognitive, and social stimuli. *(Infant-toddler Center Console Flaminio, Milan)*

Each infant-toddler center has an advisory committee responsible for making decisions and giving advice about waiting lists, budgets and expenses, opening hours, and educational and curriculum choices. In addition, there is an advisory committee at a higher level that serves the whole community (see Spaggiari, 1998, for the description of the practice in Reggio Emilia). Because of community-based management, parents, teachers, and citizens have acquired the habits and mind-set of participation, that is, the sense of having the right and the duty to participate. Times and spaces are provided, and caregivers receive paid hours in their contracts for community-based management activities. Furthermore, community-based management also provides a regular and effective way for fathers to participate, though this feature has not yet been fully examined. In the best situations, community-based management gives rise to many ways for parents and caregivers to meet, communicate, and share responsibilities.

The city of Reggio Emilia is known for the part it has played in helping create, develop to highest level, and disseminate these practices for others to understand the importance of participation. However, other cities, too, have evolved high levels of participation—even some cities that have a different, less engaged, more private outlook on childhood and family themes. Everywhere, participation has created occasions for sharing knowledge, working together, building trust, and sharing responsibilities among the adults who are part of children's lives either as professionals or as parents. The practices in different cities have some shared features as well as local variations. Thus, community-based management has led to a widespread, well-accepted set of practices supporting close parent-caregiver relationships in early childhood education, unknown at other levels of education, such as primary, middle, and secondary schooling.

All of this progress has not been without difficulty and challenge. Over the years, some advisory councils have become bureaucratic in their processes, and finding parents to serve sometimes becomes difficult. The development of parent participation is by no means always or completely successful. In practice, systems often go back and forth between allowing parent initiative and then setting regulations that undermine it.

Today, however, a new mood prevails, at least at the level of intentions and words, to involve families, particularly families coming from isolated or minority backgrounds. Early childhood services, deeply rooted in the community and closer to families than any other level of education or type of social service, are probably the best buffer and transition step in the integration process of minority families. Immigration poses novel problems for Italy, traditionally a country of emigrants. The well-established patterns of participation in infant-toddler centers, now taken for granted by Italians, are not always clearly understandable to new immigrant families.

Participating can be a difficult process fraught with contradictions, particularly in small communities and big metropolitan areas, where there is not a long-standing experience of participation or a set of shared values such as there is in the medium-sized cities. We Italian educators must reconceptualize and adjust our notions of family participation with so many new situations on the horizon. We must also meet the challenge of conveying to a new generation of caregivers, who are mostly young women of the same age as the parents whom they serve, an understanding and appreciation of the practices developed over years of history and engagement.

We know that we cannot hold rigidly to our old ideas, but at the same time we should not let them become insignificant nor let their process and history be forgotten. To return, again, to the words of a caregiver with a long, rich experience, "First there were *the* children, then *my* children, then the children and their parents; now we have to think about *our* children, though it is very difficult."

NEW TYPES OF SERVICES

The forces of change within Italian society have created great innovation within the domain of infant-toddler care. Society has witnessed an increased awareness of both children's and parents' needs. The culturally embedded tradition of civic participation has merged with attention devoted to establishing ongoing practices for professional development. This merging of practices in response to social forces has created opportunities for parents and children to embark on new experiences in infant-toddler educational services. The role of caregivers has also evolved, finding new definitions and responsibilities.

Within each city there is a growing demand for support around educational issues, not confined only to the infant-toddler center. For example, there are demands by families whose children did not get a place in a center because the mother was not employed. In addition, educators are aware of the importance of beginning a support network for parents early in pregnancy and continuing throughout the first year of the infant's life, during the times when families are most sensitive and ready to change.

In response, many municipalities have created new part-time services. A common feature of such services includes greater physical presence of parents than the full-time infant-toddler centers. They also allow flexible attendance and provide times and spaces for parents to meet. Such activities and meetings can enhance caregivers' roles in the lives of the entire family.

In 1985, new initiatives started to emerge. These were community initiatives, usually part-time services staffed by both professional and paraprofessional caregivers. As a general rule, these types of initiatives were less costly to operate than traditional full-time child care centers. Cost reduction has been an important feature in helping to cement policy makers' support for expansion of services during times of economic recession when large new financial investments have not been politically feasible.

The new services have recently received recognition and financial support through a national law passed by the Italian government in 1997 (*Legge* 285). As in other countries, the change in the law was the result of grassroots efforts by parent and citizen groups, in conjunction with advocates from nonprofit organizations and health and social departments. In Italy, one unique feature has been the important role of people from the municipal infant-toddler programs in leading and supporting these grassroots efforts. The most extensive new services have come into being in cities with the strongest systems of infant-toddler education and care, such as Pistoia, Parma, Modena, and Milan. In those cities, administrators and caregivers from the municipal infant-toddler programs have taken leadership for generating new outlooks and practices, building upon the results of past experiences and directing organizational focus toward previously underserved groups of families. They have helped develop a network of new services to exist side by side with the older services, without threatening them as low-cost rivals. Instead, the new services have now become well established and are accepted as an expansion of and a complement to the full-time infant-toddler services. The older and newer services mutually reinforce one another.

The following are examples of the types of new services currently available:

- Mother-child groups (each facilitated by a professional caregiver and located near a full-day center), serving children and parents together. An example is the Milan program, Time for Families (see Chapter 6).
- Part-time programs, offering children special activities in a setting with parental involvement. An example is the Children's Areas in Pistoia (see Chapter 8).
- Parks for infants, toddlers, and preschool children, where caregivers provide socializing experiences for children and parents. An example is found in Modena.
- Socializing and counseling centers for parents to meet, become oriented toward other services, and find culturally sensitive mediation services for minority groups. Centers for the Family in the Emilia Romagna Region are an example.
- Toy libraries and children's book libraries, intended as resource centers and meeting places for children and families. An example is found in Bologna.
- Prenatal and postnatal parent support groups, often with activities such as infant massage, fathering groups, and other special initiatives. A prototype example can be found in Ferrara.

- Special times and places for socialization serving immigrant mothers, often in conjunction with other services for new families. Examples are found in Milan and Reggio Emilia.
- Training for baby-sitters and at-home caregivers. Examples are found in Milan and Parma.

Some common features link all these different experiments. First, the public administration for early childhood services provides professional staffing, staff training, and coordination with full-time child care, as well as the physical site. Next, parents pay a small fee for operating expenses and may also be expected to provide volunteer work. Finally, these initiatives tend not to remain as single experiments but instead, when successful, to develop into a network of services for families.

Caregivers, capitalizing on their successes in organizing environments, activities, and social contexts for children and parents in traditional infant-toddler centers, are now focusing on activating parent resources and taking a more decentralized position supporting the parent-child relationship. Such a shift poses many new challenges. First, children use these new services less regularly and for fewer hours per day or week than in traditional child care. It is therefore important to provide children with the most valuable activities and to define practices of adult-child interaction that allow for significant relationships during the limited time frame. Second, parents are asked to become more active partners. They are present daily, not just during the initial transition period. The parents themselves are seen as entitled to educational services that are to be invented and constructed collaboratively. Third, caregivers, even the most expert, are called upon to rethink and retune their communication skills, observation methods, organization of spaces, and approaches to modeling behavior.

Compared to the traditional working experience, these new experiments are delicate and difficult. However, they also infuse new life into the work setting, allowing caregivers an opportunity to renew their repertoire of skills, access new forms of professional development, and meet families in order to develop relationships in ways not possible in the more common full-time centers. Evidence gained from 10 years of experience, as well as some recent evaluation studies, has demonstrated the enriching value of such endeavors and the possibilities for refinement of practices and exchange of knowledge between the two types of services. The newest emerging trend is for those involved in the older services to become consultants and trainers to new agencies and groups. They are working with parent cooperatives, cooperatives of young caregivers, and others who wish to enter the field. This kind of work is a real challenge for caregivers, as some have been working with children for nearly 30 years. Overcoming great difficulties and negative attitudes, they helped create and document a "culture of childhood" and thereby helped build trust and confidence in municipal group care for infants and toddlers.

Although sometimes the convergence of old and new services arouses ambivalence and competitive feelings, that surely is understandable. More important, these events present a great opportunity to enhance the professional role of infant-toddler caregivers and to further establish the quality of services, developed without much support over so many difficult years. The old and new services will make known the quality of the environments, the appropriateness of materials, the balance of relationships, and the sensitivity to children and parents' needs. Both kinds of services will activate support for practices that have been the achievement, and indeed the pride, of many—even if still not enough—infant-toddler centers in Italian cities.

REFERENCES

Appell, G., & David, M. (1970). *Da 0 a 3 anni, un'educazione insolita* [Between 0 and 3, an unusual education]. Milan: Emme Edizioni.

Balaguer, I., Mestres, J., & Penn, H. (1992). *Qualitè des services pour les jeunes enfants: Un document de reflexion* [Quality in services for young children: A document for discussion]. Brussels, Belgium: Commission of the European Community. (Italian version published in *Bambini*, June 1995)

Becchi, E. (1999). *L'infanzia in Italia alla fine degli anni 90: Rappresentazioni, cure, pedagogie, istituzioni, investimenti, prospettive di politica sociale* [Infancy in Italy at the end of the 1990's: Representation, care giving, teaching, institutions, and investment, social and political perspectives] (Background Report). Organization for Economic and Cultural Development (OECD), Early Childhood Education and Care Policies Program.

Bondioli, A., & Mantovani, S. (1987). *Manuale critico dell'asilo nido* [Critical manual for infant-toddler centers]. Milan: Franco Angeli.

Gerber, M. (Ed.). (1979). *The RIE manual: For parents and professionals.* Los Angeles: Resources for Infant Educators.

Harms, T., Clifford, R., & Cryer, D. (1998). *Early childhood environment rating scale* (Rev. ed.). New York: Teachers College Press.

Harms, T., Cryer, D., & Clifford, R. (1990). *Infant/toddler environment rating scale.* New York: Teachers College Press.

Lézine, I. (1981). *Interazione educativa nella prima età* [Educational interaction with the youngest children]. Milan: Franco Angeli.

Mantovani, S. (Ed.). (1975). *Asili nido: Psicologia e pedagogia* [The infant-toddler center: Psychology and education]. Milan: Franco Angeli.

Mantovani, S., & Musatti, T. (1983). *La ricerca al nido e il suo significato educativo* [Research in the infant-toddler centers and its educational meaning]. In T. Musatti & S. Mantovani (Eds.), *Adulti e bambini: Educare e comunicare* [Adults and children: To educate and communicate] (pp. 5–10). Bergamo, Italy: Juvenilia.

Musatti, T. (1992). *La giornata del mio bambino* [My child's day]. Bologna, Italy: Il Mulino.

Spaggiari, S. (1998). The community-teacher partnership in the governance of the schools: An interview with Lella Gandini. In C. P. Edwards, L. Gandini, & G. Forman (Eds.), *The hundred languages of children: The Reggio Emilia approach—advanced reflections* (2nd ed., pp. 99–112). Stamford, CT: Ablex.

Chapter 3

Change in Italian National Policy for Children 0–3 Years Old and Their Families: Advocacy and Responsibility

Patrizia Ghedini

Early childhood was long absent from the Italian government's national political agenda. But after the silence of the 1980s and the first half of the 1990s, children are the center of new interest, urged on by various social pressures and a broader awareness of children's issues. The new stature of children's issues is apparent in numerous legislative measures adopted or in the process of being adopted by the Italian Parliament. In this chapter I discuss an action plan that led to two important steps: first, a pivotal law (*Legge* 285), passed in 1997, providing support for initiatives in favor of childhood through adolescence, and second, the proposal of a much needed new law to improve infant-toddler services. This new law is being discussed at the level of the national parliamentary committee but has already been passed by various regional governments. The relevant changes in policy connected with these legislative agenda are as follows: an involvement of several different sectors of government (education, social services, justice, foreign affairs, and so forth), a movement toward decentralization that gives local government greater autonomy and responsibility, and a plan to foster collaboration with private initiatives, while retaining public control of early childhood care and education.

SERVICES FOR CHILDREN WITHIN A NEW REFORM STRATEGY

Today the climate concerning childhood services is profoundly different from what it was just a decade ago. A new season of reform has arrived, as evidenced by a proposal unprecedented in Italy: the Government's Action Plan for Childhood and Adolescence for 1996–1998, which was followed by a second plan for the years 1999–2001. This proposal was presented by the Ministry of Social Solidarity, in collaboration with all the government ministries that affect children's quality of life within their respective spheres of interest: school, health, and environment. The Ministry of Foreign Affairs also collaborated in regard to international cooperation, as did the Ministry of Justice concerning children accused of petty crimes and misdemeanors.

To ensure concrete implementation of the plan, Parliament passed a law (*Legge* 285/1997) known as *Dispositions for the Promotion of Rights and Opportunities for Childhood and Adolescence*. This law allocates 900 billion lire (about $450 million, U.S.) for three years (1997–1999), and establishes an annual sum of 312 billion lire (about $156 million, U.S.), for three years, beginning in the year 2000. According to this law, regions and cities can establish local projects and services that support children and families in serious difficulty and that address the needs of all children and youth (0–18 years old). This is part of a concept of recognizing and promoting children and their rights as a social group.

The Social Context of Legislative Reform for Young Children

In order to clarify the context for the new initiatives that deal specifically with services for young children in Italy, it is important to name some of the elements that have contributed to these legislative choices. As in the rest of Europe and in North America, there have been profound changes in the structure of society, the organization of families, and the relationship between partners. Such changes have raised new needs, amply evidenced in numerous research studies in the fields of demographics, sociology, anthropology, and psychology. They are also confirmed by surveys and reflections conducted within services for young children. This has raised new questions for those in local and national government and has made the necessity of redefining social and political interventions more urgent. Increasing demands by women, including those with young children, to be in the workforce require families and the social system to confront the problem of child care during parents' work hours. Pressure is being exerted at the institutional, legislative, and cultural level by the politics of equal opportunity for women and men. This is sustained by the European

Union's support for specific equal opportunity programs. There is also increasing pressure for a greater presence of women in political, social, and cultural life. Partners are searching for new forms of balance between freedom and responsibility based on greater parity between the sexes.

Political interest in Italy has shifted toward a new attention to families with children. This is a consequence of a greater awareness of the importance of the family for social cohesion, but also the result of the decline in births, which has deeply affected the Italian culture, social and organizational relationships, and the cost of children in family budgets. Italy has one of the lowest birthrates in the world: most families have only one child or, at the most, two. In general, these are children conceived at an older age than in the past, often when parents believe they have achieved the most favorable conditions for starting a family. Therefore, the children are the result of precise choices and the focus of especially notable expectations and desires, as well as emotional and financial investments. At the same time, the nuclear family is more and more fragmented, and this leads to a different relationship between generations in terms of sharing practical know-how about the care and raising of children, and in terms of increased difficulty in taking advantage of everyday familial assistance. In addition, longer life expectancy often leads to a different role for grandparents in taking care of children. The number of single-parent families is also growing, along with the needs specific to that condition. Furthermore, there has been a gradual increase in immigrant families with small children, who present new and different problems in terms of cultural differences, communication, and social integration.

In the current social system, the birth of a child means substantial changes to the family structure, the use of time and space, the lifestyle of the couple, and the use of economic resources. It also generates solitude, insecurity about how to raise the child, and difficulties in orienting oneself amid the many invading messages from the mass media. The solitude of young mothers and very young children is a major cause for concern. Recent research about the daily life and care of children 0–3 years old who do not attend any type of early childhood service (Istituto Nazionale di Statistica, 1998) reports that many children of stay-at-home mothers spend their time alone with their mothers, playing primarily by themselves and only for a very brief time at games suggested by the adult. They are almost always in the house and rarely outdoors, almost always without the presence of other children, and with few opportunities to interact and socialize with age peers. Watching television is becoming more and more common for very young children.

Higher educational attainment and better communication have resulted in parents having a better understanding of children's developmental needs. Consequently, they demand higher quality from the programs and assistance offered by services for young children. This understanding can also lead to uncertainty and a sense of inadequacy, which translates into a need for the same services to address and support the parents in their educational choices.

Decentralization and Status of Public Financial Support

Among the elements responsible for changing Italian politics of childhood, one must consider the institutional reforms currently underway in Italy. In recent years, reform was aided by numerous efforts toward decentralization by the State due to an awareness that the closer those who govern are to the citizens, the better they can understand the current needs and organize the appropriate responses. The debate about welfare and the limits of public finance has helped clarify the problems that exist. In Italy the benefits provided to citizens have been universal health care, 4-week paid vacation for workers, 5 months maternity leave with full pay plus an additional 6 months at half pay, retirement benefits for women at 55 years old and for men at 65, pensions for housewives, reduced work schedules for some sectors of public employment, and so forth. In order for Italy to enter the European Union, however, the national budget deficit had to be leveled. That has brought spending cuts in the general welfare system and changes as well as general trimming of social programs and all the benefits. Furthermore, workers' benefits had to be lowered to be brought in line with the other European countries. The government has had to look closely at the organization of social services and solutions that guarantee quality performance at a lower cost, as well as the relationship between public institutions and private organizations.

Until a few years ago, almost all the infant-toddler centers in Italy were managed directly by cities. The concept of exclusively public services recently expanded to other organizations, giving local officials the responsibility for directly managing public social services as well as regulating the whole system of services, public and private. This new role of managing combines appraisal and promotion of public and private resources and initiatives for the care and education of young children. The new model is based on the intention of sharing work and common responsibility while extending and ensuring the quality of responses for families' emerging social needs.

This new approach assumes a more collaborative relationship among selected public institutions, citizens, and private businesses. Along with services managed directly by the State or by cities, there is a strong presence of private preschools—primarily Catholic—which have been involved for many years in the direct management of 28 percent of the preschools nationwide. As private services such as these are faced with precise, new qualitative requirements from the government, formal agreements have been developed. Cities and regions are allocating funds aimed at supporting management expenses and improving the quality of educational offerings.

The vision that underlies this new reform strategy is founded on some fundamental tenets, which include the following:

- The politics of social services must be redefined within a framework of the rights of citizenship of all children. Preparation for education is seen as a fundamental, universal right that the system must guarantee, regardless of whether children attend public or private preschools.
- The awareness that greater complexity of social needs inevitably requires a greater variety, flexibility, and personalization of responses. Those responses can only be given at the local level, where a closer relationship between institutions and citizens exists.
- The awareness that greater social complexity, coupled with a lesser availability of public financial resources, necessitates an increased efficiency in coordinating the public and private entities with regard to their financial and human resources. This goal is eliciting new forms of citizen participation and more pervasive social responsibility.
- The belief that public institutions, based on their respective abilities, are responsible for assuring the conditions necessary to guarantee children and their parents the same rights and the same opportunities, whether the families use public or private services. This requires the public system to explain clearly its goals, intended directions, organizational standards, indicators of quality, and systems for evaluation and regulation of quality.

THE RIGHTS OF CHILDREN AND SOCIAL RESPONSIBILITY

In planning and establishing new services for early childhood, one must acknowledge both the social complexity of family life and the rights of children. Beyond rhetorical affirmations, recognition of those rights is measured by explicit policies and by programs that exist in favor of children, recognizing children from the first years of life as members of a permanent social group of citizens. Respect for the rights of children is measured by the attention that we give to children's quality of life—to their psychological and physical well-being, their potential, and their developmental rhythms—from a perspective of listening and reciprocity between children and adults.

Too often the rights of mothers are placed in opposition to the rights of children. In fact, women's rights are often presented as detrimental to the rights of children. It is a woman's right to an occupation outside the home and to motherhood that is chosen, compatible with personal autonomy and not experienced in solitude. In today's society, rights and needs are interwoven differently than in the past, and one must conceive of the rights of people or groups of citizens according to a systematic perspective, such that the rights of one do not impair those of others. One must seek solutions that are best suited to society's needs with respect to individual choices, while also keeping in mind that current limitations often do not allow parents the real possibility of making choices that are respectful of their wishes.

Infringements on the rights of children result when fathers do not participate in the care of their children. This is exacerbated when the organization and culture of the workplace is not receptive to reconciling family and professional responsibilities. Similarly, a city that does not anticipate the presence of children and the necessary forms of daily child care in its planning is disrespectful of its citizens, who are forced to improvise child care with grandparents, baby-sitters, neighbors, and so forth. Infant-toddler centers and all services for young children should be configured as places where the rights and the needs of children, of families, and of women can be recognized more broadly.

This awareness needs to include teachers' rights to social recognition of their role, to adequate preservice and in-service preparation, to work in appropriate spaces and with updated tools, and to receive, from personnel such as pedagogical coordinators, support in order to develop the necessary professional abilities. This is especially true in services for very young children, which establish their identities through relationships of reciprocity among children, parents, and educators. The ideal is interdependence among all three to the point that the well-being of one determines and is determined by the well-being of the others.

In addition to a societal vision that places the rights of children and childhood at the center of society's investment in itself, responsibility must be coordinated so that political and personal actions together produce programs that allow real reconciliation between work and family systems, as in the sharing of care and education of children by mothers and fathers, and collaboration among families, social organizations, the economic system, and other institutions.

THE NEW LAW FOR INFANT-TODDLER SERVICES: PRIORITIES AND GOALS

In the framework of the current Action Plan, all services for children 0–3 years old have been identified as a priority for two fundamental reasons. First, this is an attempt to develop an organic policy capable of responding to the rights of children from birth onward and to the needs of their families. The goal is to allow parents to choose among more options for child care and education through parental leave from work, economic assistance, more flexible work hours, adequate services, and so forth. Second, this is an attempt to update services nationwide for young children in quantitative and qualitative terms. Sensitive local authorities, educational professionals, and union organizations, along with movements and associations seeking to reclaim reform in this sector, have promoted grassroots actions, debates, and national conventions on the central topic of infant-toddler centers. For example, in 1993, a proposed new law about infant-toddler centers was presented by popular initiative, supported by the signatures of 150,000 citizens.

Because Italian social needs are extremely complex and differentiated, a variety of responses must be prepared, such that our educational services can take into account the needs of all children, their parents, and society. This means providing services and innovative programs that offer families a variety of child care solutions. It means offering options that are known for their organizational flexibility and timely attention to needs that emerge from the fabric of families and society (see Chapter 6).

The new laws intend to establish a system of educational services for young children 0–3 years of age, which also support parenting. The system is to be organized nationally, and particular attention would be given to regions where such services are lacking. The laws establish national guidelines so that all the services for young children share certain basic features, including the same degrees required of all teachers, integration of different types of services, close collaboration between public and private institutions, and families' participation in educational choices. The laws provide for guidelines that are characterized by flexibility and collaboration, and then regional governments will write laws to provide implementation.

Access to infant-toddler centers, as well as to related public and private services using public funds, is open to all children without regard to gender, race, personal circumstances, religion, ethnicity or social group, or citizenship, including those who are transient or homeless. Children with disabilities are guaranteed spaces. Continuity with preschools and other social, health, and cultural services is an equally important goal.

The educational nature of services for infants and toddlers can be seen in the qualifications for personnel and other requirements in the new law. In particular, it defines the education, skills, and abilities all early childhood educators must have. It also indicates how activities should be developed and underlines the importance of close cooperation with families.

Choosing to require a university degree that includes both 3 years of coursework and supervised professional experience shows attention to the delicacy and complexity of the work of caring for young children, attention to current experiences, and also attention to improved continuity with preschools and the rest of the educational system. Furthermore, standard qualifications for educators will enable greater mobility between different types of services, allowing more flexible and productive use of human resources. In addition, the law provides for ongoing professional development for all educational personnel.

The proposed law also provides for pedagogical coordinators nationwide to work with every early childhood service, public or private, that receives public money. It also indicates their responsibilities and requires that pedagogical coordinators have professional degrees in either education or psychology. Pedagogical coordinators, who are already in place in some cities, are typically responsible to several services in a particular area for both educational and administrative support. Teachers and other early childhood workers need to count on resources like these for planning and supervision. Similarly, they need liaisons to other services so they are not isolated in their work. At the city level, the law gives pedagogical coordinators responsibility for theoretical and technical support for teachers and their professional development. Specifically, pedagogical coordinators are supposed to do the following things:

- Collaborate with teachers to create and confirm the overall educational project and coordinate activities
- Plan and sustain the connection and participation of families as well as the connection with other educational and social services
- Promote and monitor the quality of services, including appropriate documentation and assessment
- Support the growth of a "culture of childhood" in the local community

The law acknowledges that through their simultaneous attention to teachers and administration, pedagogical coordinators play an indispensable role in guaranteeing quality services (see also Terzi & Cantarelli, Chapter 7, this volume).

Thus, the legislative proposals approved by the government and currently being considered by Parliament fit into the context described throughout this chapter. The broad intention is to promote, within a new social welfare system, a relationship between citizens and institutions that allows for shared responsibility among local public and private institutions, nonprofit organizations, and families, by inviting parents to be protagonists in early childhood care and education.

REFERENCE

Istituto Nazionale di Statistica (Ed.). (1998). *Indagine Multiscopo: Famiglia, soggetti sociali e condizioni dell'infanzia* [Multipurpose Research: Family, social subjects, and infancy condition]. Rome: Author.

PART II

VISION, STRATEGY, AND INNOVATION: EXPERIENCES FROM DIFFERENT CITIES IN ITALY

The chapters in this part describe the programmatic visions and experiences of leading educators who have helped create the infant-toddler programs in Reggio Emilia, Milan, Parma, and Pistoia. The authors highlight themes or issues that have particularly engaged the innovative energies of their city. Thus they focus on those aspects for which their systems may be especially recognized and regarded in professional circles. Together, the authors in Part II present a remarkable picture of some of the best pedagogies and practices underpinning the comprehensive, family-centered systems serving infants, toddlers, and their families in Italy today.

The part opens with Chapter 4 by Carlina Rinaldi of Reggio Emilia, well known in the United States through her writings and lecture tours, who here describes how the philosophy, policies, and practices in Reggio Emilia are intimately linked to an underlying shared "image of the child," which motivates and guides what the surrounding community expects for young children.

Chapter 5 also focuses on Reggio Emilia, through an interview (by Lella Gandini) with Cristina Bondavalli, a senior infant-toddler teacher in the *Nido* Peter Pan. The dialogue takes the reader inside a *nido* and highlights possible everyday happenings and the flow of events that create a special quality of life and relationships between children, teachers, and parents.

In Chapter 6, Susanna Mantovani addresses socioeconomic diversity in the large industrial city of Milan. She has been instrumental in planning and implementing a new type of service, Time for Families *(Tempo per le Famiglie),* to meet changing parental needs, in particular the problems of isolation and anonymity of newcomers to the big city. In describing this new service, she analyses the innovations in professional development that were gradually formulated to prepare caregivers to be particularly sensitive to their parents' situations and desires.

Chapter 7 is by Nice Terzi, director of infant-toddler education in Parma, and her collaborator, Marialuisa Cantarelli. They highlight the innovative methods of professional development that were designed by the teachers of Parma, hand in hand with administrators such as themselves, in order to support the teachers and sustain the emotionally intense and demanding in-service work that they were doing.

Chapter 8 focuses on the Tuscan city of Pistoia. Annalia Galardini and Donatella Giovannini, key leaders of the early childhood programs there, tell the story of a comprehensive and exemplary system that is deeply rooted in the local community and in the values and traditions of Tuscan culture. At the same time, the system is not static and frozen, but alive and responsive to emergent family and childhood needs.

Chapter 4

Reggio Emilia: The Image of the Child and the Child's Environment as a Fundamental Principle

Carlina Rinaldi

The implementation of policies and practices in early childhood education is inexorably linked to the pedagogical question of what the society expects from the children. This is an issue that must be raised by every generation and now is the time for our generation to address this question. The solution that we adopt and the school that we organize directly reflect our concept of the potential and rights of the children, as well as the role and tradition that our society creates for children.

It is my hope to renew pedagogical practice and legitimate the early childhood institution. The school for young children is extremely important to our understanding of certain factors including what kind of future we will build for the children and with the children, and what role we will give to early childhood institutions. Are they services for families, spaces for socialization, or places of education? There are many basic questions that force us to reflect on the fundamental idea upon which our society is based, questions such as: Who is the child? What is childhood? Does childhood simply exist, or is it created by us? Does each society create its image of childhood and of its child? How does a child learn? What is the meaning of *to educate*? What is the relationship between infant-toddler centers, school, family, and society? Are infant-toddler cen-

---

Chapter 4, previously published in *Innovations in Early Education: The International Reggio Exchange, 7*(1), Spring 1999, pp. 1–3, is reprinted with permission of *Innovations.*

ters and schools in general a preparation for life, or are they part of life? These questions have accompanied our experience since the beginning.

We want to share with you a few of our questions—questions that can describe the pedagogical, political, social, and cultural identity of our early childhood services for children 0–6 years old. In Reggio, we are convinced that these early childhood services are also places of education. *It is not impossible* to combine social services and education. I am referring to a kind of education that focuses on the child in relationship with the family, the teacher, the other children, and the broader cultural context of the society. These services are not counter to the family or substitutes for the families, but services that are integrated with the family. They are places for dialogue, places for relation, places of participation, and places of education in a process that involves children, teachers, and families.

Each of us has his or her own image of the child, which is reflected in the expectation that we have when we look at a child. The definition of *identity* played a determining role in our definition of the *image of the child,* which was developed by the pedagogy that inspires the infant-toddler centers and preschools in Reggio Emilia.

The image that you have in your life, as a citizen, as a family member, inspires your expectation when you look at children and you create schools for them. This is also true for society. Childhood is created by each society: Each society can create its own image of children. The image is a cultural convention, and there are many possible images. Some focus on what children are, what they have, and what they can do, while others, unfortunately, focus on what children are not, do not have, and what they are not able to do. Some images focus more on their needs than on their power and capacity, what the children cannot be or do rather than what children can be or do. Until children are 10 or 12 months old, they cannot speak, and some say they cannot communicate with others. Why is this? Again the image is a cultural convention, a cultural interpretation, and therefore a political and social issue, which enables you to recognize or not to recognize certain qualities and potential of children. As a result, you have positive or negative expectations, and construct a context that values or limits the qualities and potential that you attribute to children.

Your image of children is a social and cultural image that determines if you recognize their life in the quality of the social services and school that you create. The image of children is, therefore, a determining factor in the definition of the social and ethical identity of the subject. It is the determining factor in the definition of the educational context as a right for children and their families.

[illegible]ne of the fundamental points of the Reggio philosophy is an image [illegible] child who experiences the world, who feels a part of the world right [illegible]birth; a child who is full of curiosities, full of desire to live; a child [illegible]s full of desire and ability to communicate from the start of his or [illegible]fe; a child who is fully able to create maps for his or her personal, social, cognitive, affective, and symbolic orientation. Because of all this, a young child reacts with a competent system of abilities, learning strategies, and ways of organizing relationships.

In synthesis, our image is of a child who is competent, active, and critical; therefore, a child who may be seen as a challenge and, sometimes, as troublesome. In some ways, this child is not easy. This child is a person, a subject of life. This child produces change in the system in which he or she is involved, both in the family system and in the social system. Think of how much could change in this society, when a child emerges as a subject of life, a social subject, a citizen emerging on the social, political, and cultural scene as a subject of life and not only of need. To us, the child is a producer of culture, values, and rights, competent in learning and competent in communicating with all the hundred languages. (This term refers to the capacity that children have, once they are supported by thoughtful teachers, to express their thoughts, feelings, and understanding of the world through many modalities and media.)

We are talking about the child whom one meets every day in Reggio Emilia, at home, everywhere in the world. Our children need to be this way; they are this way; they are searching for a bond. Their looks show their intention of communicating, their curiosity, and their desire. We talk about the child as a researcher, trying to understand the meaning, trying to answer the fundamental question, What is life? We see that the children speak to us, even when they don't speak.

In Reggio, we have tried to develop this theory about the image of the child and to develop an educational experience that could be used to raise us to the level of this powerful new child that we hold in front of us. Children learn through the relationship with the cultural and school context. We have to try to organize a school, an infant-toddler center for this child. We have to try to organize a cultural and school context that might become an ideal place for developing and valuing children's learning and experiences. In summary, we believe that motivation and competence in learning can be developed or muted depending on the awareness and the openness of the place where the children live. A lot depends on the society, the school, and the culture. When we consider the question of whether the human being is a product of nature or a product of culture, of genetics, or of the environment—the question of nature versus nurture—we find that what is important to understand is the interconnection and infinite ways in which nature and nurture interact, and where there are parallel situations for this incredible dance of life that is the child and the life of the child.

A strong image of the child is also a strong image of the teacher and a strong image of the school. It is up to all of us to understand the real subject that we are discussing when we talk about the image of the child. Therefore, it becomes particularly important to construct a school environment—an infant-toddler center and preschool—that can offer the children a sense of security that comes from feeling accepted and welcome: A

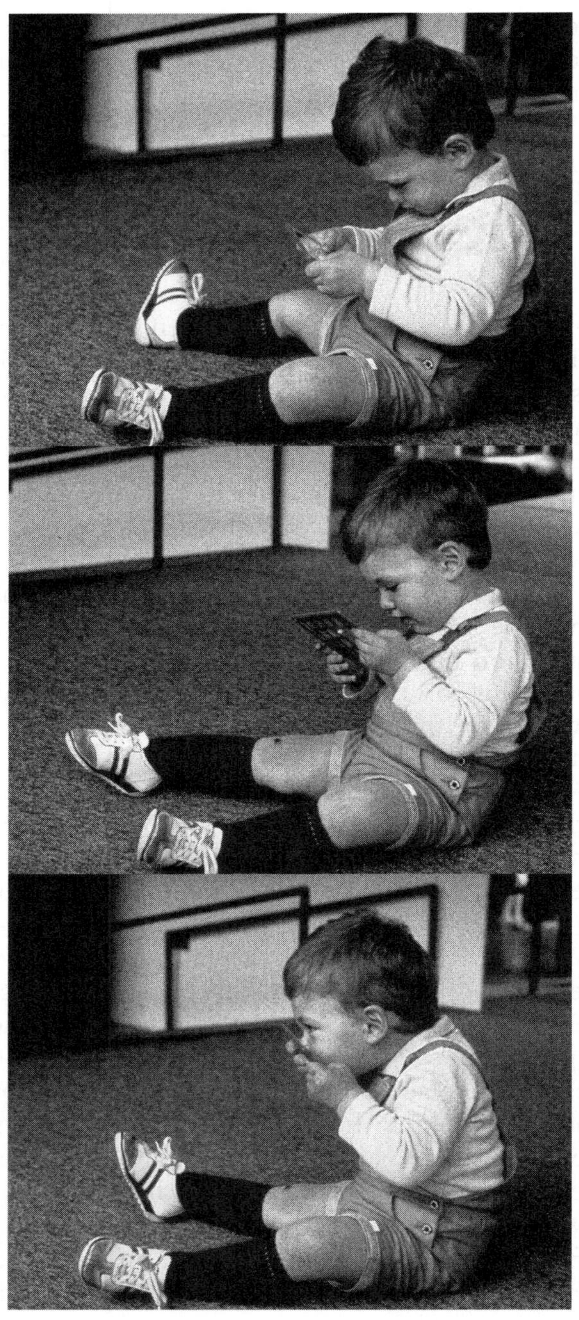

FIGURES 4.1, 4.2, and 4.3. A 1-year-old child reflecting on his image in a small mirror (*Infant-toddler Center Arcobaleno, Reggio Emilia*)

space that welcomes the child, welcomes the family, welcomes the teacher, welcomes everyone because the school is not a place that substitutes for the family but a place for a new way to educate the children and to educate ourselves, a new place for our culture. When one talks about education, one talks about culture and values of the culture.

The school environment must be a space that welcomes the individual and the group, the action and the reflection. A school, an infant-toddler center is first of all a relational system where the children and the adults not only are formally initiated into an organization, a form of our culture, but also have the possibility to create culture. The creative act is much more possible when educational creativity involves not only the children, not only the teachers, but also the parents and the entire society around the children.

For us, the three subjects of education are the children, the teachers, and the families. These three subjects are in relationship with each other and are an interconnected system. This means that everything that happens to one affects the others. You cannot have a school in which the child doesn't feel right, in which the teacher doesn't feel right, in which the family doesn't feel right. It is essential to create a school and infant-toddler center in which all the subjects feel welcomed, a place of relationships. Education is something that you try to create everyday. When you organize an infant-toddler center, a space for children, with this image of the child and you believe that the child is struggling with relationships with the other children and with the other subjects, teachers and parents, you have to organize space and time that can welcome not only children, but also the teachers and the families. When you talk about *progettazione* or "organization" (see Gandini & Goldhaber, Chapter 10, this volume), or when you try to plan things for this space, you are thinking not only about the children, but also about the teachers and the families. That means you try to provide opportunities for learning and constructing knowledge for children, teachers, and families.

I would like to share with you the complexities of this system. It is important to understand that what defines your point of view is the spaces that you create for persons, individuals, subjects—a system that is strongly in harmony with the family and the cultural background. You have the subjects—the family and the infant—and you have to begin with them. You believe in a powerful child and a powerful teacher. You have to sustain a teacher for her to become the teacher that this child needs. You have to respect the rights of the child. The school, the infant-toddler center, is a system of relationships. It is for children, but you cannot separate them from family and society, the places where they live. Children are social subjects. The school is a place for the culture, not only in which to translate the culture but also in which to create the culture of the children, the culture of childhood, and the culture of the infant-toddler center.

We have tried to interpret this message in the infant-toddler centers and preschools in Reggio. The rights of children can be our way of negotiating what we discover, our process, and our pleasure. When you look at your children, your families, and your society while creating this environment, it becomes much more than a space. It is a part of life, which cannot be copied, only created. Our interpretation of the environment is not a model. It's our way; you will want to find your own way. Each child is the center of this system of many relationships, which the young child immediately begins to have in time and space. The child is the protagonist, trying to discover and understand connections, relationships, and responses, working out his or her hypotheses and involving the other children in his or her investigations.

Given our theory of the child, one can understand why the space cannot be too static and why we design the space as warm, welcoming, stimulating, and safe. The space encourages investigation. It is able to renew itself, to recognize the need and the request but also the life of the children and the adults who live in that image. Therefore, the space has the possibility to transform itself. The space has to communicate. It can speak many different languages. The space is a powerful and fundamental language. It can welcome and exalt differences. In this way, the space can make some sort of relationship between others and us. That means that when we organize the space, we are also thinking about a way of living, the quantity and quality of relationships and possibilities. In that space, we try to organize and to guarantee encounters with others and with ourselves. We try to promote relationships and collaborations in the group, but also highlight individual identities and personal space. We try to stimulate investigations and exchange, cooperation and conflict.

For us in Reggio, the infant-toddler centers are places of life for children, teachers, and families—places not only to transmit culture and support the family, but to create new culture, the culture of childhood, the culture of the child; places in which we can offer to our society a new image of the child, a new image of childhood, a new image of the teacher, a new image of the family. All over the Western world, the family seems to feel alone from the moment of the birth of the child. The infant-toddler center is a place that supports the family and the citizens of a new century, of a new future. Our generation can help determine the future of our children. That is the reason why we not only have to work together in order to understand what to do for the children, but we also have to ask them to become good parents and good teachers and to form a good society.

Chapter 5

Reggio Emilia: Experiencing Life in an Infant-Toddler Center

Interview with Cristina Bondavalli

Lella Gandini

WELCOMING THE CHILDREN AND PARENTS INTO THE INFANT-TODDLER CENTER

Lella: As we begin our conversation, let me ask you how the relationships between the infant-toddler center and the home develop over time.

Cristina: The parents' first contact is with the registration office of the Municipal Infant-Toddler Centers and Preschools. The parents fill out the registration form with the administrative staff. Later, the selection is made according to established criteria that are used for every family that applies. For example, families with a child with special needs—or special rights, as we say—will have immediate precedence, next will be single-parent families, or with both parents who commute to work, families who do not have the support of grandparents, and so on. A list is made according to family needs. The families are then notified of their acceptance through a public posting in late spring. Once the child has been accepted, the infant-toddler center (*nido*) invites the parents and the child to visit while the children are there so that they can see the center when it is lived by the children.

Chapter 5, previously published in *Innovations in Early Education: The International Reggio Exchange, 6*(1), Spring 1998, pp. 1–4, is reprinted with permission of *Innovations*.

That is the first encounter the families have with the *nido*. In the month of August, there is a meeting of the group of children and parents that will be coming to the *nido* in September. This meeting is organized by the educators of the infant-toddler center, by the *pedagogista* (pedagogical coordinator), and is the first moment of interaction among children, among families, and with the teachers and the environment of the infant-toddler center. Then individual meetings with the families are organized in order to establish a dialogue for reciprocal sharing between parents and teachers of each child. Parents share information about the preferences, desires, and habits of their child in the course of daily life. Besides learning about the children, the teachers want to introduce the parents to the organization of the infant-toddler center in order to help them feel at home there. This is a very important encounter because it is the first time that teachers and families can have a true dialogue and begin their common history.

Before the beginning of the school year, there is also a meeting of the parents and teachers of each classroom. In this meeting, parents and teachers decide the organization and the plan for the transition into the infant-toddler center, or *inserimento* (see Bove, Chapter 9, this volume). At this time, we also try to work out some strategies, and the teachers try to understand the parents' thinking and expectations about this first beginning; in a way, we try to bring the thoughts, desires, and complexities of the parents inside our environment.

This series of meetings is a way of organizing, thinking, and predicting together how the first mornings will be shared and also a way to explore how the parents can be present from the very beginning. We require the presence of one of the parents during their child's first few days at the infant-toddler center. We also ask the parents to offer their suggestions and strategies concerning their behavior with their child during the first days in order to allow the child to have the possibility to get to know the other children, the teachers, and the space. In these first meetings, we also try to organize all families into small groups that will start at the infant-toddler center at different times. So, small groups of children and small groups of parents begin together. A small group of children and parents begins the first of September, and then, after a few days, another small group begins. The first group of children and parents have already become in some way familiar with the infant-toddler center and have a little bit more experience and, therefore, can help the second group.

The strategy of entering into the infant-toddler center at the beginning of a new school year helps children, teachers, and parents construct a context of relationships that continues to grow.

Throughout the year, meetings are planned with the clear intention to establish continuity and to consolidate relationships. Daily communication is another very important tool for knowing each other. This communication develops through encounters that occur every day between teachers and parents. We want to create a relationship of knowing each other, trusting each other, comparing notes and exchanging ideas. We want to build a relationship of participation and belonging that develops over time.

During the families' very first days at the infant-toddler center, during the period of transition or *inserimento,* we, as teachers, want to create a truly welcoming environment within each classroom and throughout the infant-toddler center. We want to communicate a sense that children and parents are welcome, expected, and considered important. We ask the parents to be present with the children at the beginning because this very first transition needs to be supported by them. We want this first beginning to be shared by parents, children, and teachers together so that we can better support the children in this very important moment when new relationships are formed at the infant-toddler center. The transition in small groups of children and families has to be a strategy that creates a sense of communication and reciprocal knowing between children and adults and among adults; teachers and parents together construct this sense of belonging and trust.

Lella: Do you have particular strategies to get to know the children at the beginning?

Cristina: I think it is very important for teachers to listen to children from the beginning and not only in terms of verbal language because many of these children have not developed their verbal language very much. It is important to listen carefully and observe what the children are communicating to us through many languages such as gestures, facial expressions, or other signals that may show curiosity, interest, or well-being (see Figure 5.1). Together we also have to share and understand signals like crying and other moments of difficulty. The importance of listening and observing is connected with the spirit of transition, which cannot be defined with a precise beginning and a precise end. It is a period in which there are pauses, times when we try something, then adjust the situation, while continually involving the parents and their thoughts. For example, do the parents think it is time that the children say good-bye to them? Should we take more time today than the day before? All these things are particular to each child. So the individuality and subjectivity of children are very important, as are the kinds of relationships that the children have and their ability to create a network of relationships. Are these children accustomed to having other relationships?

FIGURE 5.1. A soft space to "hide and seek" favors the beginning of relationship and play. (*Infant-toddler Center Arcobaleno, Reggio Emilia*)

Lella: Could you describe an experience of *inserimento* or "transition" that has particularly touched you or you think could be helpful for colleagues in the United States?

Cristina: I will tell a story about two children who began their experience at the Peter Pan Infant-Toddler Center when they were 24 months old. One of the children, Mattia, came to the infant-toddler center for the first few days with his mother. Then the teachers and Mattia's mother agreed that it was time for her to say good-bye. So one morning, after spending a little time with him, she said good-bye, and Mattia didn't like that too much. He was not happy. He didn't want to take off his jacket. He was crying. He preferred to stay by himself. He didn't want us, as teachers, to come close to him. We tried to talk to him and to take him in our arms, but at the same time we understood that we had to respect his own pace and let him decide when he was ready to be close to us or to accept our coming close to him.

Another child in the class, Francesca, had already overcome the moment of saying good-bye to her mother. She was really quite happy and didn't mind when her mother left. She was serene when she said good-bye to her mother. We noticed that Francesca observed Mattia and she understood how delicate the moment was for him and how fragile he was. Seeing Mattia crying that morning, Francesca went close to him. To our surprise, he let her come close to him.

Francesca sat next to Mattia and, with an attitude of great participation and solidarity, said, "Come on, Mattia, don't cry! You will see your mommy will come back. You will see that she will come very soon." And then we saw that Mattia accepted this moment and he really liked having Francesca next to him. He knew that Francesca had overcome this difficulty of saying good-bye to her mother. So this beginning of a friendship and Mattia's acceptance of Francesca's message helped him overcome his sense of sadness.

So, in a sense, it was Francesca who made his transition possible. He accepted her more than us adults and more than the strategies we had tried. Of course, we were close to him all this time, and he probably felt that. But it's also true that, from an early age, children seem to be able to have great solidarity, great attention to each other, and the ability to listen to each other. Therefore, on the part of the teachers, there was a great deal of welcoming and support for both children but also an appreciation for what Francesca was offering us.

THE SPACE OF THE INFANT-TODDLER CENTER

Lella: The environment of the infant-toddler center offers messages that both children and adults can "read." What are the aspects of the space to which you pay particular attention? According to your experience, which are the aspects that tend to make parents feel accepted as part of the experience? In the space of an infant-toddler center, how can one reflect and respect the uniqueness of every child and, at the same time, give value to the small community that groups of children and adults form together?

Cristina: I think it is essential for the space of the infant-toddler center to transmit a sense of expectation and welcoming to parents and children. This space should communicate, and we, as teachers, have to think very carefully about this. We want to create communication so the relationships that are beginning will continue. Spaces can truly give this sense of continuity through communication and welcoming.

For example, the entryway of the infant-toddler center is very important for communicating messages. But also, the entryway of each room should offer to parents who enter with the children something that gives ideas about what the teachers and children are doing. They should find their own children there, perhaps through the notebooks or journals of the teachers. They should also find information and images of what is happening inside the room and how the group is forming. A journal prepared by the teachers should communicate a sort of panoramic view of what is happening, the changes that are taking place in that room or section.

I'm thinking about the visual documentation that can communicate microstories or narratives about what happens among the children. Narratives can also be done visually, capturing through photographs looks, gestures, and interaction among the children. I'm also thinking about spaces and places that are capable of being transparent and transmitting what is happening when the parents are not there. I'm thinking about a physical place where parents themselves feel accepted and welcome. For example, a place where parents can stop and sit and be together, to talk with the teachers and also with other parents that come into the infant-toddler center. This is a way for them to be sharing impressions and reflections with each other. I'm thinking about the value of a place where the children can find their own photographs together with the photographs of other children. This communication on the wall enables adults and children to see visual images of the children in relationships with others from the beginning.

Other spaces, other places can also give this message of welcoming. I'm thinking now about the personal drawers of toddlers and infants where children, parents, or teachers can put things brought from home, for example. Things that come inside the infant-toddler center increase the network of relationships because these objects help form a connection between the life of the children in the infant-toddler center and at home. These drawers are usually personalized by placing photographs or symbols that the children can recognize. This is important for the children's identity. They also recognize the others with whom they can share the space. So the child becomes a subject in the relationship. The child recognizes his or her subjectivity.

I'm also thinking about the places inside the different rooms to welcome what the children have brought from their vacations—little treasures they have collected that they can share with their friends and teachers. These treasures help each child recognize himself or herself as a unique person but also as belonging to a group of friends. The calendar with the birthdays encourages the children to appreciate their own uniqueness and the relationship that they have with others. We also create folders containing individual drawings and work of the children that can be shared with the others and with the parents. So we try to create a space that welcomes individual differences and uniqueness, but also constructs this sense of relationship among children, with adults, and with the environment of the infant-toddler center itself.

Lella: Curiosity, active participation, the pleasure to play and to express oneself lead children to interact with the space and, therefore, to influence the very space that teachers have prepared for them. Could you describe some situations in which you observed infants and toddlers directly and indirectly modifying the space of the infant-toddler center?

Cristina: I think the value of space and environment, in a broader sense, is that one cannot consider it as fixed and set forever, but rather as part of a process of change and growth. Therefore, the space is ready to change in relationship with the subjects, the children who live in the space. Here is an example of an experience with the children between 18 and 24 months. We had a space in the classroom that the teachers intended for symbolic play with dolls, but we soon noticed that the children in that classroom were more interested in the space that was devoted to construction with building blocks and other materials. We reflected about the children's interest in building in discussions with other teachers and with the parents of those children. As a result, we decided to widen the space called the Construction Space that had been devoted to building. The classroom changed its appearance completely. The symbolic play area became an additional space for building. The parents started to bring material to school, such as plastic tubing, pieces of wood, and cardboard tubing of various dimensions. The classroom changed because of the children who inhabited that space.

Another example has to do with children between 24 and 32 months. A space that had been set up for symbolic play in the kitchen soon helped us to encourage the children's great interest in numbers. Some children had noticed the number of the trolley that they took to the infant-toddler center. Some of the mothers told us that the children were interested in the number of the house where they lived. After a dialogue with the parents, the teachers learned that many of the children were interested in numbers. So we made the decision to reorganize the space for kitchen play another way. After discussing this with the children, we decided to call the space the Office. Parents brought in a typewriter and an adding machine. Then we added numbers and letters that the children cut out of the newspaper.

The space should be flexible and ready to be changed. We can see that the space becomes more alive when we follow the interests of the children and new ideas that the class suggests. Then we can see that the space follows the process of growth of the children throughout the year.

CHILDREN'S RELATIONSHIPS WITH PEERS

Lella: Could you share some of your reflections and experiences regarding the capacity of very young children to enter into relationships with their peers? In your view, how can adults facilitate and support these exchanges as well as the emergence of friendships?

Cristina: This is a very important question, Lella. Once again, it is essential that adults listen to children. In my view, it is particularly important for the adults to know how to listen to all languages of the children in the infant-toddler center because their verbal language is not well developed. It seems difficult for infants and toddlers to declare without words their pleasure, their readiness to enter into a relationship, and their desires. But we, as adults, should be able to understand the desires, readiness, and capacity of these very young children to enter a relationship with others even when verbal declarations are not made. Their gestures, their look, the solidarity, and the collaboration that emerges among children communicate this to us (see Figure 5.2).

Sometimes the provocation, the conflicts that emerge during these relationships declare to us, as adults, how strong the desire is on the part of the children to enter into relationships with others. The role of the adults, the teachers, is to be aware of the great power and potential capacity of children in this regard. When the adults are truly convinced of this potential and capacity, then this way of listening, this desire to be very attentive becomes part of their way of being with children. As a result, the adults acquire a stronger capacity to recognize all types of languages as strategies for building relationships.

After recognizing and supporting these languages, it's important to consider the value of the great skills of children and to ren-

FIGURE 5.2. A 22-month-old child covers his peer who is pretending to take a nap in the doll's bed. (*Infant-toddler Center Arcobaleno, Reggio Emilia*)

der them visible through documentation of the moments that the children have with each other. The adult has to be able to capture these important moments, being present and involved in the relationship yet not slowing down or accelerating the time that the children need. The adult must be able to give the time to the children to live through a relationship. If we reflect on this, this time is often very different from the value of time that we, as adults, give to moments like this. The adult who is within or inside the situation is able to capture these moments. This adult will be able to witness this great capacity and potential that children have even when they are very young.

EXPERIENCES WITH PROJECTS

Lella: Considering the many languages that generate actions, thoughts, feelings, and images among children, what suggestions do you have for teachers who would like to begin to construct gradual and meaningful experiences for infants and toddlers? Educators in the United States often ask the following question: "Is it possible for infants to be involved in a project?" How *does* one define a project for children less than 3 years of age? Could you tell us about some of your experiences?

Cristina: I think it is essential that teachers have the capacity to recognize happenings in the infant-toddler center as events that can have the potential for children to live through. Here is an example: Alessandro, who was 22 months old, brought to the infant-toddler center some sea urchins he had found on the seaside. He wanted to share and experiment with them with his friends. I think that was a truly important occasion for the small group of children because it gave shape and voice to their curiosity, their questions, and their experimentation about sea urchins. This was a very rich moment for all the children of the classroom.

The teachers wondered how they could support the children's curiosity. Together with our other colleagues, we thought to offer the children some magnifying lenses so the children could see more closely and look inside the sea urchins. We also decided to place some mirrors of different dimensions on the table to change the points of view and to look at the sea urchins from different sides. In a sense, we were rendering the situation more complex. When it was placed on the mirror, the sea urchin was indicating the multiple aspects of its own image to the children. We teachers experimented together about a graphic language that small children could use to interpret the sea urchin. We opted for thin black markers and white paper. We realized that we were documenting this happening and that it had become a small project with the children who had started to question and investigate.

In any case, the sea urchins had given them more questions, and we had found reciprocal answers together. So each child was experiencing a personal process of self-learning in a situation that had been created by one of the children, then supported and stimulated by the teachers. The teachers had thought about situations in a context that could support the children and also give them the possibility to go on with their investigation and to modify the situation that they created in the beginning.

A project could also be proposed by the teachers, but the teachers still have to let the children find personal strategies to adopt within their own investigation or research. Once again, drawing materials, wire, and clay can become a way for the children to express their thoughts and give voice to their gestures and mental images. The questions and the personal paths of the children become a project at the moment when the adult is capable of entering and staying within this game of making suggestions and proposals, having expectations about the path to take, then revisiting and interpreting the children's personal paths with other teachers. The teacher has to be playing the same kind of games that the children play when he or she gives them the possibility to revisit, progress, and have a process within a personal investigation. So teachers should compare notes with other teachers, with *atelieristi* (studio coordinators), with the *pedagogisti* (pedagogical coordinators), in order to put into a network all that can be done to support the children in their personal research (see Malaguzzi et al., 1996).

Materials are truly important in the moment they become a language that is owned by the children and not just a technique that has to be learned or used in only one way. Materials should become languages to give voice to children's thoughts, mental images, and sense of possibility about entering into relationships with the other children. Through materials, children have a chance to collaborate, cooperate, and exchange knowledge with each other. These are the kinds of questions that adults should discuss among themselves in order to try to observe, document, and understand what the children construct or bring forward in an autonomous, personal way.

COLLABORATION WITH PARENTS AND THE COMMUNITY

Lella: How do you organize a meeting for teachers to work with families in order to support their initiatives, or the ones taken together, or to make plans? Could you tell us about some experiences?

Cristina: At Peter Pan Infant-Toddler Center, the teachers and parents decided to research the possible places in town where children could go with their parents after leaving the infant-toddler center each day. This work originated from a suggestion from the parent-teacher committees that are active in all the city preschools and infant-toddler centers. Other municipal preschools and infant-toddler centers became involved in a similar project focused on the topic of the city of Reggio Emilia. At Peter Pan, we collected data through a questionnaire sent to the parents. From these data, the teachers and the parents created a map of the city marked with all the places in the city where children, teachers, and parents could spend time. It was a very large project, and the teachers began to feel more a part of the life of the family outside the infant-toddler center because they learned about a variety of places in the city that were chosen by families. The particular interest of this project was that the data collected in several of the municipal preschools and centers were very rich in giving a picture of how our city is perceived by families. Not only that, the conversations and drawings by children served to construct a guide of the city seen through their eyes, which is now a book for all of us to remember our journey together (Davoli & Ferri, 2000).

Once again, it is important to give value to teachers researching together with the parents, not just asking them to do something. This research was a shared work that was based on a true need of families and also respected the system of the infant-toddler center, which is based on three protagonists: teachers, parents, and children.

Lella: In what ways is the neighborhood around the infant-toddler center involved in the life of the center? How does the community participate in the activities of the infant-toddler center?

Cristina: The life of the infant-toddler centers and the preschools is immersed within the life of the city and the citizens. Grandparents or relatives of the children tend to participate in the life of an infant-toddler center or preschool. Citizens in Reggio Emilia can be a part of the parent-teacher committees even if they're not parents. They can enter into the life of the school and can participate in discussions about any issue that is relevant for the parent-teacher committee to consider.

One of the possibilities for citizens who want to participate in the initiatives of the infant-toddler centers and preschools is an event called Open Courtyards. A few years ago, we began to open up our playgrounds, gardens, parks, and courtyards in the spring or summer, just before the closing of the schools for the year. This initiative creates a space outside of the building of the preschools and infant-toddler centers where there is shared participation in performances, celebrations, and concerts. Each preschool and infant-toddler center plans how it can initiate and support such an event involving various aspects of the life of the city and inviting any interested citizen to participate.

TRANSITION TO PRESCHOOL

Lella: Could you describe how you think about, organize, and live through the transition between the infant-toddler center and preschool? How do the children and parents experience this transition?

Cristina: The transition between the infant-toddler center and the preschool is very important. The experience of the Reggio municipal infant-toddler centers and preschools is for children from birth to 6 years of age. Our philosophy considers this age span one unified period, not two separate periods of a child's life. Therefore, we try to create a smooth transition between our infant-toddler centers and preschools. Children who are 2 to 3 years of age have occasions to visit their future preschools. At this time, they can encounter the new environments and their future teachers. It is not likely that an entire classroom of an infant-toddler center will go on together to the same preschool. More often, subgroups of children within a class each go off to various different preschools.

The teachers in the infant-toddler center and the preschool have meetings and exchanges about the children who are making the passage to preschool. These dialogues are consistent with the philosophy of continuing the life and the experiences of the children in the infant-toddler center. This kind of communication considers how the children have lived through the experience, not as a step that is concluded, but rather as something that has continuity. Parents have meetings with the teachers of the preschool in order to establish a dialogue, get to know each other, and begin a process that they will build together.

We believe and hope that what we propose is a continuity of philosophy—a strong image of the child that cannot be fragmented in age levels but has a long-range view and is capable of welcoming each child's differences and variety of experiences and culture.

REFERENCE

Davoli, M., & Ferri, G. (Eds.). (2000). *Reggio tutta: Una guida dei bambini alla città* [All of Reggio : A guide by children to the city]. Reggio Emilia: Reggio Children s.r.l.

Malaguzzi, L., et al. (1996). *I piccolissimi del cinema nuto: Giochi di finzione al nido fra Pesci e bambini*. [The little ones of the silent movies: Make believe with children and fish at the Infant-toddler Center]. Reggio Emilia: Reggio Children s.r.l.

Chapter 6

MILAN: MEETING NEW KINDS OF FAMILY NEEDS

Susanna Mantovani

Infant-toddler centers were the first major service offered to support Italian families with very young children, but in recent years, other services have been created to meet new kinds of family needs. In the mid-1980s it first became clear, especially in a big city like Milan, that conventional infant-toddler centers were not always adequate. For example, administrators of these centers could not reach out to families who were isolated yet who held traditional (i.e., mistrustful) attitudes toward early childhood education. Furthermore, because infant-toddler centers were an expensive service, they were limited in their potential for expansion in times of economic recession. Therefore, cities that had well-established early childhood services began to experiment with new models.

The new services had to be tailored to meet the needs of the changing Italian family. Family size was decreasing (Italy today has the world's lowest birth rate with a mean family size of 1.2); parents were becoming older (the average age of first-time mothers rose to 30). We discovered that these demographic changes had profound implications. Contact with families in centers and through surveys showed that for many families the model of the single-child family has brought about an overinvestment in their long-awaited and planned-for child (see Ghedini, Chapter 3, this volume). Furthermore, the data indicated that families in big cities were often isolated and without consistent ideas about children; for example, the family members could not agree about their child's education. Other emerging

 ISBN 0-8077-4008-X (paper), ISBN 0-8077-4009-8 (cloth).

challenges were changing models of parenthood, including the positive feature of stronger father involvement from the earliest months and different views of child rearing brought in by new minority groups. In addition, rising expectations in educational standards brought out doubts, inconsistencies, and the desire to make the most and the best of parenting, to find support from experts and peers, and to share the parenting experience with them. Conflicts seemed frequent within the families with relatively older parents, but conflict between parents' and grandparents' views of child-rearing and education presented another source of disagreement. This was common as grandparents were still major partners for child rearing, with nearly 35 percent of parents with children under 3 relying on them regularly, especially in the smaller communities.

Moreover, isolation and anonymity were high in big cities, so families had further difficulties in locating and using educational services. In many cases, family and educational services seemed to be independent systems, and the services were available and acceptable mainly to two types of families—those with "progressive" attitudes or those with serious problems. The first type were families in which mothers chose to work without ambivalence and for whom a good confidence in public group care was established. The second type—at the opposite extreme—were families involved with social services or who had needs associated with single-parent status. All considered, demands for mediation, counseling, and support were increasing. Awareness of these facts signaled that we needed new forms of educational opportunities for children and parents, and that they should be flexible and multifunctional, with strong opportunities for both adult and child socialization.

In the following pages I will briefly describe the experimental program, Time for Families, which to my knowledge was the first of its kind to start in Italy when it began in Milan in 1985. Time for Families now includes a network of centers in Milan and provides a prototype for a large and growing number of similar initiatives with different names all around Italy (for examples, see Mantovani, Chapter 2, this volume).

UNDERLYING CONCEPTS

Time for Families is based on the assumption that in order to be helpful and empowering to parents, a staff has to be trained to work with young children and also be capable of both good modeling for and developing an appropriate attitude toward parents. This attitude has to be based on respectful and interested observation of each parent-child relationship, generous and discreet listening, and the capacity to share observations and impressions with the team. The staff needs the ability to process strong feelings and challenges to their values that often emerge from daily contact with other people's family relationships. Time for Families assumes that there are no given and predefined ways to be a "good enough" parent.

The goal of the program is to help parents become more aware of their own needs and of their children's characteristics and needs (as revealed in initial interviews and observations).

Although Time for Families uses an individualized approach, it is nevertheless based on some general assumptions about families and their needs. First of all, some families have difficulties in sharing educational responsibilities. They tend to live the first year of parenthood as a private and intimate experience. Though they need support, they tend to mistrust the traditional child care institutions, which were originally intended primarily for children with working parents. It seems obvious, but at times personnel in infant-toddler centers and preschools have seemed to forget parents' desires to share ideas and intentions. Too often the caregivers impose their model without much negotiation with those families who do not already share their ideas.

We believe that a major variable determining good child development is parental satisfaction. That is, parents want the conviction that they (along with their children) can develop around their educational choice, and this becomes a powerful antidote to parental insecurity. We have tried to move beyond the sterile debate over whether center-based care or home care is better for children. Instead, we have assumed that all families have a right to make educational choices. We have tried to assess their needs and then, capitalizing on our past experience with families in the infant-toddler centers, to create appropriate new opportunities for socialization and support.

After the birth of a child, parents encounter many health and social service professionals. The parents are usually eager to find support and information. The professionals, for their part, usually present families with their regulations and norms but do not encourage families to explain their own communicative systems. Instead, they offer forms to fill in, leaflets to read, formal home visits, and health screenings. They ask questions about the child, but seldom do they ask questions about or listen to the things that families feel are important, urgent, or confusing at that time. Many families experience such questioning as external investigation and evaluation of their competence, rather than concern and interest. What parents want is help in answering the simple, everyday questions they face in raising their child.

We believe that, with some support, almost every family has a very good chance to develop secure relationships and to become an effective family. Even when they may seem deficient, they still undeniably have a unique parental relationship with their children. By denying deficiencies or sometimes by pointing them out, we can easily undermine the infinite potential of each family to build an adequate relationship with the child. With Time for Families, we tried to establish a type of service in which parents should be actively involved from the beginning, and whose basic organization should correspond as quickly as possible to the expressed needs of the family. We intended to create a good space and a good time

FIGURE 6.1. Caregivers set up a space where parents can offer experiences of massage for infants. (*Time for Families Giacosa, Milano*)

for both the child and the parents together, rather than supporting their development in isolation from each other, which we believed would not produce a beneficial outcome.

To paraphrase Maria Montessori, we intended to create a setting in which we could *help the family to help itself,* by creating a better communication between different parties, opening up opportunities for them to witness several possible behaviors and solutions, and creating possibilities for active change toward more secure relationships. As highlighted by the name of the program, Time for Families is a very "patient" service, not at all pressed to achieve instant outcomes.

ASSESSING NEEDS

Today, assessing an individual family's needs, checking our ideas and proposals with actual family requests, and adapting realistic possibilities has become a common practice. Yet before Time for Families, this was not so. We introduced a new philosophy, which is the idea that we should not presume to know what specific families need, particularly if one of our goals is to activate *family* self-confidence and positive resources. As part of this philosophy, our training practice brings the working teams together and prepares them to have an appropriate listening attitude. Each team is, from its first meeting, a group with shared ideas and objectives.

In developing our program, we conducted home interviews with 150 families of children under 3. Mothers participated more than fathers, though fathers were often present. We asked them about their lives with their children; changes in their lives; and opinions about education, needs, and difficulties. We also asked what type of resources they would want to use.

These interviews confirmed an acute sense of isolation in many senses: in time (solitude with their child), in space (restricted apartments and lack of open, outdoor spaces), and often in psychological loneliness (particularly among mothers with low schooling who had quit their jobs after the child's birth). Some mothers declared a greater intimacy with their partner after the birth of the child and a close and happy relationship with the baby. However, most complained about loneliness, mutual estrangement, their lack of experience, and therefore their uncertainty about educational choices and how to reorganize the family's life and habits. They complained that life with their child was by no means what they saw advertised by the media: ideal, happy children, always dry, easy to feed, easy to get to sleep, living in tidy homes with mothers with impeccable makeup, lean bodies, and talkative and affectionate husbands.

Most of them were good "average" mothers, but life in the city with a young child often seemed to generate a gray area of malaise, a great need for "getting out" to talk with others, and in the case of children growing older, a need to have some organized space for them to play and meet other children. When we introduced the proposal of a social space for parents and children, with no access formality and the chance to meet other parents and professional staff, most not only seemed enthusiastic, but they urged us to open as soon as possible.

The first Time for Families was opened in February 1986 in a joint effort from the municipality of Milan and the Bernard Van Leer Foundation, with supervision provided by two researchers in psychology from the University of Milan. More than 30 families attended in the first week. After one year, and after moving to a new, more appropriate site, there were 150 participating families. By 1999, there were 11 Time for Families centers, fully established as one of the city's educational services. The last three opened in city areas marked by social problems or heavy migrations, and more should open in the near future. Attendance is always very high, and there are waiting lists, although places are always available for families in special need.

DESCRIPTION AND GOALS

Each Time for Families center has one or two rooms for children's activities. There are professional and paraprofessional staff members present, and parents (or grandparents or baby-sitters) can either observe or take part. There is also another room for adults, where parents can meet and where informal or thematic discussions can be held over a cup of coffee. On certain days, the professional staff is reduced, and parents are supposed to organize their activities by themselves. Every day there is a special activity (e.g., manipulation of colors and play-dough, water play) carried on in a separate room for children in small groups.

Parents and children generally attend three or four times per week for a period of two to three hours each time. Parents can choose the days they attend, but homogeneous age groups are sometimes encouraged (e.g., designating a special day for babies, or as in one particular center, reserving the adult space one day per week for immigrant mothers from Egypt to organize the activities they wish, provided they not exclude others).

The goals of the project include the following:

- To help parents work toward appropriate autonomy for their children and for themselves
- To give the parents a chance to have time and space in which they can compare experiences with other parents, while still being accessible to their children
- To provide parents with an opportunity, through staff modeling and the observation of other parents, to see and experiment with new ways to behave and play with their children

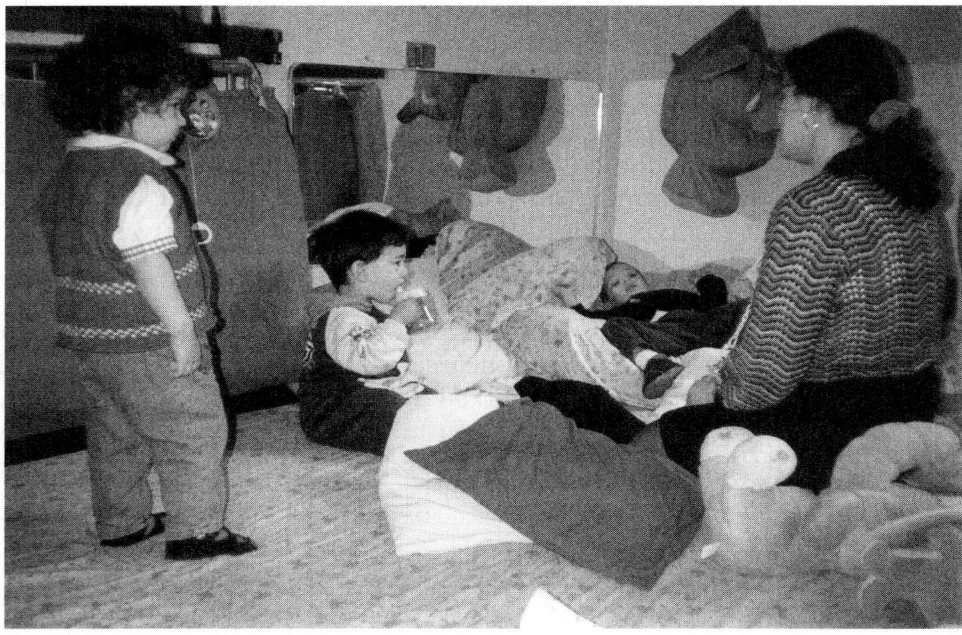

FIGURE 6.2. In a cozy corner caregivers have prepared soft toys and blankets to support closeness and a sense of well-being, among children and adults. (*Time for Families Giacosa, Milano*)

- To give parents a chance to take a break and to share responsibilities in dealing with their children
- To give the children new socialization and play opportunities
- To train staff, who may return to full-time child care services, to tolerate greater flexibility, to work with a parent-child pair and support their relationship, and to lead parent groups

In sum, our aims for the children are to foster secure relationships, autonomy, and competence in dealing with new adults and new peers. For the parents, we intend to encourage sensitivity, consistency, and flexibility.

With Time for Families, we have learned an important lesson: there are *many* various ways to be "good enough" parents. Even those ways we do not like are sometimes "working" for a particular mother-child pair. Of course, our staff is not flawless, nor immune from a tendency to react toward some parents in ways that do not always support and bring about greater self-confidence, better attention to the child, and a more secure relationship. But through continuous in-service training and supervision, we try to enhance and support what we consider to be appropriate, nonjudgmental attitudes.

PARENTS AND CAREGIVERS

In spite of our goals, the role of caregiver is a very demanding one, and the parent-caregiver relationship can often be difficult. At times there is a tendency among caregivers to make parents feel incompetent or even guilty when their child has a problem, is difficult to adjust into the group, or does not accept willingly the caregivers' suggestions. This blame or attribution of guilt to the family becomes an alibi for justifying the professional's failure, one all too common and likely to bring about conflicts or frustration.

But there are still other potential pitfalls for educators who hope to support and activate parents and to help them feel competent and secure in dealing with their children. First, there is a common tendency to overprotect and overassist the parent, and to take responsibility away from him or her. Parents may be seen as inadequate, fragile, in need of help; and the caregiver may feel more competent and superior because of his or her attitudes, pedagogical knowledge, and experience. Parents may be encouraged to be more and more passive, but later their lack of activity can be judged negatively and even be seen as exploiting the caregiver. Second, especially for young caregivers there can be a certain fear of parents, who may be seen as more experienced and the only ones entitled to know the real needs of their child. The caregiver may feel competent enough and willing to play with a child, but prefer to avoid close contact with the parent, feeling especially ill at ease when the parent observes him or her interacting with a child. This often leads to superficial communication, or none at all.

Our practice in Time for Families has allowed us to better understand the difficulties caregivers have in dealing with parents during the adjustment period, at play sessions, and in parents' groups. It has allowed us to build up training models based on observations, group discussion, and supervision. We have seen that the caregiver has the delicate task of welcoming parents, making them feel at home, modeling how to handle a child, and encouraging exchange with other parents in group work. Parents gradually feel more competent as caregivers help them observe their child, know when to engage in joint play and when to let him or her play autonomously, and ultimately reach an optimal distance from that child. In short, the caregiver's role is to support the relationship existing between parent and child, allowing a better but free development of it. To this end, the work at Time for Families has made a major contribution to understanding and practicing a model of training for work with parents—one we feel to be useful also for caregivers working in infant-toddler centers and preschools. By now more than 200 caregivers working in other services have gone through this training.

Educational Support

Seeing adult-child pairs in Time for Families and collecting adults' expressed feelings both during the home visits and during parents' groups, we have come to believe that parents not only need an informal space and an occasion for socializing but also some kind of educational support from staff. They need a calm, consistent, sensitive model—a patient but steady support to integrate into the new environment. Our staff is supposed to become a reference for the family and a way to rebuild lost social experiences. They should be ready to let themselves be observed by the parents, modeling a sound relationship with the child—not merely talking about it. It is a particular and delicate task that cannot be reduced to interventions to foster development, as was often the choice in many early intervention programs. Caregivers should model appropriately, not be intrusive, and convey the message that the parent is the basic reference for the child and that he or she is important and potentially competent. A merely instructional intervention would be ineffective for eliciting the parent's own style and competencies. In order to support the emotional and cognitive growth of the child, the caregiver has to support the child *together with* the significant family adult.

It is a unique role, and it leads to unique relationships. The caregiver has to become a reference point and a significant figure, both for the child and for the adult family member. The caregiver also encourages the parent to observe his or her child, and this creates a favorable situation both to elicit interest and curiosity in the child—discovering his or her potential—and to gain optimal distance, avoiding intrusive interventions. In an interactive context of this kind, the caregiver introduces modeling and specific proposals to parent and child. The parent can observe the caregiver, evaluate, and eventually try out similar behaviors at Time for Families or at home, according to his or her own judgment and rhythms.

Style, ways of communicating, the capacity to be very discreet and nonintrusive but to control the group situation and to contain anxieties and emotions, as well as the planning of interventions and interactions, all are crucial aspects of the caregivers' professionalism. It is obvious that such tasks require maturity, competencies in observation and analysis of the interactions taking place, and the capacity to rethink and discuss in depth observed sequences of interactions. Our training has tried to develop such abilities. It is group-based, and through the regular staff organizational and training meetings, it also aims to give caregivers a time and a space in their minds to rethink their observations. Our training intends to give caregivers opportunities to process their feelings, to define and formulate their implicit educational and family values so that they do not undermine but instead support program goals. We feel that these skills can also be useful to caregivers who, after working for a period at Time for Families, return to work at more traditional child care centers or preschools.

FIGURE 6.3. A space organized as a workshop for adults is prepared to sustain and value the competencies of parents and guide them to participate in working with caregivers. (*Time for Families Giacosa, Milano*)

Parent Groups

The second part of providing support is through parent groups. I shall not go into great detail about these because we are still experimenting with the model and our evaluation is ongoing. Our discussion is enriched by the continuing new experiences of groups with non-Italian mothers and also groups with expectant parents, which develop into postnatal support groups.

Parent groups in Time for Families are free of charge, informal, and designed for flexible participation. They are now a major feature of our programs. Family members, particularly couples, also meet in the evenings to discuss specific questions. Sometimes requests for a sequence of thematic discussions emerge from the parents. Usually these deal with parents' own real-life experiences with their children, within the context of the family and within the context of the couple. From the beginning we have been astonished by the quantity and quality of emotions and issues, and by the need to share that bubbles up in parent groups. Overcoming a phase when we basically thought families needed good professional counseling once they had had the chance to tell others about doubts and problems, we discovered that counseling was generally ineffective in bringing about change. We found that parents are great consumers of professionals' suggestions. They often managed either to put them into practice so automatically and rigidly as to immediately guarantee their ineffectiveness or to ask for them and then ignore them.

On the contrary, the mere exchange with other parents' experiences and opinions had a major impact: finding out that others had the same problems immediately demystified them and put them in a more understandable perspective. Listening to other people's solutions motivated parents to research their own solutions and gave them the confidence that a solution, no matter which one, was possible. Other parents could ask questions, make suggestions, even criticize and be ironic without putting the others in an inferior position. This elicited more confidence and activity in the group. Often concrete common initiatives, mutual support, or other forms of networking came about from groups, though the same actions had failed when proposed by professionals. The parent group seems to act the way a peer group does for young children: favoring exchange, allowing unthreatening opportunities to disagree—even strongly—and eliciting new solutions and discoveries.

Time for Families parent-group meetings can be informal or thematic in nature. There can be groups for talking or groups for doing, such as preparing materials for the playroom. An experienced caregiver with proper training and supervision can lead informal groups. Professionals in education or psychology lead thematic groups, which usually emerge after a few informal group meetings on a theme. The basic style for the leading professional is at the same time very nondirective and very directive. It is nondirective in the sense that no questions are asked, no evaluation is given, and emerging contents are paraphrased and offered for clear discussion. It is directive in the sense that the group leader always maintains control of the organization of the discussion, guarantees the possibility of exploring the theme in depth, and mediates the strong emotions and conflict that may emerge every time very intimate experiences and personal choices are being discussed.

CONCLUDING THOUGHTS

Time for Families started in 1985 with the goal of sustaining isolated parents of young children. Our intention has been to help them gain a sense of self-confidence so that they could help themselves. We have prepared professionals to be respectful and interested reference points for families in order to sustain children's secure relationships, autonomy, and competence, while at the same time encouraging parents' sensitivity, consistency, and flexibility.

Our work continues: we have tried—and to some extent succeeded—in exporting our experience and training with parent groups from Time for Families into infant-toddler centers and preschools, where families increasingly ask for times and spaces to meet and talk with other families. Sharing what we have learned is consistent with the philosophy of Time for Families as a new service embedded in the general system of the city's educational services. We are proud, and cite as a good result, that many of "our" parents have become active in their home-school relationship and in parents' committees in their children's schools, now all the way up to middle school.

Chapter 7

PARMA: SUPPORTING THE WORK OF TEACHERS THROUGH PROFESSIONAL DEVELOPMENT, ORGANIZATION, AND ADMINISTRATIVE SUPPORT

Nice Terzi and Marialuisa Cantarelli

The program of professional development in Parma has been developing over 20 years and involves three elements. The first is the organization of professional development and in-service preparation of teachers. The second is the organization of work within the infant-toddler centers, for example with regard to space, time, rhythm, materials, and relationships. The third is the organization of work between administrators and teachers, such as the tasks of pedagogical coordination, admission policy, personnel management, and so on.

In Parma we believe that the system of professional development is closely connected to the organization and professionalism of the work of the teachers. We consider our system to be one of the most important assets of our educational service. In this chapter, the system of professional development will be described, including our outreach to cooperative and private institutions serving children in the area.

ASSUMPTIONS UNDERLYING OUR APPROACH

We have worked toward an eclectic approach that can accommodate content and methods from many disciplines. It is a participatory process, one

---

"negotiated" by the personnel who benefit from it, so that its content and its very sequence derive from their needs. Professional development requires a careful and deep reading of the educators' needs. We try to respond to more than educators' usual requests to extend their technical skill and knowledge of operating procedures and theoretical foundations. We have found we must also address their deeper (perhaps unspoken) needs and help them reflect on the direction for their own work.

This type of professional development has helped define a new sense of professional identity among teachers. That identity is marked by communication with and listening to children, families, and colleagues. Our model of professional development encourages teachers to practice "reading" attitudes and emotions, paying attention to them, and understanding them. It has made teachers more aware of how delicate it is to intervene in the close relationship between children and parents. Our professional development continually redirects teachers' inquiries from "*what* to do" to "*how* to do."

We have built a program of professional development based on our concern about the many sources of fatigue, strain, and emotional tension that teachers and staff experience every day in their work. In fact, we consider that the dignity of their emotions has to be recognized and that the educators' ability to consciously control their own feelings and reactions has to be valued along with other professional skills. This has meant introducing topics into our in-service program on subjects such as children's developing ability to regulate their emotions, the significance of emotional "distance" versus "closeness" in all relationships, and the need for continually refining the delicacy of teacher interventions.

With regard to the relationship with families, our services entrust their mission to the teachers and staff who operate in direct contact with the children and families. We are all aware that there is no foolproof system of control that anticipates and prevents all problems, but instead only a system that allows for reflection afterward. Therefore, we take great care in personnel preparation and try to build a deep trust in those who carry out our overall objectives. Reaching our objectives depends on how well we succeed in preparing our personnel because most of the time educators have to decide autonomously on the most appropriate intervention in any given situation, with little or no opportunity to consult with a colleague or one of the pedagogical coordinators in advance. Corrective intervention can take place after the fact on the basis of a request by the educator, who expresses his or her doubts or uncertainties, or awareness about the need to reflect further on what happened. This intervention, with the opportunity to reflect systematically on his or her own work, enriches the educator's professional knowledge and, in our view, contributes to building trustworthiness. Trustworthiness is not built as a result of authoritative indications but rather through a personal and subjective maturation, enriched by the individual resources and the personal style of each educator.

Our in-service program begins with the assumption that people who do this kind of work, if they have a professional disposition (attitude) and motivation, will be guided by a subjective frame of mind when deciding the most useful intervention in a given situation. We have to be aware that they are guided not so much (or not only) by what they believe is better rationally, but ultimately, by what they believe is most opportune in terms of internal convictions that are deeply rooted in and intimately held by each individual.

Thus, teachers who must translate newly acquired knowledge into daily practice cannot be limited to superficial and purely intellectual learning. Instead, they must acquire an authentic habit of mind, deeply held and almost instinctive. In order for this to happen, they have to develop abilities to read and evaluate situations so that practice derives from an autonomous understanding of what is useful and why.

In fact, the goal of our in-service work involves convincing teachers not to accept other people's beliefs as if they were prescriptions to be followed rigidly. Instead, the goal is to create a culture of teaching that raises confidence, recognizes and refines individual resources, and invests in teachers' potentials. That implies a long-term effort with a focus on work with the teachers rather than on concrete planning. This focus inevitably produces some frustration, as teachers must sometimes tolerate temporary situations of partial uncertainty rather than getting immediate results. Our work together was not driven by adherence to one model of teaching, but rather by theoretical principles and clarity of proposals, goals, and motives. We allowed time for reflection and debate in order to achieve deeper understanding.

ORGANIZATION OF PROFESSIONAL DEVELOPMENT

Further issues arose as we created a structure and organization of professional development. In our discussions, we formed the conviction that teachers must assume the daily responsibility for choices and decisions in their work with children and parents. They cannot endure the schizophrenia of being in some ways autonomous in decision making and in other ways completely dependent. Instead, they need to participate in the planning of their work and also must be able to make choices about their own professional development.

Our plan for professional development provides two opportunities within the in-service program structured to sustain teachers' decision-making responsibility. The first consists of giving individuals and/or teaching teams the possibility of making choices from among the menu of in-service proposals scheduled annually. This choice is a very useful motivator, especially where in-service preparation is free and required, as in the best systems. It also balances the diverse needs and interests of all the parties, including the institution and all the various individuals (who may even have changing professional needs as they go through different phases of their lives). And not least of all, it allows us to acknowledge the dimension of personal preference.

The second opportunity concerns teacher self-evaluation. As teachers come to the end of each part of their in-service preparation, they are asked to look back on what they have learned. For teachers, this goes way beyond simple content and means "evaluating their own learning." They do this individually and also in group contexts among the colleagues with whom they shared the experience. In fact, the group can affirm the positive points from each member or bring out doubts and constructive reflection on the experience. We think that all this evaluation functions to develop teachers' abilities to self-regulate, fundamental to our professionalism and services.

ORGANIZATION OF THE INFANT-TODDLER SYSTEM

The understandings we have gained about professional development have changed the organization of work in our infant-toddler centers. We have chosen to favor continuity of educators with small, stable groups of children. We made this choice as a result of reflection by our educators, guided by university researchers. Together, they considered theoretical assumptions and also did systematic observations of children of different ages and in different classrooms. They thought about how adults could best sustain play and exchanges among children, and decided that greater continuity and stability were beneficial. They then used their decision in organizing the programs and classrooms and designing processes for the *inserimento,* or "period of transition" for new children and families.

In addition, in order to improve our capacity to address family needs, we have concentrated on providing flexible, economical services by experimenting with a space arrangement we call the "apartment" (a small center containing one or two classrooms and a kitchen). We have also created a service we call the Play Center. We presently have 16 infant-toddler centers and one Play Center in our system.

Daily Schedules and Physical Spaces

Children attending our infant-toddler centers are grouped into either *short-day* (until 2:00 p.m.) or *normal-day* (until 3:30 p.m.) rooms. This schedule is helpful also for part-time working parents. Teachers have fixed schedules so that the children see the same teacher each morning. Some children have the opportunity for *extended day* (until 5 p.m.), necessarily involving a rotating teacher schedule.

In thinking about the physical space for these groupings, we began with criticism of the quality of standard, prefabricated spaces that resemble preschools. This led us to prefer home-like characteristics within the context of rather small apartment spaces. The apartment centers allowed us to address the needs of the very youngest babies, who were being brought to us in ever-larger numbers. We also wanted to introduce into each center (spread over the zones of the city) the addition of short-day classrooms without penalizing any other age group by adding more groups of children in the same centers.

Grouping Children According to Age

Each infant-toddler center has a mixed-age group of children from the youngest to the oldest. Within this group, children may be organized in mixed-age or same-age subgroups according to their teachers' choice. Each mixed-age group has 18 children: 10 little ones (13–24 months) and 8 big ones (24–36 months).

We had begun with the educational goal of allowing children mixed-age exchanges that would be rich both relationally and cognitively. In particular, the apartment infant-toddler centers allow the older children to be "teachers" of the younger ones. The older children are supported in their good nature and tenderness toward the little ones. The older children are rewarded by admiration from the younger ones and develop their ability to take different perspectives. For the younger children, these centers encourage a natural, imitative attitude, and allow an active response to the older children.

Groupings of Children with Adults

Each mixed-age group is subdivided into two subgroups of nine children, each with a primary caregiver (reference person) and homeroom space. The subgroups are stable throughout the year, though they are flexible and involve progressively more time spent together with the whole group. The primary caregiver assumes the responsibility for the subgroup of children and the relationships with them during each child's transition (*inserimento*) into the group. Transitions take place individually or in small groups, little by little throughout the year.

Because we are aware of how an individualized relationship facilitates the child's autonomy from the teacher and within the group, the teacher gives attention to both personal and group relationships, thus constructing a sort of "mental map" of the relational life of the group.

REFLECTIONS ON PROFESSIONAL DEVELOPMENT AND ORGANIZATION OF SERVICES

During the years when we were creating and modifying our approach to professional development, we were also reorganizing the ways in which we delivered our infant-toddler services. We brought issues of organization into our in-service discussions. In fact, as individual teachers and teacher teams made small experiments in their programs, we brought some of their thinking into wider discussion. Thus, before the local experiments were stabilized into permanent components of the overall organization of services, other teachers had the possibility to decide if they would try an innovation, to evaluate its advantages for children and for themselves, to consider its practical and emotional difficulties, and to modify it.

For example, with regard to using a primary caregiver system, two teachers from the same classroom (who had validated the usefulness of this strategy during their professional development and who had worked for a long time with all the children together in the same room) decided to experiment with working in two rooms with two subgroups for a year. Then they assessed the positive and negative aspects of the experience. They described more emotional fatigue and more intensive attention and responsibility, but also more satisfaction, deeper knowledge of each child in the subgroup and of the relationships within the larger group, and, furthermore, greater clarity about their own roles.

The method we used during professional development meetings was to move from theory to practice by inviting teachers to try certain new experiments in their settings: "Anyone who is interested, try it!" We left it for each individual teacher or teaching team to decide. Ours was a journey composed of reflections and successive adjustments, sometimes on the part of the teachers, and other times on the part of the administrators. We passed through phases of rigidity before finding a balance that includes leeway for personal autonomy. Above all, it was a journey that required many years from the first experiments to the expansion through all our centers.

The journey with teachers involved a parallel journey with families. Families must always participate in the evolution of programs and services. In our case, they were involved on formal occasions, such as steering committee meetings, and informal occasions, such as the numerous meetings held at the classroom level.

THE TOSCANINI PLAY CENTER: TEACHERS AND PARENTS IN A COMPLEX SYSTEM OF RELATIONS

We can illustrate how close work with families affected the process and outcomes of teacher professional development by looking at the story of one program. The Toscanini Play Center opened in 1988 and is located within the infant-toddler center of the same name. The program is open every day from 7:30 a.m. to 2:00 p.m. and serves families with children under age 4 who do not attend other city services. The program serves two goals. The first is to offer young families a type of program that could respond to the changing developmental, educational, and socialization needs of their child in a flexible way. The second goal is to create a space for communication, socialization, and discussion among adults, including educators, parents, and grandparents.

During a series of professional development meetings on these new types of services, we first addressed the demanding role of teachers in more flexible services. Teachers suggested that their role was a constructive challenge for them. Working with both children and adults together was uncomfortable for them and seemed to require exceptional professionalism, as they had to be simultaneously teachers, activity leaders, consultants, and social workers. If they concentrated on only one of these roles at a time, they seemed to lose the big picture of what was happening, as if they were on a bus with no driver. They felt there was the risk that they were the ones picking up the pieces, dealing with the fragments of superficial relationships involving the children and parents. Meanwhile, they were not satisfying the parents, who were communicating their own uneasiness to the teachers and to the administration.

The teachers attempted various solutions as they tried to deal with their feelings of inadequacy and make some sense of the situation, but none of these was wholly satisfactory. Sometimes they tried to find an educational style that mirrored the particular style of a parent but yet was comfortable to the teacher, in the interest of keeping everything under control. At other times, they maintained responsibility for the group of children but let pedagogical coordinators take over the group of parents. On still other occasions, they would let the group of parents become completely dependent on them, leaving them feeling fatigued, professionally isolated, and emotional overloaded as a consequence of dealing with both children and their dependent parents—who seemed, at worst, insecure, argumentative, and uncooperative.

In order to solve our problems, we had to reexamine the situation searching for clarity, organization, and coherence. We had to redesign a unifying role for the teacher as a flexible mediator and find ways to eliminate teachers' anxiety, feelings of inadequacy, and professional isolation, and address parents' uneasiness. To achieve these goals, it became critical to prepare a long-range plan of professional development and to hire additional personnel on-site (such as a pedagogical coordinator or a social worker). All these processes supported the teachers as they continued their observations and made decisions about interventions.

From the time we first began to plan the Play Center, we had assumed, in line with the rest of our thinking, that teacher professional development would be the linchpin of the new service, even if we were not yet completely clear what was needed. Looking back, that was the right assumption. On the explicit level, we were faced with the problem of trying to understand what was happening within the new program. On the implicit level, however, the deeper problem was to define the process of preparing teachers to work in this new program. We had to redefine old roles and job descriptions. We had to answer the question that teachers kept asking, Who does what and with whom?

FIGURES 7.1 and 7.2. Children are involved in activities while parents and teachers converse. (*Play Center Toscanini, Parma*)

To get to the answers, we all had to become a working group of researchers. Together, we searched to clarify our goals and find what we could all feel were "good" solutions, gradually coconstructed for the Toscanini Play Center. As a group, we all became simultaneously teachers and learners. From that point on, we were able to develop useful approaches to the professional preparation relevant to realizing our objectives and plans for the Play Center.

ORGANIZATION OF WORK BETWEEN ADMINISTRATION AND TEACHERS: THE ROLE OF PEDAGOGICAL COORDINATORS

Now we arrive at the role and the function of the administration. All the goals and strategies outlined up to this point rest on the existence of highly qualified pedagogical coordinators who work closely with the city director of services for children under 3 years of age. The coordinators perform two fundamental tasks for the system: administration and professional development.

These tasks do not coexist easily, as they encompass some partly contradictory aspects. The duties of administration and organization of work include both management and control functions, tasks that often are characterized by interventions after the fact and that tend to evoke defensive reactions.

Our approaches to technical support of teachers and professional development do not fit well into a pattern of top-down bureaucratic control. Instead, they are based on strong professional responsibility of all staff, activation of internal resources, nonjudgmental attitudes, and a strong alliance between administration and teachers. This implicit "contract" with teachers makes it possible for them to trust the administration. Teachers can confront and discuss the difficulties of their work without fear, rather than covering up problems and making it seem that everything is just fine.

In order to limit, as much as possible, any confusion between roles, we chose to separate the tasks of management and on-site supervision. First, certain tasks having to do with the management and organization of services are clearly distributed among the pedagogical coordinators, in an explicit way that keeps vital information accessible to all. Second, each coordinator, besides having precise management tasks, serves as the pedagogical consultant for a specific set of the infant-toddler centers. In this environment people become accustomed to listening, attending, and allowing emotional checks and balances. As pedagogical consultant, each coordinator tries to facilitate cooperation in the assigned group of teachers and staff in order to understand the issues that they encounter from time to time. Those can be difficulties the educators present from their work with children, parents, or colleagues. The pedagogical coordinators also share various experiences and opinions with the teachers, and they sustain and promote overall planning and evaluation. For more general professional development (i.e., continuing education), we turn to outside experts, such as university professors or administrators from other cities.

All this requires time and predictable occasions for teacher meetings within each classroom, team, and center. Such meetings become truly functional places for exchange and communication, for creating continuity among fragmented experiences. Each coordinator meets with all the teachers in the infant-toddler center twice a month as a collective team. In addition, the coordinator meets with each classroom group of two or three teachers once a month. These meetings allow us to connect real-life experiences with the knowledge we have acquired from professionals inside our system as well as outside. Through this process, we have gradually constructed our approach to professional development with a collective memory. Both become the legacy of our services.

But the core of the coordinators' and city director's roles is to be mediators and to maintain an open dialogue with those who work in the centers, to assume responsibility for what both coordinators and director suggest, to be willing to give and take criticism, and sometimes also to deal with moments of resentment and anger. Strong negative emotions are part of the life of institutions and relationships. Unless people are given opportunity to express frustration and resentment, they can fall into negativism, misunderstanding, absenteeism, and burnout. In contrast, when they have safe places, times, and procedures for open expression of emotion, within the limits of courtesy and civility, then they can control damaging impulses and reinterpret them in a constructive manner.

Pedagogical coordinators also, like teachers and staff, need safe places and times for themselves. And it is necessary, even obligatory, that they too continue their in-service process of professional development. The city director of the infant-toddler services is responsible for carrying out a continuous program for the professional development of the pedagogical coordinators. This takes the form of a meeting held every two weeks, and it provides a space for sharing reflections on ongoing work, discussing difficulties in the operations of the center, or discussing issues involving a single child, relations with parents, or among staff. These biweekly meetings sustain the richness of a group effort with all its potential for collaboration. They represent professional development for everyone involved and are included in the work schedule.

In addition to these meetings, another type of regular meeting occurs. The city director of services and coordinators meet in order to make decisions and plan the overall development and organization of services. It is an important opportunity within the administration and coordination function itself. The pedagogical coordinators explain and listen to each other's reasoning, achieve consensus or air dissent, and understand their colleagues' positions. These meetings constitute the basis for constructing and revising plans that are sufficiently shared to move ahead.

We must not forget that the coordinators, just like the teachers and staff, tend to act on and communicate to others that which they actually have played a part in planning. We should not underrate this group decision making, because it is a tool to guarantee tranquility and autonomy at each step in accomplishing the work entrusted to us. Furthermore, everyone continues to feel "ownership" of work done by both self and others.

OUTREACH

This whole system of professional development and its accumulated knowledge are now at the disposition of private citizens who work with young children. They have grown to trust the services and make requests to continue their education. For many years we have offered professional development courses for staff at the infant-toddler centers that receive part but not all of their funding from the city, as well as at nonprofit child care cooperatives that operate in our territory.

We have made this choice for several reasons. For one thing, we are convinced that raising awareness and sharing information are unique responsibilities of the public sector. For another, we wish to experiment with public-private collaboration, as the staff of these different institutions now participate in professional development with our personnel in mixed groups. This also encourages "cross-pollination" and exchanges among people who work in the two contexts. The plans for professional development are now drawn up in cooperation with the other institutions, which raises issues that are emerging from their sphere of action, and they participate with us in assessments at the conclusion of each cycle of professional development. Finally, we believe that it is vital to help create a common language about children and a high level of quality of care and education throughout institutions, while maintaining a diversity of experiences.

Chapter 8

PISTOIA: CREATING A DYNAMIC, OPEN SYSTEM TO SERVE CHILDREN, FAMILIES, AND COMMUNITY

Annalia Galardini and Donatella Giovannini

This chapter about infant and toddler centers in Pistoia has two main divisions. In the first section, Donatella Giovannini, pedagogical coordinator, speaks about creating favorable spaces for children, including the teacher's role in making the environment meaningful and constructive for children. In the second part, Annalia Galardini, director of the early education system of the city, describes how relationships are created and sustained with families and the local community.

CREATING FAVORABLE SPACES FOR CHILDREN AND FAMILIES

It was by no means an easy task to develop the educational identity of our services and to clarify the educational intent for institutions directed to very young children. Our challenge has been to invent and perfect new strategies and to construct new environments for children that promote experiences of relationship and learning. Today, we have accumulated a wealth of knowledge and pedagogical practice that are in a constant process of adaptation and organization.

In particular, we want to focus here on how to create meaningful opportunities for exploration and play in infant-toddler programs, in order to stimulate children's social and cognitive development during the course

---

of every day. These goals require the preparation of a physical and social context that is rich and predictable for children.

The quality and organization of space and time in the educational setting can encourage exploration, support the development of abilities, help maintain concentration, and give a sense of belonging and well-being to a young child.

Clear and Evocative Prepared Spaces

The quality of the space within the infant-toddler center can be improved, in order to support children's action and autonomy, by creating specialized places that respond to the different ages of children and their different activities. For example, for infants under one year, we prepare spaces by constructing soft and supporting structures created by long, snake-like stuffed pillows (covered with washable cloth) that can be placed in different configurations. Our teachers design these pillows and make them working together with parents (see Figures 8.1 and 8.2). For toddlers, who like to move in and out of enclosed spaces and put objects in and out of containers, we provide a small house-like structure where the children can hide or take some of their favorite toys. For the children between 2 and 3 years of age, we design spaces for painting, looking at books, explor-

FIGURES 8.1 and 8.2. Teachers and parents together prepare soft spaces for infants under one year. (*Infant-toddler Center Il Sole, Pistoia*)

FIGURE 8.2.

ing the natural world, engaging dramatic and symbolic play, and so on (see Figures 8.3 and 8.4).

These spaces can be made *evocative* so as also to encourage imagination and expression. For example, the puppet theater always has a central place in every infant-toddler center, and through puppets and fairy tales, teachers and children explore imaginary roles together and confront emotions. This environment evokes the creation and re-creation of imaginary characters: the Little Gray Mice, Rainbow Magician, and Prezzemolina ("Little Parsley"), among many. These give life to a collective imaginary world that can easily be found in a community of young children. The characters create a familiar place, a secure psychological space around the children that is particular to each center. This special space becomes a sort of affective and cognitive envelope that renders the environment of the center more enjoyable. We could tell of many characters who came for long stays at the centers and became part of the life there. They have tied together a large variety of play experiences and have actively stimulated the children. For example, the witch, Nerina, a character who came out of the dark in one center when teachers and children were playing together, became a connecting theme for a series of projects, dramatizations, and play activities. Although this character was nourished by children's fears, such fears within the group of peers and adults could be controlled and almost enjoyed.

The Constructive Messages of Objects and Materials

When materials and tools are available in large and attractive variety, infants and toddlers take pleasure in handling objects, placing them in and out of containers, or combining them in many ways. In fact, young children like to be in charge of their own small realizations and discoveries. The types of objects that they find guide their reflections. Every object brings out different play behaviors and different forms of thinking. Objects contain messages in the possible ways in which they can be combined and in their variety. Objects can encourage children to experiment actively, make connections, and act on their own thoughts.

Furthermore, the diversity of materials offered makes it possible to repeat activities in a more varied way. In fact, for an activity to be truly formative and meaningful, it should be offered more than once. Children absorb the implicit possibilities when an experience is consolidated and repeated. The adult should introduce new levels of play only when previous levels are consolidated. When there is a balance between what is known and what is almost ready to be known—not far beyond the knowledge and competencies that the children possess—then proposals become interesting, pleasant, and intriguing (as defined by Vygotsky's concept of *zone of proximal development*, discussed in Bodrova & Leong, 1996).

We pay great attention to the presentation of materials as a way to offer children an intense, absorbing experience. What we call a *generous*

FIGURES 8.3 and 8.4. For children between 2 and 3 years of age the space is prepared to engage them in a variety of play, exploration, and construction activities. (*Infant-toddler Center Lago Mago, Pistoia*)

environment is one in which the generosity derives not only from the richness and the variety of materials provided but also from the teachers' attitudes, implicit in the care with which materials have been sought out, selected, and offered to children. It is a generosity of attitude characterized by attention and listening by adults who know how to observe, offer things, and pace their offerings at the right moment. In this way, teachers sustain children's attention and coinvolvement, reanimate their interest when necessary, and value what they do.

We also try to make the environment clear and predictable—what we call *legible.* It becomes understandable and meaningful, even to children younger than 2, through the use of colors and images. For children between 2 and 3, symbols can also be added to indicate functions. For example, with children between 2 and 3, we like to prepare an "ecological area" that contains natural materials, such as pebbles, twigs, seeds, and leaves, organized on open shelves and ready for manipulation (see Figures 8.5 and 8.6). Children begin to construct an understanding of symbolic language by using containers distinguished in color and labeled with symbols signifying their contents.

This kind of organization also supports neatness, tidiness, and autonomy. Young children find it difficult to organize paths for the construction of knowledge in situations that they do not control. When they can work without constant intervention, their autonomy increases. Their capacity to focus improves, not through verbal requests from adults but because of their own motivation. For example, in our ecological area, children themselves contribute to the order of the environment in their desire to find things they like or to make room for special objects brought from home.

Connected play experiences allow children to extend and continue experiments, which become enriched and more complex over time, integrating new knowledge (see Musatti & Mayer, Chapter 13, this volume). Many proposals for play engage the children for several days. This teaches the children tenacity in the realization of a project. What prevents this process from becoming repetitious? It is not merely that they encounter new stimuli, and not simply that they gradually grow in their skills and ability. Rather, it is that teachers consciously select experiences and materials that have potential for creating connections. They enrich children's experiences over time by planning ahead. Teachers then recognize the persistence that children demonstrate as the result of their support over a long period of time. Furthermore, when children are engaged in such connected, coherent experiences, they gain a sense of control, understand what is taking place, and secure the keys for reading their own actions.

Environments that are predictable and organized encourage children to share their action and play in a conducive and emotionally positive way. In fact, a favorable environment creates a positive climate that becomes evident in gestures of cooperation and kindness among children. In contrast, when materials are scarce, activities monotonous, objects uninteresting, or there is chaos, then the harmony of play is inhibited, children

FIGURES 8.5 and 8.6. An experience with natural materials that went from gathering, exploring, and organizing to creating a personal interpretation through a collage. (*Infant-toddler Center Il Faro, Pistoia*)

FIGURE 8.6.

tend to move impatiently from one thing to the next, and competition and conflict may increase.

The Role of the Teacher

For the environment to be set up skillfully, attention must be given to the roles of teachers and their abilities to construct together a flexible, organic plan of work. One great risk that must be avoided is to allow everyday life—the cadence and rhythms of routine—to overwhelm the building of meaningful new connections. Certainly, the routines of arrival, meals, activities, and rest offer familiar support, but if we become inattentive and unreflective, we begin to miss the richness that is inherent in everyday life. When we rely too automatically on familiar actions, the running of the center becomes too much like domestic management.

Without thoughtful organization, teachers fall into mechanical repetition of actions rather than making productive new connections. However, when equipped with good planning tools (such as observation and documentation), they can get to know their group of children and the children's interests and propose spaces and activities, without having to improvise the composition of the group and the proposal every morning. Our experience demonstrates that when teachers work with stable groups of children whom they know well, that builds the quality of the program. Such a practice allows teachers to predict the children's preferred repertoire of activities and to create opportunities for play that are both socially and intellectually attractive and stimulating.

The role of the teacher is not limited to preparing and organizing the environment in anticipation of projects and activities. It also includes becoming involved in children's actions. When the teacher is attentive and closely involved in children's play, this increases the significance of children's gestures and words. As the teacher comments on what is happening, she supports children's curiosity, perceptions, and emotions, and helps children to recognize their thoughts and share them with the group. In fact, the teacher can repeat what one particular child said, making the meaning clearer. Thereby, she supports those strategies and actions of the child that are most effective and integrates them with contributions from other children. The teacher assumes an important tutorial role and becomes the director of the entire educational happening.

Many people consider it difficult to maintain a consistent attitude of involvement and emotional sharing with children, and this is a legitimate concern. But in our view, what usually makes a teacher uneasy is not a fundamental lack of personal caring and sensitivity, but rather bad past experiences of having set up situations that are not favorable for children. This can be corrected through professional development. We want each teacher to be able to enter into a sense of genuine closeness or "complicity" with children, which should not be confused with a general benevolence. Rather, complicity is an attitude constructed over time and based

FIGURE 8.7. The teacher participates with children in play with percussion instruments. This was part of a long sequence of exploration of sounds. (*Infant-toddler Center Lago Mago, Pistoia*)

on a commitment toward getting to know the children well and recognizing their serious and tenacious way of engaging in play.

As the teacher attends to the role of "partner-in-play," she can develop an attitude of empathy toward children—not too demonstrative, not too cold and indifferent. Empathy means the "right time." The important thing when we share daily life with children (in particular when we share moments of play) is not necessarily to reach an important "truth," but instead to be able to encounter one another, listening without misunderstanding, without overriding the other's meaning, in harmony based on deep, mutual familiarity.

To be able to put oneself in this meaningful situation allows a teacher to be open to the communicative style of each child. She can offer individualized attention not only to those who do very well or those who misbehave, but instead to each child and each unique style, without indulging in quick evaluations or incorrect assumptions. The teacher can respect the time and rhythm of each child, learn a nonintrusive attitude, and take account of individual temperaments. For example, some children enter into play right away, while others wait and find pleasure only after watching, sometimes for quite a while, what the others do. All together, the teacher's role in the infant-toddler center is complex and never boring. The teacher creates a favorable context for opportunities of playing and learning, for listening to children, and for becoming a witness to children's experiences, through competent documentation.

The role of witness to the experiences, along with the role of director and the role of observer of children, carries the teacher far from the traditional role of showing children what to do and how to do it. In this multifaceted role, the teacher becomes truly involved in what the children are doing. She becomes a partner in play and gives value to the children and their actions, always extending and supporting their expressions (see Figure 8.7). The children come to have positive feelings about how their initiatives will be received, and they learn to trust that special grownups will be present and available to help them when they need it.

FAMILY AND COMMUNITY RELATIONSHIPS

The care and education of young children, as we have seen, involves a dynamic mix of human relationships and careful organization. In this section, we will address issues of participation, responsibility, and community belonging as necessary steps to creating a favorable culture of childhood in Pistoia.

Throughout Italy, we have found that public systems work best to serve young children and families when they are deeply rooted in the local community. Therefore, public administrators have tried to establish community relationships based on connections, debate, and collaboration. Educators have become very effective at bringing about innovation at the local level. Municipal governments have planned and established interventions and practices that have stimulated change and advanced solutions later introduced into national legislation. Other European countries have come to look with interest at the work done in Italy, and in particular at the fact that many cities have created integrated, efficient, and culturally appropriate systems of children's centers.

In Pistoia, we take it as our starting point to base our work on the principle of establishing meaningful relationships in the centers for young children. We try to guarantee that our centers are closely connected with the surrounding community and are part of an overall educational project that gives children a sense of greater belonging (Galardini, Giovannini, & Iozzelli, 1999). Therefore, we must try to determine and respond to family needs and match them with services and programs. We must not only maintain high-quality services, but also we must constantly improve and add to them so that they come to better fit changing local conditions.

Constructing an Alliance Between Home and Center

To achieve our vision, we continually try to construct an alliance and coherent connection between the two worlds in which children live: home and infant-toddler center. The crucial point is to create harmony on the part of the adults (parents and educators) who have different responsibilities, emotions, feelings, knowledge, and attitudes toward the children.

Each child needs to feel enclosed in a network of relationships and solidarities that are a source of security and protection (see Figures 8.8 and 8.9).

This careful attention to relationship is consistent with the latest research in child development. We have moved from theories focused narrowly on individual development to ones addressing children in context. Child development is now considered a process of social construction that takes place in the context of close and meaningful relationships with adults and peers. There is no doubt that a rich, integrated network of interpersonal relationships represents for children a great potential for growth. Thus, in our services for young children, the construction of the relationship between family and center has taken a rich and varied path, tightly woven with that of the overall educational project.

There are three ways in which we can describe our strategies for building relationships between children's centers and families: organization, communication, and exchange.

Organization. The first way of promoting relationship concerns various organizational aspects of the center (schedule, admission, fees). In each center, parents elect a committee of representatives responsible for providing direction to the center and promoting opportunities for parents to meet. Parents participate in this committee as a way to guarantee the center's connection to family needs and as a democratic check on the management of services. The parent committees of various centers work together and are recognized as the citizens' cumulative voice in defining general objectives for the organization of services for young children. By supporting parental involvement in financial and organizational choices, the public administration shows how it values the involvement of families.

Communication. The second way to support connection between families and centers more properly expresses the educational scope of the programs. The children's centers are repositories of knowledge and accumulated value as places of learning. They are places where educators meet parents to explain and communicate the beautiful, interesting, and important things that children do. The adults share ideas about children and reflections on the educational task. To this end, our educators have expanded their commitment to creating different forms of documentation, thereby preserving memories and making the journeys and products of each child's effort visible so that they can be shared with others. For example, they offer parents information through posters, panels, booklets, videos, slide documentaries, and journals, in which the experiences of children and the most meaningful events are recorded. The space itself becomes legible through documentation (as many chapters in this book make clear).

Documentation is not only something that educators offer to families, but also a way in which they call upon parents to participate directly and offer their own points of view with regard to the experience the chil-

FIGURES 8.8 and 8.9. Taking turns in serving lunch expresses care and concern and supports relationships. (*Infant-toddler Center Il Sole, Pistoia*)

dren are living. For example, the centers often use two-way notebooks, starting with the first entry of infants in the center, for collecting photographs and comments about home- and center-related events. Such documentation creates an orchestration of points of view that can be reinterpreted by families, by teachers, and by the ones who are invited to observe closely, giving everyone a more complete vision and a more complete reading of the children's experience. It includes many voices and multiple listeners; it shows another way by which the center speaks of itself to families and remains transparent to the community.

When educators make a service truly known to the families that use it, they accomplish a complex undertaking that has both cultural and political value. It contributes to the dissemination of knowledge related to childhood. It makes participation part of the wider exercise of democracy on the part of citizens. It encourages a larger number of people to take on responsibility toward the new generations.

Exchange. The third way of building connections between parents and the center involves everyday collaboration and exchange linked to particular moments, such as celebrations, birthdays, excursions, and so on. Educators look for a practical contribution on the part of each parent to the life of the community, for example, through joint work in building furniture, playground equipment, games, or toys. Even more important, they also expect parents to interact with them in everyday ways. These social exchanges are often very positive and useful occasions that build ever more meaningful relationships and that bring life and color to the center. Parents often bring to the center little gifts of toys or food, just as children often carry small presents home. Such giving is a symbolic expression of the value each side gives to the exchange. The little gifts involve both the giver and the receiver, and the exchange guarantees the reciprocity that binds the community together.

However, the contribution of families to the enrichment of life at the center is not limited to social exchange and cooperative work. Families also contribute their own knowledge about their children, and this helps improve the quality of the overall educational project. Within a service that is especially dedicated to quality through the use of reflection and professional sensitivity, room is made for parents to be protagonists. In order to truly hear and welcome parents' messages, teachers rely on their professional skills. They are fully aware that it is not only they who give the family the means to better understand their child, but also the family who offers resources and contributes understanding based on the experience of being parents. Each family, with its particular culture, has many things to communicate if only educators listen, and many resources to invest if only educators can create a space for true dialogue. It follows, therefore, that this kind of participation—sharing of knowledge between parents and teachers around the educational experience—is an integral part of our educational approach. As such, we regard it as a valid end in and of itself.

The Responsibility of Public Administration

Educators are not the only ones who have a responsibility to create ways and means for family participation in educational services. Administrators share the tasks of creating and maintaining welcoming and personalized pathways to communication with families. Such communication even includes the organizational choices that take place prior to the admission of children to a center, for example, the ways in which the infant-toddler centers are made visible to the city and community and how applications are processed.

The fruits of such communication can be seen in the fact that families come to our services with expectations that mirror the image we have projected of our services. Indeed, the administration's work is to make our goals clear to the public and to make visible the work done with children that takes place inside the centers. It is a matter of activating channels of communication with parents in order to make them aware of the possibilities the infant-toddler center can offer. For example, it has been particularly useful to offer citizens designated "open house" days for visiting the centers during the period of preenrollment. Moreover, it is important that the office personnel who process enrollment requests not only demonstrate administrative skills but also explain the educational aspects of the service and that they listen and understand each family's needs from the very first contact.

The Community's Responsibility Toward Its Children

The relationship between families and an educational center must be understood in the wider context of childhood and community. Thus we come to the third aspect of our reflection, the community's responsibility to its children, entailing choices about policies and politics for childhood.

This is a complex issue that reveals itself in the ways that the society views its children, invests in them, and creates expectations surrounding childhood. We must ask how a particular community assumes its responsibility to younger generations, how it interprets their requirements, and how it constructs responses to families' needs and children's rights.

In Italy today, with respect to services for young children, we find ourselves pressed by demands that push us in two directions. The first seeks expansion of services, especially for children under 3 years of age in urban centers where families have less support from extended kin. The second challenges us to find or create new types of services that are flexible with respect to hours and organization. Throughout Italy, public administrations are called to organize centers and programs that serve children, others that serve children and parents together, and still others that serve families by offering education and information directed to parents. These requests remind us of the right of children to have spaces and opportunities of their own, and they also affirm the challenge to the community to share with families the responsibility for the growth of children.

Traditionally in Italy, services for children were provided from a perspective that saw children as fragile creatures to defend and protect. Only recently have children been recognized as persons with their own rights within society. Therefore, public administrations should create services that parallel the functions of families by respecting children's rights to play, have friends, and develop all their cognitive, affective, and social potentials.

But when we speak of community responsibility, we must also consider how services are rooted in a particular territory, in a particular culture. We submit that the task of adults—teachers and parents—is to transmit to children a sense of belonging to a community with a history. This applies inclusively to all the children in the city, including all the new arrivals. Here in Pistoia, these roots are visible because educators have tried to create a pleasant closeness between children and the city, with its culture and history, which is then reinterpreted in the schools and centers through each child's personal story, imagination, knowledge, and life.

The centers and schools, in fact, open the world to children. Sometimes they invite the surrounding world into the space of the center where there are evident traces of local artifacts and furnishing coming from children's homes. For example, in the rooms of the youngest infants, the sleeping area has wicker cradles woven by local craftsmen. Sometimes one sees teachers pushing strollers, along with 2-year-old children, walking slowly to go out to visit meaningful places and landmarks around our city (museums, churches, public buildings, gardens, markets, and ancient city walls). The older children investigate the architectural characteristics, patterns of use, and the historical events that distinguish one from the other. Educators value the community's cultural heritage as well as the individual cultures of each family coming into the community. These family traditions include narrative and symbolic aspects as much as factual events. People pass along their cultural heritage through myths and stories, and the sense of tradition becomes the pleasure of memory. Children thus come into contact with happenings far from their present, everyday experience. Fables, tall tales, fairy tales, and rhymes are often retold in the living voices of grandparents who participate in community life.

To support and build upon this intergenerational transmission, and continuity of our programs from infancy on, we have created a laboratory in one of our Children's Places (*Area Bambini*) where we tell stories drawn from the rich oral tradition of Pistoia. Preschool and elementary children bring and share stories, tales, and nursery rhymes they have heard from their parents and grandparents. As children become familiar with local history, they realize a continuity of past and present that enriches and colors the present with shades of the past and encourages growth.

CLOSING REFLECTIONS

From everything that has been said, it can be seen how important it is to help children build their individual identities and, at the same time, find a sense of belonging. To be and to belong: these become one in defining growth. Thus, it is not by chance that in the repertoire of traditional tales, there are several about children lost in the woods who learn to find their own path back home. Indeed, to grow means to free oneself from the fears of being lost and being alone. We must help children form active relationships with the places of their lives. Then they can set out on their own adventures and find a path of growth, strengthened by the sense of security that comes from an identity that is recognized by others and in which they recognize themselves.

Ernesto De Martino (1995), an Italian anthropologist, reflects on this sentiment in the following way:

> Those who do not have roots, who are cosmopolitan, bring about the death of their own passion and humanity. However, in order not to be provincial and stay in one place, one should keep a living village in one's memory, an image to which the imagination and the heart return over and over. (p. 20)

REFERENCES

Bodrova, E., & Leong, D. J. (1996). *Tools of the mind: The Vygotskian approach to early childhood education.* Englewood Cliffs, NJ: Prentice Hall.

De Martino, E. (1995). *Storia e metastoria: I fondamenti di una teoria del sacro* [History and metahistory: Foundations of a theory of the sacred]. Florence, Italy: Argo.

Galardini, A., Giovannini, D., & Iozzelli, S. (Eds.). (1999). *L'immaginario bambino* [The imaginary world of the child] (Dual language Italian and English edition). Bergamo, Italy: Edizioni Junior.

PART III

NOTABLE PRACTICES: STRATEGIES, REASONS, AND NARRATIVES

This part of the book moves the discussion beyond particular systems and their programs, to consideration of some of the most innovative and important strategies or practices found within them, recognized by outside educators as well as by Italians.

One such strategy, eloquently described by Chiara Bove in Chapter 9, is the *inserimento,* or "period of transition" and settling in, with its distinctive processes for delicately introducing new children and families into the infant-toddler center.

Another is *documentation,* described by Lella Gandini and Jeanne Goldhaber in Chapter 10, a tool for supporting coconstruction of knowledge among all the protagonists in the infant-toddler system.

Chapter 11, by Donatella Giovannini, focuses on the *diario,* the "diary" or "memory book," a way to collect traces, memories, and interpretations of each child's personal journey through the program, prepared by teachers as a parting gift to the child and family.

In Chapter 12, Gabriella Magrini and Lella Gandini focus on the *inclusion* of young children with special needs. They draw on Gabriella's documentation to tell the story of a little boy named Dario and the growing closeness and dialogue between his mother and teacher.

Chapter 9

INSERIMENTO: A STRATEGY FOR DELICATELY BEGINNING RELATIONSHIPS AND COMMUNICATIONS

Chiara Bove

Italian society has made an investment in high-quality education for children less than 3 years of age. The care and education of very young children has come to be seen as the responsibility not only of the family but also of the broader community (New, 1993, 1998). The public has come to accept the existence of the services and to trust that they will be good for parents and children. As described in this book, general principles of pedagogy and organization have been laid down in several cities in Italy, allowing for gradual evolution of new services and continued quality improvement of existing services.

In recent years, a widespread debate throughout Europe about how to define and describe "quality" in early childhood services has stimulated Italian educators to reexamine what they do. One particular issue upon which we have focused concerns the *inserimento,* the time during which the family and the professionals first meet and begin to work together.

THE CONCEPT OF *INSERIMENTO*: THE ITALIAN PERSPECTIVE

Inserimento (which can be roughly translated as "settling in," or "period of transition and adjustment") is our term for the strategy of beginning relationships and communication among adults and children when the child is entering an infant-toddler center or a preschool program for the first time. The Italian concept of *inserimento* indicates the initial process of the child's adjustment into the new community. Interpreted as a delicate event in the child's and family's life (Mantovani & Terzi, 1987), the practice of *inserimento* is primarily based on a great variety of strategies aimed at encouraging parents' involvement, and it begins even before the child's first day at the center or preschool.

The presence of someone who is very well known to the child for the entire duration of the *inserimento* is highly valued and supported. After a series of communications and visits between the family and the center, parents are invited to spend some time at the center with their child. During the first days, the parent and the child will remain for a few hours playing, observing, and communicating with the teachers and other families. Day by day, parents and children increase their stay in the center until their full schedule is reached. The center provides flexibility in the way parents can respond most effectively. With a great range of variation covered, parents' full-time presence may last from a minimum of a few days for some families to a maximum of several weeks for others.

Thus, during the period of *inserimento,* the center staff provides for children to be cared for and nurtured by their parents in the out-of-home context. Although this privilege will not last forever, it gives young children an initial feeling of familiarity and emotional security that usually carries over when the parent is no longer present. These practices also aim to give teachers the opportunity to learn about individual patterns of interaction and about differences in parental style.

Gradually, as parents begin to reduce their presence, parents and children will experience the first separations and reunions. Most of the time, educators facilitate a positive initial separation by offering a context strategically designed to support and show delicately beginning relationships.

The process of *inserimento* requires a carefully designed and prepared environment, which immediately conveys messages of welcome and respect to parents and children. Such messages must be evident in the care given to the physical space, in the positive attitudes and behaviors of the educators during this process, as well as in the great variety of personalized responses to each family's requests. The main indicator of *welcoming* to parents is that they are seriously invited to spend as much time as possible in the center. At the same time as the mother or father is getting to know the teacher, the teacher has the opportunity to socialize with the parent. Eventually the child will benefit from the relationships growing between parents and teachers.

Furthermore, while the child is offered the opportunity to gradually familiarize him- or herself with the teacher, the other children, and the environment, the parent may assume a more relaxed approach to infant care. As the center provides new children with a prepared space that invites them to play with peers, it gives parents many opportunities to ob-

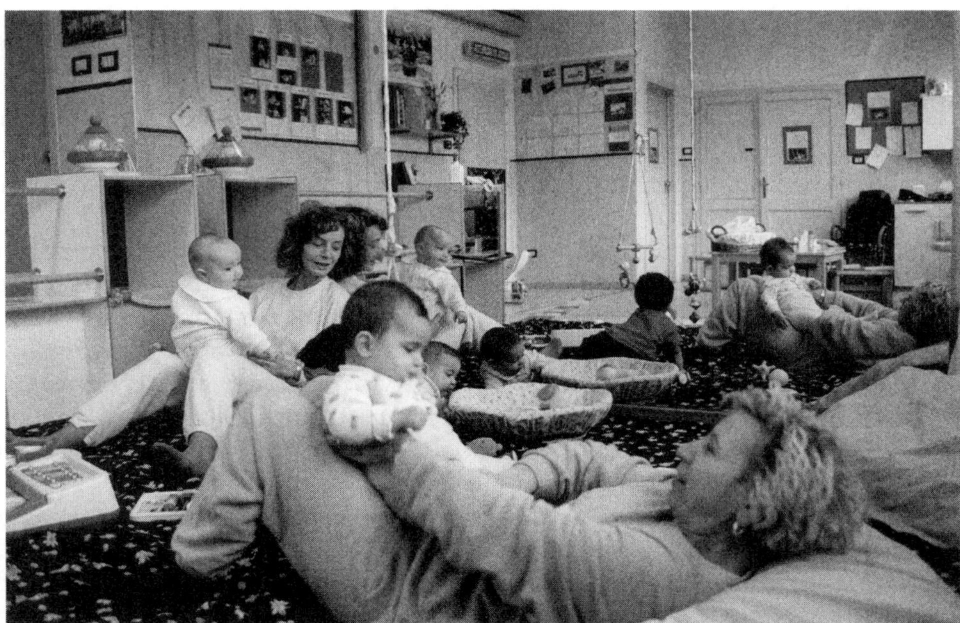

FIGURE 9.1. Teachers hold and play with infants in a way that imitates the style of parents. (*Infant-toddler Center Sagittario, Modena*)

serve their own child's behavior in a social context. The teacher, acting as a supportive figure for both adults and children, facilitates reciprocal observations.

During this period, some specific group experiences with other families are offered in order to give parents the opportunity to learn that other parents share their concerns about entering infant care. The practice of sharing among adults may reduce individuals' anxiety and at the same time provide them with a context for autonomous reflections on their own style of relationships.

GUIDELINES FOR *INSERIMENTO*

Over the years, by practicing *inserimento,* educators (both teachers and professional development coordinators) have defined some general guidelines for this transition. They have devised models of gradual, predictable, and recognizable ways of welcoming and interacting with new families. Based on these general models, a wide variety of educational strategies have been developed to facilitate this experience. These include teacher-parent interviews and home visits before the child starts at the center; parent-teacher meetings before, during and after the initial transition process; various forms of documentation; large or small group discussions with parents; and daily communications between parents and teachers.

Through these various strategies, centers have attempted to meet each family's needs, to sustain parental involvement, and to respond to the parents' requests for emotional support in caring for their young children. Each center aspires to offer a thoughtful and personalized adjustment into the new setting for each family involved, with the intention that each dyad of parent and child will have the opportunity to receive individual attention.

There is no longer debate about whether or not it is appropriate to provide a gradual separation with the adult's mediation. Instead, the question is what is the best way to support the first transition of the child from the family to the infant-toddler center. Approaches to *inserimento* vary as a function of each community's practices and preferences, but because it represents an important indicator of high quality, almost all infant-toddler centers and preschools must now give more attention to this aspect of their service.

In Italy, two main alternatives have been worked out. In some centers educators focus their attention on the individual child and family *(inserimento individuale)*. In others, they emphasize group practices where a few families participate together in the transition process *(inserimento di gruppo)*. In the first case, each parent-child unit enters infant care at a different time, so that the teachers can focus on that new family without jeopardizing attention to others. In the second case, the process of *inserimento* involves a small number of families together. This provides adults, as well as children, with opportunities to socialize and relate to each other during this initial phase. In this situation there are still plenty of opportunities for individuals to experience their own particular transition. And in both cases, teachers must have had appropriate professional development in order to successfully facilitate both individual and group communications and interactions.

The ultimate goal in both strategies of *inserimento* is to support and value relationships between children and adults and, as it has been recently thought appropriate, to extend the value of relationships among all adults.

THE ROLE OF ADULTS

When thinking about the role of the adults in this relationship, it is important to consider the close attention that is required of them, as I described above. Some theoretical frameworks are useful to understand the complexity of *inserimento,* which is considered a critical and delicate event for both children and adults.

Theoretical Frameworks

In former years, when educators were more focused on the child's experience of "separation" upon entering the center, they embraced the significant theoretical contribution offered by attachment theory. They used this theory to study and understand the early mother-child relationship. From this perspective, they focused on the child's separation experience at the time of entering the infant-toddler center. They sought first and foremost to provide the child a safe and secure environment to facilitate separation from the mother and thereby to prevent negative consequences for the child's development (Ainsworth, Blehar, Waters, & Wall, 1978; Bowlby, 1988).

However, through repeated experiences and sustained attention to *inserimento,* educators developed further concepts and ideas especially addressing the context of out-of-home care. In contrast to the first attachment theorists who looked at mother-child dyads in the home context, they now focused on relationships within center-based care. They realized that the center context involves, right from the moment of the family's first contact, other adults and children beyond the focal family; it is the site of many interpersonal exchanges, all relevant for the process of *inserimento.* For the educators, therefore, there emerged the critical issue of recognizing that each individual transition is mutually defined with other adults, children, teachers, and even the environment.

In addition, educators became aware of other relevant contributions recently provided by social constructivism theorists. These contributions led to a focus on the intersubjective and relational aspects of development and suggested more new ways of thinking about *inserimento.* A critical aspect arising from this theoretical approach is recognizing the interpersonal construction of one's own development and the coconstruction of knowledge (Rogoff, 1990). This is of great interest for understanding *inserimento* because it gives attention to both adult-child and peer-peer interaction as contexts of learning (Dunn, 1993). As educators address these complexities and give growing pedagogical attention to adults as protagonists along with their children, they have contributed to developing a balanced model of *inserimento.* The model includes a balanced focus on the child's well-being, the parents' needs and resources, and the broader system of relationships in the child's life at home and at the center.

When educators encourage parents to be an active part of this transition, they allow the child to experience the new context with more security. At the same time, they give parents the opportunity to adapt to the new context gradually. This is an important point because scientific evidence highlights the interdependence between the quality of life of the primary caregiver and that of the child (Emiliani, Gelati, & Molinari, 1989; Musatti, 1992). The child's well-being is strictly linked to the well-being of the mother (or primary caregiver) and the support of the father, extended family, and institutions. This emotional framework effectively influences the whole transition process. The importance of the mother's well-being, whether she is *with* or *away from* her child, is validated and taken seriously during the process of *inserimento.*

Recent research studies highlight the complexity of the process of becoming a mother, which implies the development of a new identity.

The "mother's mind-set" (Stern, 1995; Stern & Bruscheweiler-Stern, 1998) emerges even before the child's birth and continues to develop in relationship with the child as the child develops. In recent reinterpretations of attachment theory, the mother's mental and representational world is considered an important factor in her relationship with her child (Main, Kaplan, & Cassidy, 1985). Her relational style reflects her personal history and experiences as a child and as a woman, as well as her internal world (Ammanniti & Stern, 1997). From this perspective, the mother-child interaction is perceived to be in dynamic interdependence with the mother's childhood experience (Main, Kaplan, & Cassidy, 1985).

Inserimento as Opening Oneself to Others

At this point, *inserimento* has come to be viewed as an experience of building new relationships, rather than one composed around separation from the mother. A range of recent interpretations based on research and local practice now associates the experience of entering into infant care with opportunities for constructing a broader social world rich in relationships. In the infant-toddler center, it is necessary to build closeness with the family, always considering the complex nature of human relationships so that the relationships created will be characterized by genuine curiosity, suspended judgment, and an attitude of respect and attention toward one another. By observing each infant-adult dyad, professionals develop new patterns of relationships that are predictable, recognizable, and stable in their development. Thus, the transition experience is no longer only about ensuring each single child's adjustment, but instead is also concerned with ensuring a more extended and interpersonal transition.

As a result of such attention to *inserimento,* several strategies have emerged to support the interpretation of separation as opening oneself to others. Both researchers and educators involved in practice related to infants recognize the value of parents' involvement during the process of transition. Moreover, most recently emerging is an interpretation of parents' involvement as a professional need for the teacher. This includes the interpretation of *inserimento* as a period that should not be rushed but instead a time for listening, observing, and discovering. *Inserimento* can be a time when all involved value the pleasure of getting to know one another closely.

Constructing Adult Partnerships

Building close relationships entails complex emotional involvement for both parents and teachers directed toward the goal of transforming emotions into guidelines for behavior. That is to say, if we recognize emotions and consider their strength, then we can develop new ways of activating their positive potential. In fact, adults can create spaces, strategies, and attitudes that provide a place and a time that is a thoughtful "holding environment" where people can express their full range of emotions and feelings.

Adults achieve a sense of security by discussing, sharing, and understanding their own feelings connected with leaving their child in someone else's care or, in the case of teachers, with taking on someone else's child. The experience of entering infant care can develop into a time and a place in which adults, gradually opening up to one another, can be partners rather than antagonists. In this situation they can share knowledge rather than showing off competencies.

INSERIMENTO OF VERY YOUNG CHILDREN: RECENT DEVELOPMENTS

All of this new thinking about *inserimento* holds implications for both teachers and the people involved in teachers' professional development. By broadening the focus beyond the single child's experience, we make way for practices that welcome the parent-child dyad into the life of the infant-toddler center to become something more: an opportunity for professionals to experience the intense learning involved in inquiring into and observing human relations.

The attention to very young children (under 12 months of age) is an emerging issue in Italian care and education. Several infant-toddler programs in Italy, which in the past received mostly children over one year of age, now are asked to welcome very young children. This requires each program to develop new strategies to respond effectively to the new demands. What does it mean to welcome a child just a few weeks old, as opposed to an older one, into the infant-toddler center? What about a child of 3 months? Once again we must examine the connection between high-quality care and continuing investment to respond to the increasing demand for care of very young children.

It is well known that a mother's relationship with a very young infant, especially soon after birth, is intense, deep, and exclusive. Therefore, when a very young infant first enters the infant-toddler center, all the adults are asked to become completely involved, both physically and mentally, as they strive to support the infant's ability and developmental accomplishment of feeling united even when separated from the parent or primary caregiver. This process represents a meaningful professional opportunity for educators. What follows is the interpretation of *inserimento* as a context for research and further professional development.

Action Research: Welcoming Very Young Infants

One recent experience of high-quality care in contemporary Italy involves an action research project currently going on in Modena, a small city of the Emilia Romagna region. The project aims to promote a deeper understanding of the *inserimento* of the youngest infants and to define new strategies to facilitate this experience. The research, designed in cooperation with Susanna Mantovani of the University of Milan, was funded by the Modena municipal administration. It was promoted by Laura Saitta of Modena, noted for her admirable efforts to promote good-quality settings for young children both in the past and today. This project has brought about a deeper understanding of the first transition process, which we consider to be a complex interpersonal event that involves parents, teachers, and children in the process of getting to know one another.

New strategies of professional intervention have emerged from our partnership with teachers and pedagogical coordinators from the infant-toddler centers that enrolled an increased number of young infants. During the research, we videotaped the child-mother entrance, the first separation experience, and the very first reunion. We did the first videotape during the first week and the second one two weeks later. Then we conducted interviews with both the mothers and teachers who were videotaped, including two more interviews at the end of the process. These final interviews were videotaped to produce other material to promote further collective discussions. Both interviews and videotapes were discussed with mothers and teachers in large groups. The process of looking at the videotapes with parents and teachers gave value to all of the protagonists' interpretations and also was helpful in defining supportive strategies for early intervention with parents.

The result of this work, based on intense teacher involvement, was to increase our attention to the parent-child interaction, along with emerging competencies in observing relationships. In addition, we carefully considered the teachers' emotional involvement. For teachers, their already existing professional skills in observing and recognizing different patterns and styles of relations were further enhanced by this collaborative research project.

During this research, we asked the teachers and educators to construct—as a professional competence—a mental place in which each child could be contained, recognized, and considered in relation to the adult. It is a mental place in which the adult can think of the child, in which the adult can keep in mind each child's emotional effort, remembering the child's, as well as the mother's uniqueness (Pawl, 1995). This requires teachers and professionals to have strong in-service professional development as well as space and time to reflect, interpret, and discuss their own interpersonal involvement. Furthermore, professional development depends upon the group of teachers working together. By collaborating, they become resources to one another when they discuss, share, rethink, and conceptualize in a new way their experiences, expectations, and interpretations.

An Illustration of *Inserimento*

The following account of a child and her mother entering an infant-toddler center in Modena is not a complete story, but it illustrates the complexity of the beginning of new relations among three important people: an infant, a mother, and a teacher. The passage points out the richness of the process of getting to know one another, the intensity of the emotions, and the delicate buildup of the relationship. The *inserimento* unfolds slowly and gradually, and the passage reveals how the new relationships develop and lead mother and child to be in the center "naturally." Above all, the passage highlights how much attention and professional skill the teacher must have in order to observe, support, respect, and facilitate these important experiences in the lives of children and parents. The account, based on a videotaped observation, is divided into three short scenes.

I. First Day. A mother and her child attend gradually to the new experience of entering into the infant-toddler center. They look around and explore the new environment, trying to understand what is happening and how to become a part of it. The scene describes their behavior and way of attending to something new; it describes their unique style of approaching the *inserimento*. At the same time, it describes the beginning of the relationship of mother and daughter with the teacher, based on delicate sequences of observing, listening, and getting to know one another.

> A mother and her child Luisa, 5 months old, enter the room and sit in a comfortable chair. The mother holds the child so she faces outward toward the teacher, who is sitting on the floor. Looking at the teacher, the mother says, "Good morning! Today we rushed!" "*Buon giorno,*" responds the teacher. Holding the baby's hands in her own, the mother notes, "Now we are paying attention. . . . " And she greets other children in the room: "*Ciao,* Matteo. Is Giovanni here?" The teacher responds, "No, he will be here later, and Franco will come back on Monday." The mother glances down and asks, "Luisa, are we comfortable? Are we ready?"
>
> After looking around for a few minutes Luisa smiles and looks directly at the teacher. The mother stands and carries Luisa to the floor where the teacher is waiting for them. A game of "getting to know you" takes place. The child is placed on the floor between her mother and the teacher, and the adults begin to talk, sharing their ideas about the baby's entry into infant care. Luisa turns from one to the other as she lies quietly between them. (Bove, 1999, p. 32)

II. One Hour Later. The mother, child, and teacher take the first steps in their new relationship. Here it is important to note the link between the mother-child relationship and their new relationships with the teacher. During this sequence, the mother leaves the room for a short time while the teacher continues to build her relationship with the child as they await the mother's return (see Figure 9.2).

> The teacher has Luisa in her arms. The mother is still in the classroom, observing from the other side of the room. The teacher (seeing the mother's image in the mirror) positions Luisa so that she too is looking in the mirror. The teacher asks, "Can you see your mother?" Luisa

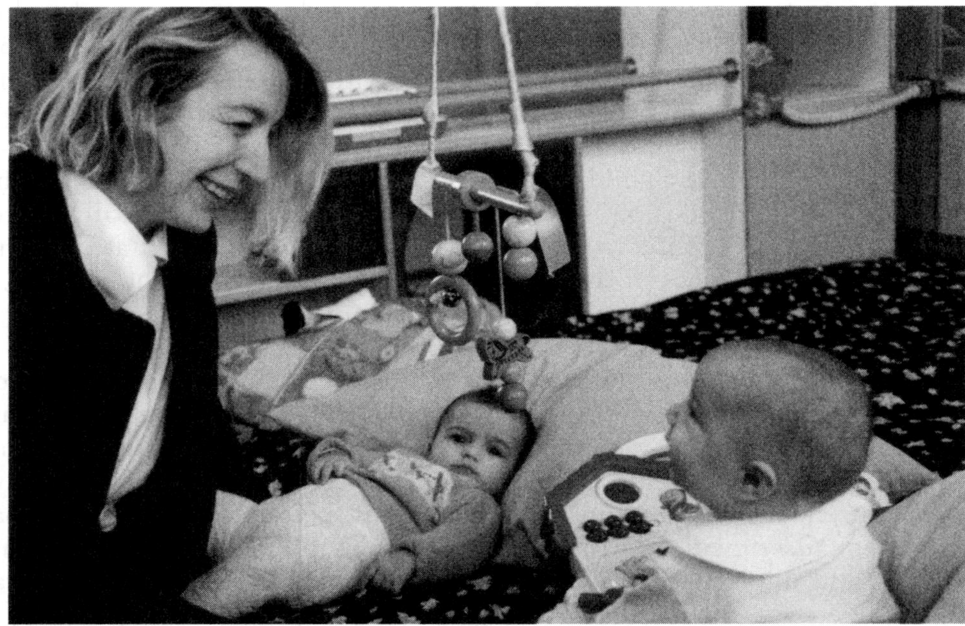

FIGURE 9.2. When the mother returns to pick up her child, the two of them greet each other with smiles. (*Infant-toddler Center Sagittario, Modena*)

> looks at the mirror and smiles. The teacher turns so that they can both face the mother. The mother approaches, all the while looking at her child, and the teacher gives Luisa back to her mother. Now the mother gets down on the floor and begins to play with Luisa. This time the teacher watches from a distance. When the mother leaves the room for a brief period later in the morning, the same play routine takes place between the teacher and Luisa. (Bove, 1999, p. 32)

III. Two Weeks Later. The mother and child enter the infant-toddler center and prepare to separate. The sequence provides clear evidence of the evolution of familiarity between child and teacher. It also reveals the mother's increased security about both *being* with the child in the center and *leaving* her child with the teacher.

> Luisa and her mother enter the room. The teacher greets them with a cheerful, "*Ciao,* Luisa! How are you?" The mother responds "Hello. We are fine this morning." They sit down in the same chair that they sat in two weeks earlier, and the teacher asks Luisa, "So, are you coming to play?" The child smiles and puts her arms out toward the teacher. The mother says, "Look, she is reaching for you!" "Are you ready?" asks the teacher. "Come here. Let's try. . . . Have you seen Matteo and Giovanni?" The teacher takes the child and kisses her

> while they move to the floor where another child is waiting. The mother watches from her chair for a few minutes and, as soon as the infant begins to respond to the teacher's playfulness, goes there and asks the teacher if it is appropriate for her to leave. After a brief conversation, the mother —watching her daughter—says, "Bye-bye, I am going. Mom is going." Then looking at the mother, the teacher says, "Watch. Luisa is following you with her eyes." At this point, the mother leaves the room. (Bove, 1999, p. 32)

LOOKING AT *INSERIMENTO* AS A CULTURAL CONCEPT

Assuming that the notion of *inserimento* is a theoretical issue as well as a practical concern, this final section will discuss the concept of *inserimento* as a dynamic, culturally constructed interpretation of the child's entrance into out-of-home care.[1]

Contemporary understanding in Italy values high-quality infant-toddler care as a pleasant and desirable experience for both parents and children (New, 1993, 1998). For some time, the child's experience in the infant-toddler center has been considered appropriate, as well as beneficial for the child's development, but it is evident now that it is also supportive for parents. This reflects our understanding of infant care as a complex relational experience in the early years and suggests that infant-toddler care is a "system of relationships" in which the emotional, social, and physical well-being of the protagonists are interdependent (Edwards, Gandini, & Forman, 1998).

Changes in the Child-Rearing Support System

The interpersonal system of each infant-toddler center is today replacing the traditional supporting system that once was represented by the extended family. The debate has progressed far beyond considering mainly the needs of working mothers. We see evidence in the fact that there is a continuing discussion about providing high-quality care for children under 3 years of age (Musatti & Mantovani, 1996) and that there is agreement that such care is an effective response to children's developmental needs as well as to the needs of parents.

Traditionally, the notion of well-being for individual children involved a broad picture including extended families, relatives, friends, and neighbors. Child rearing was shared, involving all of these participants from the very beginning. In our society today, the traditional support system has in part been replaced by new strategies for sharing the experiences of motherhood (and parenthood). These are especially helpful for first-time parents. To extend the natural intergenerational experience of sharing one's pregnancy and motherhood with one's *own* mother, efforts have been made to create other contexts in which to share also the process of "becoming a mother" (Byng-Hall, 1995). These sometimes take the form of prebirth and postbirth interventions. There may also be group sessions in which women share the experience of "becoming" and of "being" a new mother with other women in the same conditions. Usually these programs are promoted by the local hospital or by the local health unit *(consultorio).*

Many Images of Parenthood

The *asilo nido*—conceptualized and practiced as a place open to families—provides these adults with a variety of opportunities to share, debate, and discuss the major issues of their parental roles. At the same time, it provides them with a variety of occasions to observe others interacting intimately with their children. This affirms and reassures them and offers them a model of appropriate behavior.

The infant-toddler center is, for Italian parents, a place where one's image of parenthood can be supported and validated or modified through relationships with others. This requires teachers and professionals to be aware of the wide variety of ways of being a parent of a young child; that is, to be aware of a thousand different images of parenthood. Once again, *inserimento* represents the initial phase of this process of building new relationships among parents, children, and other adults.

A variety of cross-cultural studies of child development and education point out the relationship between culture and education (LeVine, Miller, & West, 1998; Sharma & Fischer, 1998) and highlight cultural relativity: what is important, fundamental, and reasonable for one community may be unimportant, nonfundamental, and unreasonable for another. Working with children and families requires teachers and professionals to be prepared to recognize and respect the tremendous variety of cultural systems that families present.

The notion of flexibility—a key concept in planning the *inserimento*—helps professionals respond to such cultural variations. How can we adjust the center schedule to everyone's needs, desires, and expectations? How can we deal with a mother who has to be back at work very soon? Careful observation and inquiry will indicate the best way to proceed with each family; teachers will be able to define flexible strategies rather than fixed protocols. Eventually parents and children will show us how to enter into relationship with them.

Our practice of *inserimento* represents the process of transition into an infant-toddler center in the Italian cultural context in which the idea of family generally represents a stable context of growth. The ideal Italian family has always centered on close, intense, and daily relationships among family members (nuclear and extended). In other cultural contexts, different ideas and values about the family and child growth and development pertain. For example, in North America greater geographic mobility gives rise to an earlier transition to autonomy for children and young people than in Italy. There is a greater value given to individual independence in the United States than in Italy (New, 1999).

In Italy, therefore, the best way to provide a smooth separation into infant care is through building close, intense, and daily relationships with child and family. *Inserimento* occurs as a culturally relevant answer to a culturally determined need. For Italians, the idea of *inserimento* refers to a complex event that reflects the mother's status in modern society as well as her possible multiple roles. The strong expectation to be a "good" mother might describe both *being close to the child* and *being independent.* For example, at the moment of transition, the expectation for the good mother to be good at leaving the child and for good teachers to be professional in taking care of the child is connected to our cultural notions of maternal role and professional role.

But the emerging attention to the experience of mother-infant separation as an adults' shared responsibility, rather than an exclusive responsibility of the mother in her role as the primary caregiver and of a teacher in her role as an expert, opens the possibilities for a more complex view of both roles. Is a mother *good* in leaving a child in someone else's hands? Is a mother *good* when she is not having a hard time separating from her child? Or, is she *good* when she is showing less pain than what we expect? Is the teacher *good* when the child doesn't cry? Rather than focusing on defining *good* or *bad* in evaluative terms, we should concentrate on the idea of constructing positive relationships for both mothers and teachers. Efforts to involve parents as active participants during the *inserimento*—both in the process of thinking and planning the event, as well as experiencing it—represents a constructive and helpful answer to the strong pressures that characterize the mother's condition and multiple roles in modern society.

A FINAL CONSIDERATION

Inserimento can be seen as a cultural concept that reflects the larger Italian interpretation of childhood and education, and that functions to further the child's sense of belonging to the society (Mantovani, Saitta, & Bove, 2000). We need to remember that no educational strategy can be transplanted directly from one cultural setting to another. However, continuing to examine cultural practices and to sustain reciprocal, cross-cultural understanding may promote further development of high-quality of infant-toddler care in each cultural context. This requires a serious commitment to establishing relationships between families and educators even before the official entrance of the child into infant care. *Inserimento* is a never-ending process of growth, transformation, and getting to know each other.

NOTE

1. Reflections on *inserimento* as a culturally constructed notion and practice are based on a cross-cultural study on the child's transition experience from

family to out-of-home care in Italy and North America. The research was funded by a scholarship awarded by the University of Milan and conducted by Chiara Bove under the scientific supervision of Susanna Mantovani (University of Milan) and Rebecca New (Tufts University).

REFERENCES

Ainsworth, M. D. S., Blehar, M. C., Waters, E., & Wall, S. (1978). *Patterns of attachments: A psychological study of the strange situation.* Hillsdale, NJ: Erlbaum.

Ammanniti, M., & Stern, D. N. (Eds.). (1997). *Rappresentazioni e narrazioni* [Representations and narrations]. Rome: Laterza.

Bove, C. (1999). L'inserimento del bambino al nido [Welcoming the child into infant care]: Perspectives from Italy. *Young Children, 54*(2), 32–34.

Bowlby, J. (1988). *A secure base.* New York: Basic.

Byng-Hall, J. (1995). *Rewriting family scripts.* New York: Guilford Press. (Published in Italian as *Le trame di famiglia,* 1998, Milan, Italy: Raffaello Cortina.)

Dunn, J. (1993). *Young children's close relationships: Beyond attachment.* Newbury Park, CA: Sage.

Edwards, C. P., Gandini, L., & Forman, G. (1998). *The hundred languages of children: The Reggio Emilia approach—advanced reflections* (2nd ed.). Stamford, CT: Ablex.

Emiliani, F., Gelati, M., & Molinari, L. (1989). *Il bambino nella mente e nelle parole delle madri* [The child in the mind and words of mothers]. Florence, Italy: La Nuova Italia.

LeVine, R. A., Miller, P. M., & West, M. M. (Eds). (1998). *Parental behavior in diverse societies* (New Directions for Child Development No. 40). San Francisco: Jossey-Bass.

Main, M., Kaplan, K., & Cassidy, J. (1985). Security in infancy, childhood and adulthood: A move to the level of representation. In I. Bretherton & E. Waters (Eds.), Growing points of attachment theory and research (pp. 66–103). *Monographs of the Society for Research in Child Development, 50*(1–2, Serial No. 209).

Mantovani, S., & Musatti, T. (1983). *Adulti e bambini: Educare e comunicare* [Adults and children: To educate and communicate]. Bergamo, Italy: Juvenilia.

Mantovani, S., & Terzi, N. (1987). L'inserimento. In A. Bondioli & S. Mantovani (Eds.), *Manuale critico dell'asilo nido* [Critical manual of infant-toddler day care] (pp. 215–230). Milan, Italy: Franco Angeli.

Mantovani, S., Saitta, L., & Bove, C. (2000). *Attaccamento e inserimento al nido: Stili e relazionali* [Attachment and transition in the infant-toddler center: Relational styles and stories]. Milan, Italy: Franco Angeli.

Musatti, T. (1992). *La giornata del mio bambino* [My child's day]. Bologna, Italy: Il Mulino.

Musatti, T., & Mantovani, S. (1996). New Educational provision for young children in Italy. *European Journal of Psychology of Education, 11*(2), 119–128.

New, R. (1993). Italy. In M. Cochran (Ed.), *International handbook on child care policies and programs* (pp. 291–311). Westport, CT: Greenwood Press.

New, R. (1998). Social competence in Italian early childhood education. In D. Sharma & K. W. Fisher (Eds.), *Socioemotional development across cultures* (New Directions for Child Development No. 81, pp. 87–104). San Francisco: Jossey-Bass.

New, R. (1999). Here, we call it "drop off and pick up": Transition to child care, American-style. *Young Children, 54*(2), 34–35.

Pawl, J. H. (1995). The therapeutic relationship as human connectedness. *Zero to Three, 15*(4), 1–5.

Rogoff, B. (1990). *Apprenticeship in thinking.* New York: Oxford University Press.

Sharma, D., & Fischer, K. W. (Eds.). (1998). *Socioemotional development across cultures* (New Directions for Child Development No. 81). San Francisco: Jossey-Bass.

Stern, D. (1995). *The motherhood constellation: A unified view of parent-infant psychotherapy.* New York: Basic Books.

Stern, D., & Bruscheweiler-Stern, N. (1998). The birth of a mother. (Published in Italian as *La nascita di una madre,* 1999, Milan, Italy: Mondadori.)

Varin, D., Riva Crugnola, C., Molina, P., & Ripamonti, C. (1996). Sensitive period in the development of attachment at the age of entry into daycare. *European Journal of Psychology of Education, 11*(2), 215–229.

Chapter 10

TWO REFLECTIONS ABOUT DOCUMENTATION

Lella Gandini and Jeanne Goldhaber

This chapter is divided into two parts. In the first part, Lella Gandini examines various facets of the complexity of documenting. She looks at documentation as a cooperative process that helps teachers listen to and see the children with whom they work, thus opening the possibility to construct meaningful experiences with them. Documentation, interpreted and reinterpreted with other educators and children, gives the option of drafting scripts for action that are not arbitrary but instead respectful of all involved. In the second part, Jeanne Goldhaber reflects on experiences with documentation at the Campus Children's Center at the University of Vermont. She examines documentation as a process that furthers understanding of children's concepts and theories with the conviction that for both children and adults documentation supports their efforts to understand and to be understood.

DOCUMENTATION AS A TOOL FOR PROMOTING THE CONSTRUCTION OF RESPECTFUL LEARNING

Documentation is an indispensable tool for educators in constructing positive experiences for children and in facilitating professional growth and communication for adults. It seeks to attest to something we consider

---

 ISBN 0-8077-4008-X (paper), ISBN 0-8077-4009-8 (cloth).

relevant, to give proof, and to communicate. In early childhood education, when we document, we make the deliberate choice to observe and record what happens in our environment in order to reflect and communicate the surprising discoveries in children's everyday lives and the extraordinary events and happenings in places where children are cared for.

Documentation is not considered here as the collecting of data in a detached, objective, distant way. Rather, it is seen as the interpretation of close, keen observation and attentive listening, gathered with a variety of tools by educators aware of contributing their different points of views. In fact, our views about childhood and our personal theories influence what each of us sees and hears; that is why we need to compare interpretations among colleagues.

The observers are "participant-observers," who have an interest in recording thoughtful pieces of information. Their intention is to construct a shared understanding of children's ways of interacting with the environment, of entering into relationships with other adults and other children, and of constructing their knowledge.

American educators have recently become very interested in documentation, not only from learning about the practices in Reggio Emilia (see e.g., Rinaldi, 1998; Vecchi, 1998), but also from certain American experiments with authentic assessment, creative display, and other related activities (Carter & Curtis, 1996; Helm, Beneke, & Steinheimer, 1997). However, many of these writings placed most attention on the final steps of documentation, such as the preparation of panels, portfolios, and other forms of communication and display. My intent here is to focus instead on the reflective processes of flexible planning that documentation makes possible and that, in turn, motivate the documentation process and give it meaning.

What follows is the result of many years of studying and reflecting on documentation, of learning from Loris Malaguzzi (1998), Carlina Rinaldi (1998), Vea Vecchi (1998), and Paola Calliari (1999). Furthermore, it is the result of working closely with Amelia Gambetti and observing several other educators in Reggio Emilia and Pistoia. It is also the result of close and long-term exchange and collaboration with educators in schools and child care systems and universities throughout Italy and the United States.

All children have the potential, albeit in different ways, to learn and to develop their own ideas, theories, and strategies. All children also have the right to be supported in these endeavors by adults. Teachers and parents, therefore, should observe and listen to them. In my view the most powerful tool for giving that support, in a way that respects them as individuals, is documentation. The documentation I am discussing here is, in fact, a "pedagogical documentation" as Gunilla Dahlberg has recently defined it (Dahlberg, Moss, & Pence, 1999). Vea Vecchi (1998), *atelierista* in Reggio Emilia, has expressed a similar concept:

> All of this documentation . . . becomes an indispensable source of materials that we use every day to be able to "read" and reflect critically, both individually and collectively, on the experience we are living, the projects we are exploring. This allows us to construct theories and hypotheses that are not arbitrary or artificially imposed on the children. (pp. 141–142)

In fact, we owe our growing understanding of the potential of documentation to the educators of Reggio Emilia. They have continued to refine both their way of creating complex and pleasurable ways for children and adults to construct learning together and their means of studying these experiences. They have also interpreted and presented these processes by preparing clear and beautiful documentations. Loris Malaguzzi (1998) writes:

> Our work on documentation has strongly informed—little by little—our way of being with children. It has also, in a rather beautiful way, obliged us to refine our methods of observation and recording so that the processes of children's learning became the basis of our dialogue with parents. (p. 74)

If documentation is a daily practice that should be woven into all activities of an infant-toddler center or a preschool, we should analyze some of its essential aspects to help us to understand its meaningful process.

Observing and Recording

By observing and listening to children with care and attention, we can discover a way of truly seeing and getting to know them. By doing so we also become able to respect them for who they are and what they would like to communicate to us. We know that to an attentive eye and ear infants communicate a great deal about themselves long before they can speak. Already at this stage, observing and listening is a reciprocal experience, because in observing how the children learn, we learn. At the October Study Group in Reggio Emilia, Paola Calliari (1999) said: "Observation, interpretation, and producing documentation are the structure of the work of teachers also with very young infants; these actions are not final and are not only for large projects."

However, to be able to examine and reflect, we have to record what we saw and heard, we have to leave significant traces of our observations. These could include using notes that we jot down or write in an extended way, or making audiotapes that gather the voices and words of children in their dialogues or in our conversations with them. We can take photographs and slides, or make videotapes that show children and teachers in action. The children's work itself, and photographs of the children's work, must be considered essential traces along with these.

Educators in Reggio Emilia remind us that teachers have to invent and rethink instruments for notation and for gathering traces that are relevant for their particular context. Each of these traces is already a document because it conveys a potential version of what has taken place (Rinaldi, 1998). As Loris Malaguzzi (1998) has said:

> Teachers must leave behind an isolated, silent mode of working, which leaves no traces. Instead they must discover ways to communicate and document the children's evolving experiences at school. They must prepare a steady flow of quality information targeted to parents but appreciated by children and teachers. (pp. 69–70)

Tools for Observing. The tools that we use to gather the traces have specific characteristics that can broaden, but also limit, the scope of what we record. We should take time to practice and get to know our tools well. Each documentation choice (be it written notes, photographs, videotapes) has its own bias, potential, and limitations. For example, written notes are essential, but they capture only what we are quick enough to write (although we should take time later to complete them); audiotapes carry the sound of words, but also the noises of the environment, the pauses and silences. Each modality leaves out something or adds something. Furthermore, the way we use each medium is highly subjective; think for example, what we could include or exclude in a photograph or a videotape depending on our focus. Sometimes, we can combine ways of gathering our observations to make a more complete record. For example, we might write some quick notes while simultaneously tape-recording a conversation, so we can later integrate our notes with the words spoken. Or we might choose different methods of writing our notes, depending on how we expect to share them. The way we are planning to examine our observations should be taken into account when we decide how we are going to collect them.

Preparing Recorded Observations for Analysis Together. Once we have gathered our observations, for them to be effective we need to edit and prepare them before we share, discuss, and interpret them. Notes need to be carefully read and organized; recordings need to be transcribed, and the transcript read and highlighted; photographs and slides need to be selected (in part) and set up in flexible sequences; videotapes need to be reviewed with an eye to selecting certain excerpts for viewing. In doing these preparatory tasks we are beginning to reflect on what we have observed and—among other eye-opening experiences—we are becoming aware of our own way of relating to the children.

Sharing, Reflecting, and Interpreting Observations. Our observations can serve as the basis of communication. We can reflect on them together with our colleagues and compare points of view in order to construct a multifaceted interpretation of what we saw and heard while observing the children. In a curriculum that is not set in advance, we can use documentation to construct our understanding of the children's actions and thoughts. This is a recurring process in the course of experiences that we coconstruct and live with children.

In my view, this is one of the aspects of documentation that is most constructive. Through this reflective practice, educators experience continuous professional development along with the pleasure of cooperating and learning together. In a similar vein, Jerome Bruner (1986) discusses with clarity and eloquence the importance in education of having an active discourse with other minds and of working as a community of learners.

A Complex Way to Consider Flexible Planning: *Progettazione*

By examining the recorded and prepared observations together, we can make predictions and develop hypotheses about the children's and our own interests, questions, and understandings. We can examine the directions in which the children seem interested in going and how, or if, we think we can assist them. Having respect for children does not mean that, as teachers, we should blindly follow all their ideas. We should think about them to determine which ones should be pursued and how they might be supported in the context of flexible planning and a flexible curriculum. That will enable us to make appropriate preparations and to be flexible during the course of our work with the children.

Educators in Italy use the term *progettazione* to define the complex way in which teachers plan together. In Reggio Emilia in particular, it refers to the work done in infant-toddler centers and preschools (Rinaldi, 1998). The curriculum is seen as emerging from the teachers' observations of the ideas and interests of children, but it is also shaped by what teachers think will contribute to the children's growth. Therefore, teachers and children construct a flexible plan together (coconstruct). *Progettazione,* therefore, is a dynamic process based on communication that generates documentation and is regenerated by documentation.

Furthermore, there are elements of the context within and around the infant-toddler center or preschool that become part of the planning. In fact, *progettazione,* or "flexible planning," takes into account the overall educational project of a city. It implies considering the schools as a system, where collegiality and collaboration support relationships among the children, educators, and parents; relationships between the school and the community; organization of work; and opportunities for learning and well-being for all protagonists (Rinaldi, 1998).

Communication Through Documentation

The documents discussed and examined above become tools for communication when we, as teachers, work together to select, organize, arrange, and identify them so as to give meaning (or new meaning) to the experience that first produced them (see Figure 10.1). As discussed above, the preparations required to make them readable and available to others allow us to revisit the material we have produced. It is as if we are seeing and listening again to what happened before, thereby gaining further understanding (see Figures 10.2 and 10.3).

Documentation can be presented in many effective ways, including not only panels, but also handwritten or typed materials such as books, notebooks, letters, and flyers, as well as shadow boxes, weaving, installations, and other works. They may be presented in all possible versions and combinations. An important part of documentation comes directly from children's two- and three-dimensional work, either finished or in-progress. It should be accompanied by the reflections of teachers and, when possible, by children's dialogues or thoughts. Also slide and video documentaries communicate in a powerful way both children's and adults' meaningful experiences.

The Experience of Revisiting Documentation with Children. Looking again at documentation with children, or revisiting it, allows us to help them become aware of their own learning and to learn how to learn. Also when children revisit documentation together, they tend to remind each other of their ideas. This gives them a sense of value and belonging (see Figure

FIGURE 10.1. A photograph such as this can help teachers analyze the process of children's experiences.

FIGURES 10.2 and 10.3. Teachers want to communicate to the parents how children explore a new play structure. They observe the children, take photographs, and place them on a panel next to the structure itself. (*Infant-toddler Center Il Faro, Pistoia*)

10.4). In general, through documentation children feel that their work is valued, and they feel part of the community of the center or school.

Potential for Authentic Assessment. When we revisit documentation, we can compare our predictions with newly emerging ideas. It is also possible to note the process involved in children's exploration of their world, their experiences, and their projects. When we do this, we are assessing a work-in-progress. We can assess not only what the children understand and know but also how they come to know. The children are in fact demonstrating their understanding by means of a flexibly constructed curriculum, which is based on observation and dialogue with them even when they are too young to speak.

Communication with Families to Sustain Participation. When parents enter the infant-toddler center or the preschool where their child spends many hours every day, they feel welcome when they see documentation that describes the part of the children's day that they usually do not witness. These children are far too young to tell their parents of their experiences directly. In too many situations, without documentation the life of a child in the center and the life of the child at home run a parallel, silent course.

FIGURE 10.4. When a brother or sister visits from preschool, their younger siblings proudly show the books that teachers have compiled to tell the story of special or daily events that involve each child at the *nido*. (*Infant-toddler Center Lago Mago, Pistoia*)

When documentation is used to show parents how teachers carefully listen to and observe their children, and nurture their children's sense of well-being and developing interests, the parents are more likely to form a sense of trust toward the educators and the infant-toddler center or the preschool. The documentation invites the parents to feel close to their children's experience away from home and contributes importantly to building this trust.

Documentation, Community, and Advocacy. As teachers, we can also use documentation to let the community around us know what happens in our space. We can make the school transparent to parents and a visible presence in the larger community. We can give strength to the voice of the children and teachers by communicating what we have understood and heard. We should find effective means to communicate on an ongoing basis what is happening in the center or preschool to the people who can and should support us in the community. We can be advocates for care and education of young children based on deep respect and commitment. Loris Malaguzzi said that programs for young children distort and assault their own nature if they do not connect to the families, to the culture, and to the local issues, and if they are in some way prevented from having a free and democratic dialogue with the environment in which they operate. He also said that support should go to a school where educators realize how their work is enriched if they join hands with both families and the people in the community (Mantovani, 1998).

Enduring Feature and Memory

We would like to make one more point about the many enriching aspects of documentation. By documenting the life of children at an infant-toddler center or a preschool, we construct a story of that particular center bit by bit. That documentation will provide invaluable memories for the people that live there many hours of their lives, for the people who pass through it during the cycles of growth of their children, and for the people who have worked hard to make it a good place. Too often centers for young children seem to be impersonal and without a trace of history. With documentation we can give each center an identity that will mirror the people who have been involved in it and offer to the ones who enter it a sense of continuity.

In other chapters of this volume (e.g., Chapters 11 and 12), various authors refer to or construct documentation as a means of responding to and accomplishing the complex task of educating infants and young children.

In the next section of this chapter, Jeanne Goldhaber describes how—in a particular setting—educators have reflected upon, developed, and taken ownership of important aspects of documentation.

DOCUMENTATION AS A PROCESS FOR UNDERSTANDING AND BEING UNDERSTOOD

Our story, like most stories, is only meaningful when placed in its context—the University of Vermont's Campus Children's Center. The experiences of the center's children and families, teachers, university students, and faculty are shaped by who we are, where we are, and, for that matter, when we are. Therefore, we believe it's important for you to know that Campus Children's Center provides year-round child care to approximately 40 children (divided into the following groups: 6 infants, 7 young toddlers, 9 young preschoolers, and 18 preschool-aged children) and is housed at the University of Vermont, a medium-sized, primarily undergraduate university. The center is located in a building that combines student living quarters, classroom space, and academic program offices, including those of the Early Childhood Pre-K–3 Teacher Preparation Program.

We believe our size and physical location have played a significant role in our development as a program and community. Being somewhat small and geographically isolated has promoted a sense of interdependence at both the relational and intellectual levels. We look to each other for emotional support and intellectual stimulation, and, I suspect, experience a certain sense of freedom to take risks and make mistakes, knowing that we are in the company of those who share our views and values.

The Campus Children's Center's physical proximity to Early Childhood faculty and staff is also significant because of the very close ties that exist between our academic and children's programs and the extent to which each supports and informs the other. The center's mission is twofold: it provides on-site child care to faculty, staff, and students, and it is also the laboratory school for the Early Childhood Pre-K–3 Teacher Preparation Program. Consequently, the academic courses and center's curriculum reflect a shared social constructivist perspective. The head teachers of the Infant-Toddler and Preschool Programs and Early Childhood faculty coteach courses and share responsibility for supervising students during their practice in the center. The teachers mentor Early Childhood students during their lab experiences and practica in their classrooms and are often invited to early childhood classes to discuss issues relevant to their group of children.

Investigating the Reggio Emilia Approach: A Brief History

Over the past nine years, faculty, staff, and students of the Early Childhood Program and Campus Children's Center have been engaged in a joint investigation of the Reggio Emilia approach. Several of us participated in our first delegation to the early childhood programs of Reggio Emilia in 1991. When we returned from that visit, we were overwhelmed by the challenge of interpreting what we had seen and learned into our own context. We made a number of minor changes to our physical environment, experimented with the use of projects and documentation as curriculum-planning mechanisms, and felt relatively unsuccessful in our attempts to apply what we had experienced in Italy. Three years later several of us returned to Reggio, but this time with the decision that we would limit our focus to the practice of documentation. We decided that documentation, with its emphasis on observation and analysis, would help us address our program's unique mission as a teacher preparation site. Since that second visit, we have been investigating the role of documentation in teacher preparation and staff development. More specifically, we have been interested in the extent to which documentation can promote practice, which is characterized by teacher reflection and inquiry at both the preservice and in-service levels.

Notwithstanding the number of years we have been engaged in this investigation, I do not want to suggest that we think of ourselves as experts. We do not. We think of ourselves as learners—slow but steady learners, as is evidenced by the number of years it has taken us to get to the level of understanding I am reporting in this chapter. I also do not want to suggest that our experience has reached closure, since even in preparing this chapter I found myself yet again rethinking our experiences and, as usual, posing as many new questions as we have answers. Above all, I do not want to portray documentation as something static or as a final product, a panel if you will. Rather, it is of vital importance to me to convey our belief that documentation is a search for understanding.

Documentation: A Search for Understanding

For adults, the documentation process furthers our understanding of the concepts children are building, the theories they are constructing, and the questions they are posing. The process of documentation brings us together as a learning community and challenges us to express our thinking articulately and publicly, and to accept the responsibility, as Carlina Rinaldi suggests (1998), of listening closely to understand other points of view.

We believe the documentation process also invites and supports children's efforts to understand and to be understood, by allowing them to revisit their thinking about their encounters with the physical and social world, to reconsider their theories, to reframe their questions, and to listen closely to each other as they coconstruct meaning and relationships. These views reflect our unique experiences and context and have resulted in a conceptualization of the documentation process that serves as a guide for our teaching practices in both our children's programs and in our academic courses as well. We believe this search for understanding is a complex and multifaceted experience. The remainder of this chapter will highlight the various components that contribute to our conceptualization of the documentation process.

Documentation as a Cycle of Inquiry

First, we have come to see the process of documentation as a cycle of inquiry, which goes through a number of steps or phases in its progression. We have learned a great deal about each phase of this cycle. However, I must caution the reader that this cycle is neither linear nor tidy. While Figure 10.5 suggests an orderly progression, our experience has been that we move through this cycle in fits and starts, sometimes jumping forward, sometimes dropping back. Nevertheless, as this cycle repeats itself in an upward spiral, all its participants build an understanding that grows more meaningful and deeper over time.

Framing Questions. More and more, we are beginning the documentation process by framing our questions. For example, two years ago, the preschool teachers began the year by asking what emerging interests, concepts, and theories the children would be bringing into the classroom in the fall. Out of that question emerged a curriculum that investigated the preschoolers' interest in and thinking about babies. Last year, all the teachers decided to frame their inquiry with a shared question that asked how young children develop the ability to represent and communicate their thinking and feelings.

Throughout this chapter I will refer to an investigation led by Dee Smith, the infant-toddler head teacher, which focused on our toddlers' interactions with clay. Dee framed her questions as: How will young children's exploration of clay become more intentional? How will it evolve into more symbolic efforts? What are the roles of the physical and social environments? We believe that formulating questions such as these helps us focus our efforts and thinking, and results in richer and more in-depth experiences for both children and teachers.

Observing, Recording, and Collecting Artifacts. We have learned that the choice of observation and recording strategies must be carefully considered in the context of the setting, the questions if they have been previously identified, and the goals. For example, in the toddler clay investigation, Dee decided to rely solely on a video camera—a decision that had both its rewards and limitations. This decision reflected her goal of getting as accurate an audio and visual record as possible, the availability of video equipment in our program, and a student staffing pattern that allowed someone to be behind the camera while someone else supported the children's interactions with clay.

Because we are a university-affiliated program and lab school, we do have these resources. To be honest, however, these very resources initially

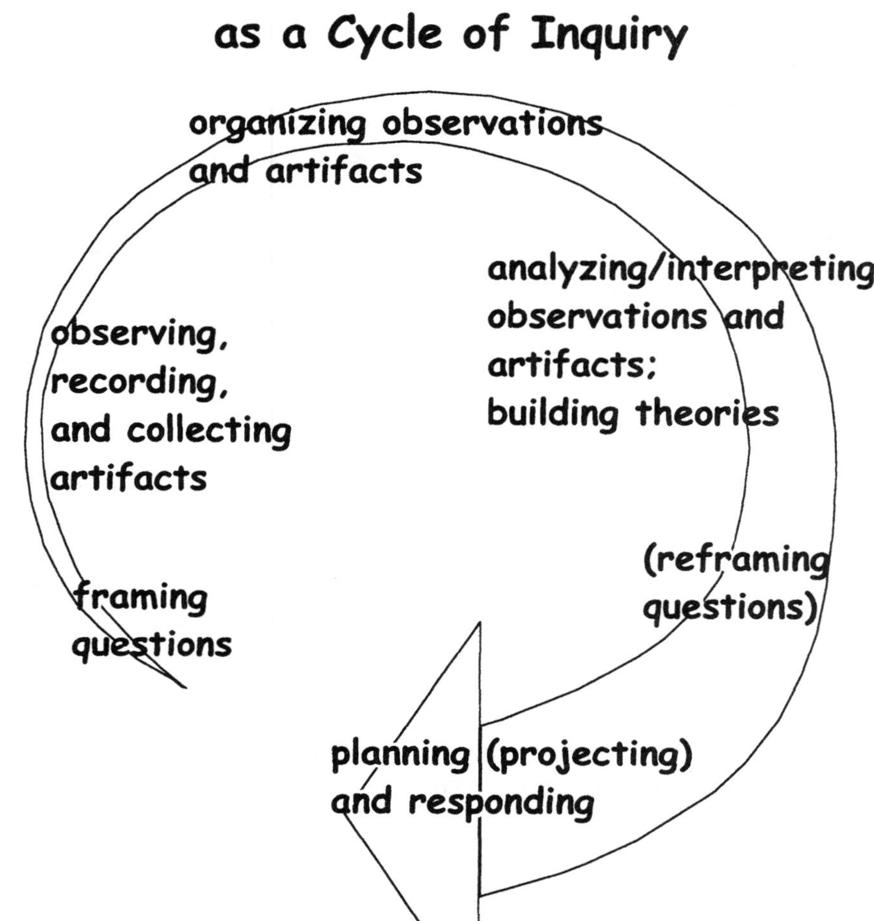

FIGURE 10.5. The documentation process as a cycle of inquiry.

pulled us away from the primary purpose of documentation, which is, as Carlina Rinaldi suggests (1998), to get closer to the child, by leading us toward a concern over documentation as a panel. Please do not assume that without access to video, digital cameras, computers, and scanners, you cannot engage in the documentation process. We have learned that pencil and paper are two of the most portable and flexible observation and recording tools available to classroom teachers.

Organizing Observations and Artifacts. The perceived need to organize came late in our experience. We had always been active observers in our classrooms, but once we recorded the observations we had no system in place that allowed us to use them productively or to share them with our colleagues, families, or children. Finally two years ago, we put a system into place, which we still use today. All classrooms have a central basket that serves as the receptacle of the day's observations, artifacts, photos, and so forth. The classroom teachers discuss the basket's contents and then organize them into loose-leaf binders. Each binder contains documentation specific to a particular "thread of inquiry," a term we use to refer to an investigation that may reflect questions framed by a teacher (as in the clay investigation) or questions that have emerged from the children (as in the case of the preschoolers' investigation of babies). The binders are kept in the classroom as working, public documents.

Further organization depends on the particular question being asked. For example, if Dee had been interested in looking at similarities and differences between boys and girls in regard to their interactions with clay, she could have reorganized the video clips in order to look at the influence of gender. In fact, the issue of organization was relatively straightforward for Dee, since she was primarily interested in the progression of children's use of clay over time, and all of her information was recorded chronologically on video. Since Dee was also interested in the influence of such factors as group size and tool use, she developed a log that reflected these variables as well.

Analyzing Observations and Artifacts, Building Theories. For us, one of the most challenging and intellectually and emotionally engaging aspects of the documentation process involves analyzing or interpreting what we have observed, recorded, and organized. Out of our analyses come theories and hypotheses about the meaning of the children's behavior. We have found that the process of analysis can involve a great deal of disequilibrium—that is, it often generates the discomfort that accompanies knowing when you do not know or do not understand.

Creating a climate that allows its protagonists (children and adults) to take risks and to be wrong is critical yet in itself an ambitious goal. For example, at various times in the clay investigation, Dee and the teachers who were working with her became overwhelmed by the complexity of the phenomena they were studying. During staff meetings, and in more informal and impromptu conversations, Dee and the toddler teachers shared segments of tape as well as their thinking about the meaning inherent in the children's exploration of the clay. Conversations such as these play a pivotal role in moving beyond using observations for descriptive purposes to using them to deepen understanding.

Reframing Questions. We have found that we reframe our questions at various points in the cycle. These reframed questions are often more specific and allow us to be more intentional and better observers. While not always the case, we typically find ourselves reframing our questions as a result of our analyses of observations, which would then lead us to a decision to observe again, but with a revised question. For example, while Dee did not start the clay investigation with any questions about the effect of group size on the children's clay exploration, our analyses of the children's interactions led us to observe the social context of the children's clay experiences with more intentionality, which in turn led to plans that included presenting the clay in smaller groups.

Planning, Projecting, and Responding. It has taken us years to understand how to use our observations and analyses to guide our planning and to shape our projections for what we might do next. For example, after repeated viewings of Dee's tapes, decisions were made that reflected our understanding of the questions the children were asking through their interactions with the clay. More specifically, in several sessions we watched the children heft the clay, break it into smaller and smaller pieces, and line up coils in parallel positions. We were struck by the degree to which their actions suggested an interest in mathematical concepts or what Sinclair and her colleagues (1989) refer to as "prelogical mathematical thinking."

This awareness led to subsequent sessions in which we made a point of presenting the clay in smaller, more pliable pieces that the children could more easily manipulate and change. We also invited pairs of children who were indicating an interest in mathematical concepts to work together. These presentations provoked further mathematical language (the use of words such as *two, more, big,* and so forth) and exploration of mathematical concepts such as one-to-one correspondence (making holes in a clay slab and systematically filling each hole with a poker or a small clay ball). Our awareness of children's interest in mathematical concepts also led to an increased alertness to the ways in which the children were investigating mathematical concepts with other materials in the classroom.

The Role of Context in the Documentation Process

The context in which teachers and children work and play, as well as the personal expectations of all involved, needs to be examined.

Documentation Must Be Embedded in a Collaborative Process. Collaboration among teachers, among teachers and the children, and among the children themselves leads to deeper understanding and richer, more meaningful relationships. The conversations we had as a staff about the clay investigation as well as conversations with other teachers about their work contributed to our professional development and kept us engaged in our work. Similarly, children clearly built on each other's ideas throughout the clay investigation, both directly through offering suggestions as well as indirectly through example.

Professional Literature Informs the Documentation Process. We are members of an academic community, so it is not surprising that at some point in an investigation, we always turn to the professional literature. Dee and the toddler teachers looked to the work at Ohio State (Ice, 1993) to guide their thinking about how the children interacted with clay. They consulted Sinclair, Stambak, Lézine, Rayna, and Verba's work (1989) for insight about the children's prelogical thinking, as well as books and articles related to constructivism by George Forman (Forman & Hill 1984; Forman & Kushner, 1983). Belsky and Most's research (1981) also offered a helpful discussion of the progression of play, as did various publications from Reggio Emilia (Edwards, Gandini, & Forman, 1998).

Time Significantly Influences the Documentation Process. It takes time to observe, to collaborate, to think, to organize your thinking, and to make your thinking public. This is as true for the adult as for the child. How to carve out that time depends on the particular setting, and most certainly requires a very high level of discipline and commitment to the process. In our case, we finally adopted the format of a graduate course for our staff meeting time in order to discuss teachers' and children's investigations, such as those of toddlers' use of clay. Certainly, this meant that some issues related to center management were not addressed in as timely a manner as they could have been, but we have found that the benefits of spending an hour and a half a week thinking out loud and together about our and the children's theories and questions far outweigh whatever is lost in terms of the typical staff meeting agenda.

Like adults, children also need time to observe, to collaborate, to think, to organize their thinking, and to make their thinking public. The daily lives of children must respect this process: children are by nature inquisitive and eager to explore; they are by nature theory builders and meaning makers; they are in fact scientists, philosophers, and artists (see Figures 10.6–10.9). And like scientists, philosophers, and artists, they simply must have long uninterrupted blocks of time to pursue their questions, to formulate and test their theories, to consider and reconsider their theories in light of conflicting or supporting data, to engage in dialogue and debate. We are convinced that the toddlers' experiences would have been significantly compromised had we limited their time because of misconceptions about short attention spans of young children.

Space Too Plays a Significant Role in the Documentation Process. While we have many resources, space is not one of them. In fact, this fall the teachers of our program decided to transform what is our staff room to a studio. This decision reflects their growing need for a well-equipped protected space for the children to engage in their investigations and use of materials (but may well underestimate the need of the teachers for a similar protected space to be together!). The clay investigation would certainly have bene-

FIGURE 10.6. Derek's expression registers the weight and size of the piece of clay.

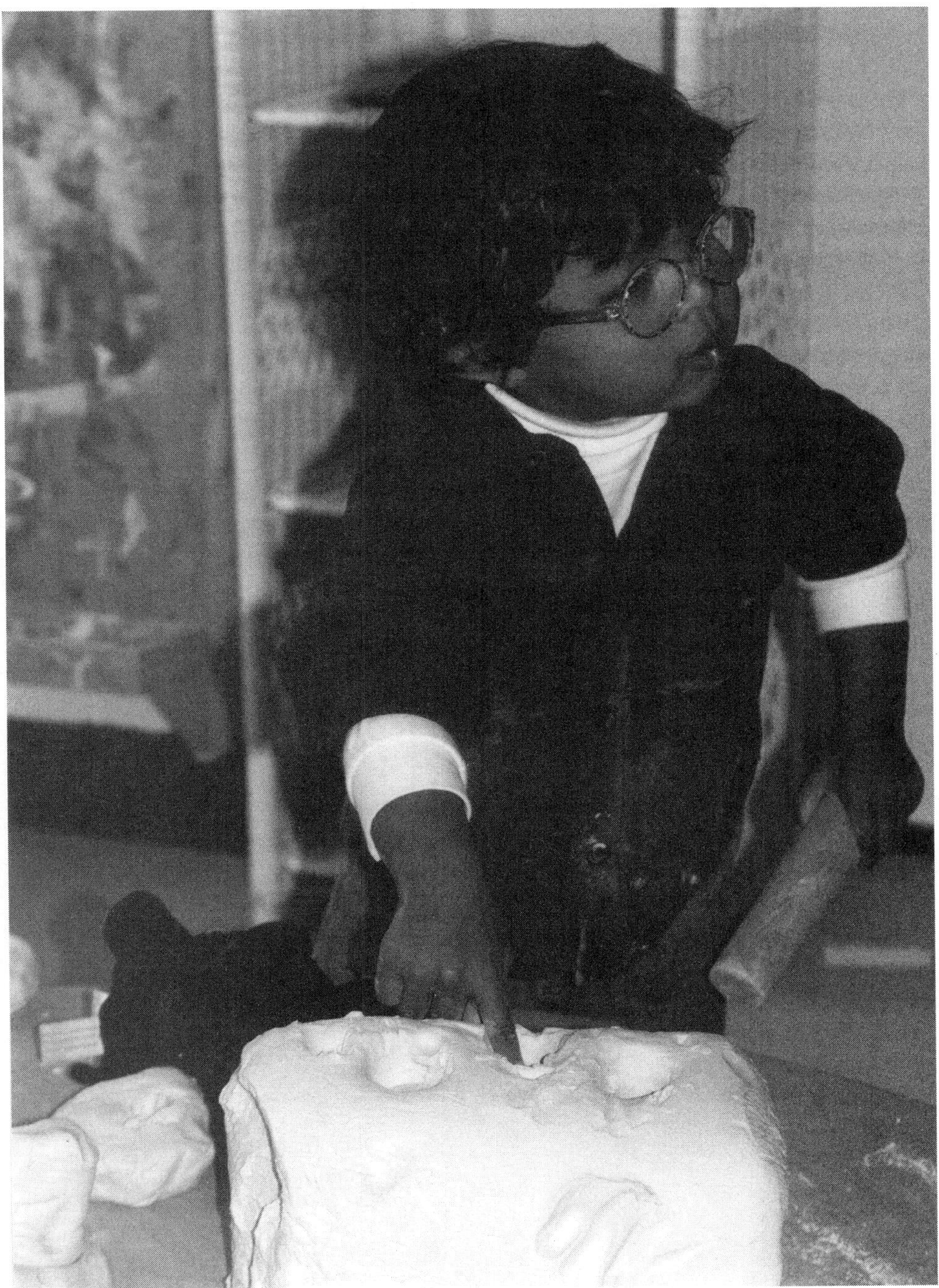

FIGURE 10.7. Andrew looks to his teacher as if he is asking a question about the holes in the clay.

FIGURE 10.8. Ethan inspects a hole created in his clay piece. "A tunnel—" he says, "train come through." As he rechecks the hole, he says, "You can't see it."

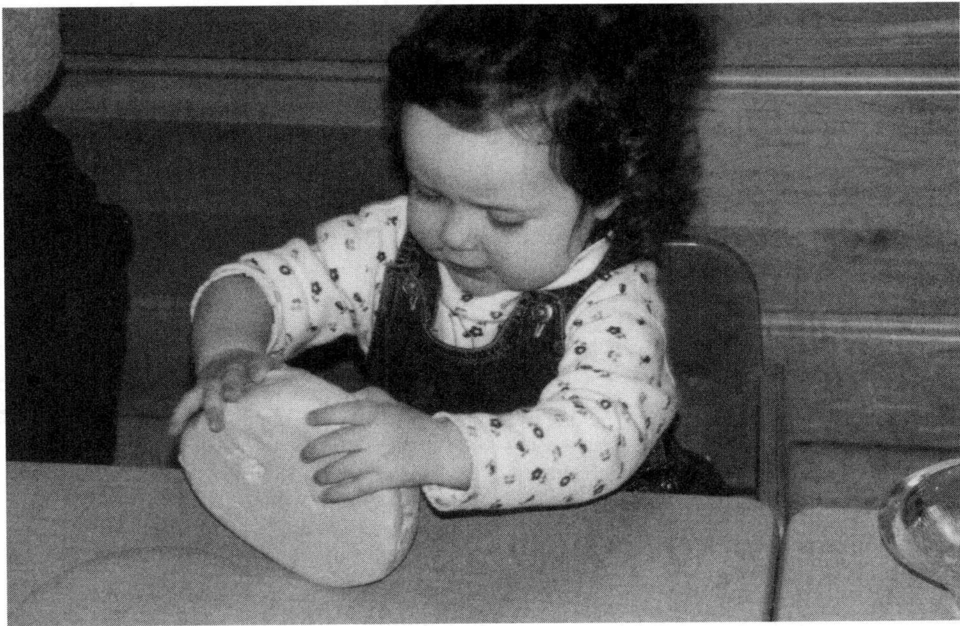

FIGURE 10.9. Maria pokes holes in the clay and then lifts it, pausing to observe the underside of the slab. After inspecting the smooth surface she turns the clay over.

fited from such a space, but even within the confines of the toddlers' room, Dee and her colleagues were constantly negotiating how to make the best use of their physical environment.

Reaching Out with Documentation

Documentation is a form of advocacy. Again and again, we were struck by the extent to which individual toddlers persisted in their own particular investigations related to the clay. By documenting and making our observations of the clay investigation public, we invited parents and students to join us in our inquiry and to celebrate children's developing knowledge and skills. We are currently exploring the use of public documentation to engage our larger community in a city and statewide dialogue about improving our early childhood programs and services. Clearly, the documentation process provides us with a forum through which we can give voice to the competence and rights of young children and their families.

Documentation is also an agent of change. Dee's willingness to share the clay investigation with the professional community at various meetings is a prime example of the extent to which the documentation process can widen and enrich our professional world. Indeed, we believe that the process of documentation has the potential to change how we early childhood educators see ourselves as professionals. It certainly requires that we expand our identity from nurturer and caregiver to include theoretician and researcher. We have found that documentation demands a high level of intellectual commitment and curiosity and a passionate engagement in our work. Documentation redefines the role we play in our professional community by its reliance on continuous dialogue and collaboration.

Finally, documentation engages the head and heart. Dee's sharing of the clay investigation with other professionals was clearly spurred on not only by what she had learned, but also by the strong feelings and emotional engagement she had experienced throughout. Children too experience the joyfulness of true intellectual engagement, discovering in themselves their competence and potential. This then, for us, is the power of documentation in that children and adults become partners in an intellectual and emotional enterprise that builds our identity as individuals and as a learning and loving community.

REFERENCES

Belsky, J., & Most, R. (1981). From exploration to play: A cross-sectional study of infant free play behavior. *Developmental Psychology, 17,* 630–639.

Bruner, J. (1986). *The culture of education.* Cambridge, MA: Harvard University Press.

Calliari, P. (1999). *The meaning of documentation in the infant-toddlers and preschools of Reggio Emilia.* Presentation at the October Study Group in Reggio Emilia, Italy.

Carter, M., & Curtis, D. (1996). *Spreading the news: Sharing stories of early childhood programs.* St. Paul, MN: Redleaf Press.

Dahlberg, G., Moss, P., & Pence, A. (1999). *Beyond quality in early childhood education and care: Postmodern perspectives.* Philadelphia: Falmer Press.

Edwards, C. P., Gandini, L., & Forman, G. (Eds.) (1998). *The hundred languages of children: The Reggio Emilia approach—advanced reflections* (2nd ed.). Stamford, CT: Ablex.

Forman, G., & Hill, T. (1984). *Constructive play: Applying Piaget in the preschool.* Menlo Park, CA: Addison-Wesley.

Forman, G., & Kushner, D. (1983). *The child's construction of knowledge: Piaget for teaching children.* Washington, DC: National Association for the Education of Young Children.

Helm, J. H., Beneke, S., & Steinheimer, K. (1997). *Windows on learning: Documenting young children's work.* New York: Teachers College Press.

Ice, E. (1993). *Projects and action research with infants and toddlers: The reciprocal nature of action and thought.* Unpublished master's thesis, Ohio State University, Columbus.

Malaguzzi, L. (1998). History, ideas, and basic philosophy. In C. P. Edwards, L. Gandini, & G. Forman (Eds.), *The hundred languages of children: The Reggio Emilia approach—advanced reflections* (2nd ed., pp. 49–97). Stamford, CT: Ablex.

Mantovani. S. (1998). Incontri, confronti, dissensi, nostalgie [Encounters, debates, disagreements, nostalgias]. In S. Mantovani (Ed.), *Nostalgia del futuro: Lib-*

erare speranze per una nuova cultura dell'infanzia [Nostalgia for the future: To set free hope for a new culture of childhood] (pp. 3–10). Bergamo, Italy: Edizioni Junior.

Rinaldi, C. (1998). Projected curriculum constructed through documentation—*progettazione*. In C. P. Edwards, L. Gandini, & G. Forman (Eds.), *The hundred languages of children: The Reggio Emilia approach—advanced reflections* (2nd ed., pp. 113–125). Stamford, CT: Ablex.

Sinclair, H., Stambak, S., Lézine, I., Rayna, S., & Verba, M. (Eds.). (1989). *Infants and objects: The creativity of cognitive development*. San Diego, CA: Academic Press. (Original work published 1982)

Vecchi, V. (1998). The role of the *atelierista*. In C. P. Edwards, L. Gandini, & G. Forman (Eds.), *The hundred languages of children: The Reggio Emilia approach—advanced reflections* (2nd ed., pp. 139–147). Stamford, CT: Ablex.

Chapter 11

TRACES OF CHILDHOOD: A CHILD'S DIARY

Donatella Giovannini

Certainly, sharing the first years of a child's life is a serious responsibility for an adult, but it is also an experience rich with feelings of affection, and with discoveries. It is an experience that strongly involves you as a teacher because you feel that you are weaving together something with a child that, somehow, will go beyond the time you spend together. To raise a child within an early childhood service, alongside other children and with colleagues, asks something extra of the adults who work with the children—something beyond assuring each child a rich and stimulating, safe and welcoming environment.

It calls for a generosity of attitude and a will to give back to the individual child—and to his or her parents—the events, thoughts, feelings, and ideas that tell the story of the days at the infant-toddler center. It calls for the ability to retell, to place events and small personal anecdotes within a broader history so that a memento of childhood can be given to each child. Beyond that, building such documentation about a single child is a way to offer individual attention and to value and identify individual differences and styles. It allows the teacher to make each child's experience unique and special.

CONSTRUCTING THE DIARY

Constructing a *diario* (diary) requires a great deal of time, continuity, and determination in gathering the materials for such a document, which is

---

 ISBN 0-8077-4008-X (paper), ISBN 0-8077-4009-8 (cloth).

made of words, images, and texts. The work begins the day the child enters the infant-toddler center with his parents and ends with his passage to preschool. In order to be sustained over time, this work requires tools that facilitate gathering data and observations. Some of these working tools must be easy to use so that they allow a teacher to make short, quick notes about a meaningful event. When the teacher later reflects about what has taken place, these notes can remind her of the whole scene. Without such a cue, the passing of time pushes the event inexorably into the past. Memory needs supports. We can use the help of photos and writings of every sort, papers, notebooks, letters, newspaper clippings, and other materials.

Tools and Strategies

The preparation for a diary is about building an archive. It is about having a container for each child to store photos, notes, observations, folders for paintings and drawings, and a box containing the child's three-dimensional work. But it may also entail using tools such as a "notebook for two voices," in which parents and teachers record a child's developmental progress (see Magrini & Gandini, Chapter 12, this volume). In addition to encouraging cooperation that allows parents and teachers to work with the child with greater confidence and trust, such notebooks for two voices offer a unique way of reconstructing together the child's growth process. These are composed of notes and anecdotes, generally short and quick, which pertain to the child's growth and development, as well as other reflections or any ideas.

Other invaluable tools are personal calendars for each child and reflective observation notebooks, both of which provide an excellent support for memory. A calendar, as soon as it is marked with a few words and letters, becomes indisputably the calendar of a *particular* child, while observation notebooks are the heart of a good diary. In fact, no sooner do the teachers begin to reflect on what they have recorded than the events and reflections that exist as notes in the notebooks and in calendars flow naturally into the diaries.

So over the course of three years, as teachers stay with the same group of children for that cycle, they accumulate and select a rich collection of materials that are stored daily in a way that is both accessible and visible to families. Making the collection visible to parents is important. It implies that this material will not be consumed in the moment, but will be carried to its fullest value in a diary, where all the material woven together creates a true biography of each child. Then, during the end-of-the-year party, when everyone says good-bye to the children who will be going to preschool, the teachers surprise those families with their diaries. It is an emotionally intense moment as parents realize that they are being given something that so strongly sums up three years of their own child's life.

Characteristics of a Diary

We hold frequent meetings between teachers from our various infant-toddler centers in order to exchange ideas and compare the ways they have developed to make these diaries. Through these meetings, we share better and better solutions. Because we have borrowed from each other over the years, the diaries from our various infant-toddler centers now have a lot in common, in addition to their inevitable differences.

First of all, we have agreed that attention to the aesthetic tends to value and give greater emphasis to what we are telling in the diary. These must be books that both young children and grownups can appreciate, so they must be beautiful. Beauty enriches and gratifies both those who have prepared the book and those who read it. We try to make our diaries beautiful through the composition of the page, the balance between written text and images, the choice of colors, and the overall compilation and construction. Making a beautiful book also demonstrates a respectful image of the child, whose story is not told through a string of platitudes but rather through good taste, showing that someone took time and gave the child's story serious attention, understanding, and respect (see the *diario* examples in the color insert in this volume).

Another characteristic of our diaries is sturdiness. In fact, since these books are meant to be read over and over by children, it is essential that they be robust (a bit like board books), made with heavy paper and bound in a way that allows easy, confident use. Parents themselves tell us that their children look at their diaries over and over, each time finding something new that sparks different stories to be told.

THE VOICES OF THE DIARY

All of our diaries are characterized by the possibility of multiple readings—by parents and by children. Thus the diary is an unusual sort of children's book, in which text and images enter into a dialogue and together reinforce the meaning. Observations and notes are linked together by a text, in which the teacher talks directly to the child in an intimate way, evoking his or her experiences: "At the table, we sang our songs, we celebrated your birthday or we told about when we went to take a walk in the park."

The colorful string of memories begins to unwind. It flows among stories of friendships with other children, playing with water and clay and taking care of plants and animals, birthdays and parties, and other moments of intense personal significance. The child is invited and encouraged to remember and to use the book actively, as a real book-game. Often the diaries contain envelopes to open, with all sorts of things inside: little messages and surprises, photos to glue, songs to sing, names of friends to look for in the pictures, strings that measure how long the child was when he or she arrived at the center and when he or she left. The pages are like windows that open to a variety of connected messages.

On the pages of the diary, each voice—the child's and the adult's—is of equal import but is dependent, and emphasis so that one becomes weak without the other and loses its meaning. Thus, for example, the teacher might present the analytical observation of an activity, a transcription of dialogues, and a corresponding sequence of photographs next to it. Another page might include a brief note beside the child's drawing, or a vacation postcard next to a photo of the child preparing his "vacation box," along with a series of remarks by the parents. The vacation box is a small cardboard box that travels with the child over the summer, providing a place to store summer treasures and memories that are then brought back in September to the infant-toddler center.

The diary offers something for everyone in the sense that there are many ways of communication and many styles of recording information—from the punctual and precise, such as records of what the children do and say; to the more descriptive, to convey an emotional atmosphere; to the sequences of photographs, which like a short film show us action in progress. It is the adult's narrative flow that connects the verbal to the nonverbal message.

In general, we shun the two extremes: the all-too-common habit of resorting to slogans and sound bytes, which only serve to diminish children's work, and information overkill, for fear of not saying everything. We have the variety of choices described above, and we know there are many more possible. For us what determines the success of a technique or tool is whether it helps us to produce texts that are useful on many levels. These are merely some of the ways we have been able to make diaries that do not constrain the readers to one single reading, but permit them to choose their own itinerary.

What Do the Diaries Tell?

Deliberately we choose to record not just special events and annual celebrations (Christmas, parties, Carnival). To the contrary, what emerges from the diary's pages is the power of the everyday, the force of normalcy. Historians know that they must record not just unusual and grand events. History should be told, sometimes more profoundly, by narrating microevents, by describing marginal contexts and small happenings. Thinking of children, Christa Wolf (1992) wrote: "We know how negligent children's memories are, caring to save only the radiant, colorful, or fearful happenings, but not the daily repetitions that are life" (p. 86). The same negligence often affects adults who are not convinced that there is richness of meaning in everyday practices, and who are therefore scarcely inclined to celebrate daily events. This is why what unfolds in the pages of a diary are the words that emerge every day, first saved, and then given back at a higher level because they have been mediated by the thoughtful and attentive adults. The "journey" of the child in the infant-toddler center, through the diary, shows a richness of small things and a taste for emotions and affectivity that meshes with the pleasure of doing things together. The diaries show a curious child, for whom growth is indicated by discoveries, by small explorations, and by strong ties of cooperation and friendship.

A Child Among Children

Being above all the witness of each individual child's experience, the diary nonetheless shows how the story of each child is interwoven with the story of the group of other children and teachers at the center. It shows how this web of relationships becomes an instrument for growth, in which identities are formed. Through each child's biography, we define the life of this little community that is the infant-toddler center. For us, the diary represents a high point professionally because personal attention to an individual child is written into the social history of a particular infant-toddler center, during a particular period of time. The diary expresses the particular culture of that center—the personal culture created by and known to all of its members.

This is why the diary includes many observations, dialogues, and testimonies that relate to the life of the small group of children. It contains the experiences that cemented their relationships and that created, therefore, that sort of shared vocabulary made up not only of words but also of gestures, play with words (word games), and reference to shared situations, rules, and encounters with imaginary characters. Similarly but more concretely, each diary contains all the other children's addresses so that they can stay in touch and these tender but important friendships are not interrupted.

From the moment they assume the function of intellectual "envelope," capable of giving back to children and parents a connected memory of fragmented experiences, the adults who compile these diaries thus become the privileged witnesses of the child's growth. The children's inability to speak directly and fully about their experiences makes it necessary for others to tell the story for them in all its richness. The infant-toddler center's educational projects risk being flattened to the lowest quality if the services lack strong means of communicating and ways of promoting relevant aspects of its experience, beyond what the child can tell in the first person.

SUPPORTING THE MOVE TO DETACHMENT

We must still address the meaning that these books have for the teachers who make them. In the life of the child at the infant-toddler center, the diary represents the ultimate gesture of attention to the child, and in our experience this form of documentation is the one that teachers take on with the greatest enthusiasm. Even though it requires a lot of their time, they do not want to renounce this challenge. This commitment from teachers is the result of their authentic and strong attachment to the children with whom they have shared a piece of life. Without a doubt there is also the desire to share with the families their children's path toward autonomy and to show how the infant-toddler center helped their children's physical and psychological growth.

But alongside these motives, it seems that we can add another. It is inevitable that people who establish relationships of great empathy with children sooner or later have to bring them to a close. Writing and preparing these diaries gives the teachers a chance to settle their thoughts and feelings, to see them mature and take form, and to detach them from the immediate context. That is, the diary is a mirror that reflects and amplifies back what has happened in the opposite direction. The teachers will put into the diary the same attention they had given from the moment the child entered the center. Making a diary is a way to take one's leave, to process the separation that will come soon, and to give one's work a sense of completeness and conclusion.

REFERENCE

Wolf, C. (1992). *Trame d'infanzia* [Childhood Plots]. Rome: Editori Riuniti.

Chapter 12

Inclusion: Dario's Story

Gabri Magrini and Lella Gandini

I, Lella, heard the beginning of Dario's story at a meeting of teachers who were working with children with special needs in their infant-toddler centers. The purpose of the meeting was to exchange experiences and ideas, to find support from each other and from the pedagogical coordinator, within a plan of professional development.

The meeting took place not long after the beginning of the school year. Gabri, a teacher in the 2- to 3-year-old children's classroom, had just welcomed Dario and his mother to the center. She explained how she felt: Dario's mother had asked her to promise that Dario would be able to speak like the other children by the end of the school year. Gabri felt at once the mother's suffering and the complexity of her role as a teacher. Naturally she did not promise what the mother had asked, but she helped her notice how much Dario liked the rich space of the center and proposed that they work together to support his growth.

INCLUSION IN ITALY

Inclusion of young children with special needs has been common in Italian centers and schools over the last 30 years. This commitment has been supported by specific legislation at the national level and appropriate policies at the local level. In 1971 the Italian parliament passed the first law concerning education of children with disabilities. In 1977 and in 1992 further national laws specified strategies of inclusion. A maximum of two children with disabilities may be integrated into any one class, and integrated classes are limited to 20 children. At the local level, administra-

---

 ISBN 0-8077-4008-X (paper), ISBN 0-8077-4009-8 (cloth).

tions made policies such as establishing the limit to one child with disabilities per class and providing a support teacher if needed. The support teacher works with the regular teacher, the particular child, and the class as a whole, in order to achieve integration. The philosophy has progressed through the years from physical integration to full inclusion. The child included, according to the law of 1992, is made part of the class, with the object of developing the potential for learning communication and social relations (Smith, 1998).

To integrate any child into the classroom implies the recognition, acceptance, and management of diversity, with the awareness of the importance of education and the social construction of the identity and individuality of each child. This—as Dario's story will show—requires a great deal of professional awareness, sensitivity, flexibility, and respect (Gandini & Gambetti, 1997).

In Italy, in the most developed educational situations, a collaborative team is put together to support the child and the family. This team consists of the teacher, the supporting teacher, a pedagogical coordinator, the child's parents or family members, and the representatives of the local health unit (such as physicians, psychologists, social workers, nurses, or

FIGURE 12.1. A little girl with special needs is welcomed to her *nido* by the teacher. Soon she will be sharing play with her group of friends. (*Infant-toddler Center Il Grillo, Pistoia*)

therapists of appropriate specializations). The support team designs an educational plan that focuses on the child's strengths and motivations rather than on the child's limitations or deficiencies and involves other children as much as possible.

A DIALOGUE BETWEEN A TEACHER AND A MOTHER

Dario's story is presented here in excerpts from the dialogue taking place between Dario's teacher Gabri and Dario's mother in a "notebook for two voices" (see Giovannini, Chapter 11, this volume) and from the teacher's own "observation and reflections notebook." This story was documented through the construction of a book that included photographs and drawings done by Dario, as well as pages from the two notebooks (Magrini, 1997).

From Gabri's Reflection and Observation Notebook

September 1996. Dario arrived at our infant-toddler center *(Asilo Nido Lagomago)* with his mother, who presented him right away as a child with serious relational difficulties. Up to that point, he had attended a municipal play center, called Children's Area *(Area Bambini Blu)*. Dario's experi-

FIGURE 12.2. Gabri points to a "notebook for two voices" in the entryway of her classroom.

ence at the Children's Area had been very positive and important (notwithstanding one small incident—a bite) because it provided a transition into the infant-toddler center. In the first meeting with Dario's mother, I immediately felt that the first thing to do was to deal with her fears. These were understandable since she had just become aware of the diagnosis of her son's autism. I knew it was a sensitive time for her. Dario arrived at the infant-toddler center at 3 years of age. He could not express himself in speech. In personal relationships he did not take an aggressive stance, but he demonstrated difficulties with physical and visual contact. He had a strong interest in using his hands to do things.

My anxiety had more to do with his mother's expectations and worries than with her son's adjustment to the center. During the *inserimento* (transition) period, at first Dario did not even realize that his mother had left, and he was calm. Thereafter, I followed the advice of Dr. Lupi, the consulting neuropsychologist from the local health unit who works with children, families, and schools. I suggested to Dario's mother that she should tell Dario good-bye, explaining to her that it was important for him to experience the separation in a constructive way. She did, but it threw her into crisis because at the moment of separation, he cried. Soon, though, she understood that this crying was a positive sign because it meant that Dario was progressing in his relationship and his differentiation from her, and that that was fundamental for his healthy growth. Slowly, as his mother grew calmer, Dario consolidated and internalized the maternal presence within himself, and he cried less and less at their separation until finally arriving at the center he was pleased to come into my arms and to greet me.

From the "Notebook for Two Voices"

Dario's Mother, September 1996. I was very anxious as I waited for the meeting about Dario's entrance into the infant-toddler center. Then came the much-awaited call from Gabri, in which she told me that the new parents meeting would be the afternoon of the same day that my older daughter Alba started preschool. During this introductory visit, which was Dario's first encounter with the infant-toddler center, he was very curious to discover and explore all the spaces and materials. Every now and then, when he slowed down, he played. The rest of the time, he was always running to find out more and more about this beautiful place that was so new to him. I sought to involve him in no matter what game with other children, but I didn't always succeed. However, I was still happy that he wasn't afraid of the other children. Even if they didn't play together directly, their presence didn't bother him, as I knew it had in the past.

Gabri, September 1996. The first day, you came with your mother, and you immediately began to explore your new environment. The young toddlers' section attracted your attention the most. You toured every corner of this space, and then you sat down on the big cushion. Your mother, slowly, brought you upstairs to the older toddlers' space where you, too, will play this year. Here, being a very large area, it was difficult for you to linger in any one corner. You seemed always to be searching for something. At a certain point, you found the coffee cups in the housekeeping area very interesting. You took them with you to the toddler's room and then you offered them to your mother. You stayed for a while to look at that room that had fascinated you so. Your mother then tried to involve you in playing with the other children; she wanted to end your walking around and around, but you reacted by having a tantrum.

Gabri, September 24, 1996. Today your mother stepped away for a longer time, though she stayed in the center so that she could observe your reaction for herself. You looked for her with your eyes, but you remained calm in every way. With your teacher Roberta you tried to make a tower with the small cubes, and then you wanted to continue your exploration of our rooms. You came to the manipulation room where children were making dough, but it didn't seem to interest you much. Therefore, I led you down to the young toddlers' area. You were momentarily free and happy. You stayed there until your mother came back in to join you.

Gabri, September 27, 1996. We went out into the garden, and your mother went home. We organized our terrarium and cracked the nuts Francesco brought in. In the meantime, you took with you two Mickey Mouse toothbrush covers that had captured your interest all morning long, even when we went in strollers to the park to see the large turtles. You were calm, however, and in the park you seemed to observe many things.

Dario's Mother, September 30, 1996. I tried to stop his usual running from one room to the other, but he fell into a fit of crying and yelling, as I've never seen him do before. A moment before intervening, I thought and understood that it was not yet the right time to stop him. However, I could not help but stop him. Very little time had gone by, and *he* wanted to continue to explore. After that day, I stayed with Dario the whole morning, but I did not interfere much. His teacher Roberta was looking after him. Then I took him home before lunch for three or four days. On the 7th, we tried to have him stay for lunch, but without much success, because I was a bit agitated. It was Alba's birthday, and I had a thousand things to do at the house. So I made a mistake those days, not because of disorganization, but because I was not yet very familiar with Gabri and I didn't dare say "no" when she suggested that he stay for lunch. Maybe that happened also because I was anxious to see how it had gone and how he had reacted. At home he was calmer, maybe because I was calmer too.

Gabri, September 30, 1996. This morning when you arrived we were in the reading room. We played for a little while with your mother, and then

FIGURE 12.3. Dario's mother tries to calm him down by holding him close to her.

you turned toward the movement room. I followed you to see what you were looking for, and in fact you approached the blocks. We brought them to the other children, but you weren't especially convinced of the idea of playing close to them so you left again. To my "no" you did not have a tantrum, but you slapped me first and then the children who happened to be nearby. This reaction showed that you recognized our presence. I began to play like I would catch you, and I took you in my arms and cuddled you. You smiled. When your mother returned, she was shocked by your behavior and seemed worried about the reaction the other children might have toward you.

From Gabri's Reflection and Observation Notebook

October 1996. Another important experience was the relationship with other children and the necessity of placing limits in order to live peacefully together. In particular moments of crisis, in which Dario tended to spin about frenetically from one room to the other, refusing every contact with others, it was necessary sometimes to say, "NO!" always explaining, however, the reasons for the limitations. To these first "NOs," he reacted energetically. He got mad, pulling at his hair, biting and slapping. This reaction only lasted a short while. More and more often, Dario noticed the other people and realized the consequences of his actions. All this facilitated the process of developing trust and attachment with me. Furthermore, in Dario's first contacts with the other children, he reacted in the same ways: he didn't want to be touched, nor kissed, nor caressed. Their presence at a distance didn't disturb him, though, and in time he moved from solitary play to parallel play. Placing limits, therefore, helped both Dario and the other children. For him, it helped with regard to the improper use of objects and to participation in the various experiences of the day (play, lunch, and stroll). For the others, it helped them to respect Dario's particular "world."

From the Notebook for Two Voices

Gabri, October 7, 1996. Today for the first time you and your mother stayed with us for lunch. We let you pick the dishes you preferred, even if you didn't want to taste anything. Your mother encouraged you, holding you in her lap, but you were interested in other things. In fact, you did not want to sit at the table but preferred to walk around.

Gabri, October 10, 1996. Today at lunch you ate a piece of bread with olive oil, all alone at the big table. Your friends were sitting at the small table, and you played at moving from one chair to the next at the big table. We tried putting your plate at this table, too, and in fact you went over to it and ate all your bread. Having finished eating, you continued for a little while playing your game of moving from chair to chair. Then you went into the infants' room, where as in the toddlers', you like to play.

From Gabri's Reflection and Observation Notebook

November 10, 1996. I see Dario as calmer now. He arrives in the morning and wants to go directly to his room to play. He has established a good, trusting relationship with me. He distinguishes me from the other teachers, though he hasn't had any difficulties with them. He allows me to cuddle him in moments of crisis, and he calms down immediately afterward. He often looks in the mirror and smiles, making me think of an identity game. He likes playing with the Legos and other building blocks for long periods of time, especially if we play music in the background. I notice that his glance lingers on different things more than in the beginning, and he is less agitated when the room is in a bit of disarray. In the infants' room where he loves to go at lunchtime, he is more collaborative with the other youngest children. They are experimenting with their first exchanges of objects, and the experience is more connected for him. Before lunch, he washes his hands with the other children, but then he doesn't want to eat with us at the table. He prefers to eat things he brings from home.

The other children have accepted Dario easily into the group. They call out to him, and if they don't see him, they ask where he is. Every now and then one of them approaches him to give him a kiss, but he does not always accept this gesture—especially from Francesco, who has a decisive manner. If, instead, I ask if I can give him a kiss, he comes closer and offers me his cheek.

November 11, 1996. Dario is calm in the housekeeping area. From here he moves toward the little bedroom, takes a can of hand cream, opens it, and then takes it into the kitchen. He goes over to the mirror, looks in it, smiles, and turns around. Every now and then he stops to watch the other children, and he returns to explore the objects around him. There are several spoons and forks on the ground. He takes them in his hands, looks at them, and tries to bend them. Matteo takes them away from him, and Dario reacts well.

He looks for other objects, still in the midst of other children, but differently than in previous times, he looks more attentively at what the others are doing. He is no longer afraid of physical contact. At a certain point, he gets bored and he comes to look for me. He takes my hand and wants to change rooms, but he doesn't fall apart when I do not consent. He returns calmly to the housekeeping area.

From the Notebook for Two Voices

Dario's Mother, December 1996. Before, every morning when I told Dario it was time to go to the center, to his teachers Gabri and Lorena, he smiled. Now, in December, when I tell him, as I do every morning, he cries huge tears. He doesn't want to go to the center, and when the car turns in to park at the center, he wants to stay in my arms. He cries and pouts. I try to remain as calm as I can, and I wait to leave the center until I can see that he has settled down. Otherwise, he is relaxed at home. However, I have to say, my son has changed a lot, compared to a year ago. My husband Angelo and I are calmer than before, and more positive, because our child is making progress. We are anxiously awaiting this Christmas vacation because we will be more free and relaxed (I hope). We will have all of our time to devote to our children, who already occupy 99 percent of our life. See, Gabri, I really have made a huge confession to you. I would never have written it before, but now I've done it!

From Gabri's Reflection and Observation Notebook

Gabri, December 1996. In the past few days, Dario seems to be reenacting his transition into our group. He is more agitated than usual when he arrives at the center, and he doesn't want to separate from his mother. When he does, he cries. This behavior—even if it worries his mother—is a positive process because it means he is differentiating situations and people. Furthermore, in the past few days we see already a change toward a greater calm, and when Dario goes from his mother's arms to mine, his mother and I comment on the separation and how Dario is more peaceful.

From December 25 to January 30, Dario and his sister Alba, with their mother and father, went on vacation to Lima, Peru, and some other cities where his grandparents and aunts and uncles live.

From the Notebook for Two Voices

Dario's Mother, January 30, 1997. We came home by plane, a bit withered from lack of sleep but otherwise fine. When we got to our house, Dario did not want to go into the house. He cried. We managed to bring him in, and in the end, he was happy to see his toys, his room, his sister's room, and his parents' room. I let him explore the whole house, explaining to him that finally we were home and that we wouldn't be going away again for a long, long time. We lingered with the things that were most dear to him. My son *has completely changed*. He is very attentive to people and seems pleased to see people he knows.

Dario's Mother, February 5, 1997. Dario pushes himself on the little tricycle, and then also on his little car. A month ago he would have waited tearfully until I pushed him. Now he does it all by himself and recognizes when there are obstacles and moves them out of the way. I am pleased.

From Gabri's Reflection and Observation Notebook

February 6, 1997. Dario came back this week from a long vacation in Peru with his grandparents. He returned calm. In the morning he whined

Teachers begin to gather material for the *Diario* starting at the time the child enters the center, but they compile it only toward the end of the child's stay.

There are many ways of preparing the cover, but the identity of the child is always highlighted.

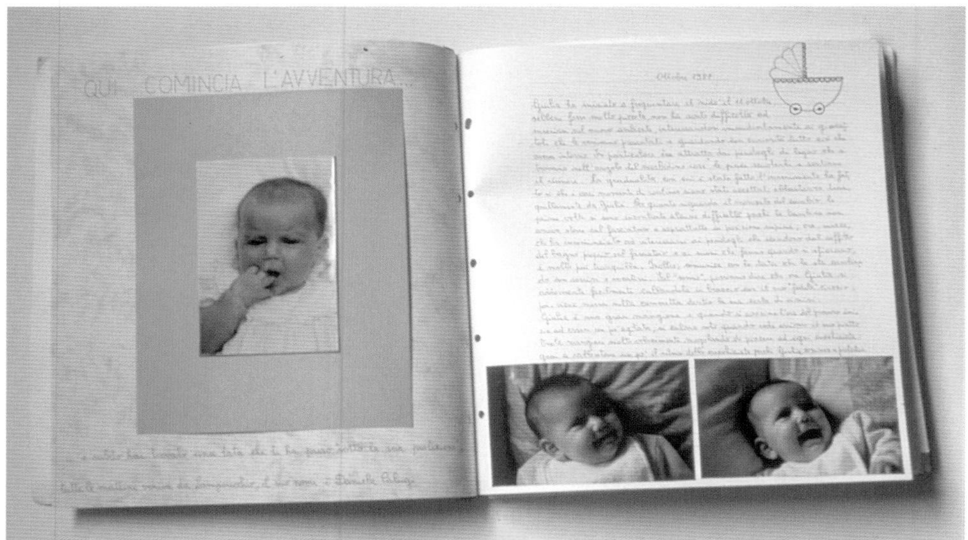

The first pages usually contain notes by both the primary caregiver and the parent concerning the earliest encounter, and the accompanying images show the infant or toddler at that time.

Words, images, text, and small creations made by child and teacher can all be included among the pages.

The continuity between center and home has a strong presence in this book. Messages sent by the family, correspondence, and photographs are included.

The moment of offering parents the *Diario* is rich with emotions and gratitude. Even if the parents expect to receive a diary, the particular one that they are given is a complete surprise.

This mother savors by herself the pages that tell the story of her little girl's three-year experience at the center.

Here, Beatrice's mother shares the pleasure of looking through pages and pictures with her daughter and with Daniele, who has been in the same group with her since they were six months old.

a little, but then he separated from his mother and was relaxed for the rest of the morning.

Today *something exceptional* happened. For the first time, Dario came to lunch, sitting in my lap, at the table with the other children. He ate ravioli, first with his hands. Then he wanted me to help him. Taking my hand, he brought it over to the plate. We took the fork, and I helped him get the ravioli on it. He guided the fork to his mouth and ate with great enthusiasm.

Week of March 14 to 18, 1997. This has been a truly "special" week for Dario. In the morning he arrives calmly at the infant-toddler center, and the important thing is that he throws his arms around me and then says good-bye to his mother with a kiss. He knows that I am in Seventh Heaven.

Even lunchtime has become a calm time: Dario sits at the table with us for the whole time. Sometimes he gets up when there is something new that is not his usual plain pasta. At first he shows no interest in the food, but then he is encouraged and he tries it. During our lunchtime we respect as much as possible each child's sense of time, and Dario is learning to respect that, getting up only a few times and returning to the table right away.

During the day he is more present and even participates in the life of the group. Now the children can hug him and give him little kisses, which he accepts without hitting anyone. He participates enthusiastically in some activities including making play-dough and playing with flour, chickpeas, and sand.

March 25, 1997. Today for the first time Dario came with us into the paint room. He was enthusiastic about the new space. He left his mother without any difficulty and set to exploring. Every thing was interesting, and the temperas were *fascinating*. Initially, he took two small containers and ran with these to add them to the colors that had already been dumped in larger containers. In the meantime, I put a piece of paper on the ground near him, along with a paintbrush full of paint. That is how he began to paint. He came over to the paint cart. He took red. He poured a little of it on the paper and with the paintbrush continued to make marks. When he realized that no more color was coming out of the brush, he put the paintbrush in the jar and played this way for a long time, getting his hands completely in the paint. This time, he didn't seem to look for help. He was happy, smiling, and having fun. He also watched closely what was going on around him. When the time came to wash up, he went into the bathroom and then came right back out.

April 24, 1997. Dario plays more and more willingly in the housekeeping area with the coffeemaker and little coffee cups, exploring them with his eyes, hands, and sometimes his mouth. He watches the other children;

FIGURE 12.4. Dario finally started to eat lunch sitting on Gabri's lap. He enjoyed feeding himself with his fork and his hands. (*Infant-toddler Center Lago Mago, Pistoia*)

he smiles. He turns toward the little bedroom area, takes an empty baby stroller, and pushes it around. I take a doll and put it into the baby buggy. He watches it and continues to push it around. He pauses at the little market area. He takes some fruits and vegetables, fills the buggy, and stops to look at the scale. He goes into the kitchen area, and on the counter seems to experiment with balancing the coffee cups on a tray. Finally, he moves the tray so that the cups no longer fall down. He is much more involved in the play than before. He is starting to play with the doll and puppet, which he did not even want to touch before.

End of the Year Reflections on Dario's Progress. It's May, and Dario is truly changed! His expression is more attentive and tuned in. His relationships with his peers are progressing. He watches them, smiling, and he lets them approach him. With me, he communicates in an ever-closer way. He caresses me, hugs me, and kisses me. Together we play with the repetition of sounds that he makes, and he smiles with contentment. With his mother, too, he has established a more positive relationship. He says good-bye to her when she leaves, and he hugs her when she returns. His mother is so much calmer.

Even his play has changed. From repetitive play with the same objects (toy cars, little cups), he has moved to a more goal-oriented play. He's beginning to show the first signs of symbolic play, and he does not demonstrate difficulty or resist messy activities.

Our meetings as a threesome went beyond the infant-toddler center. Dario's mother brings Dario to another play area *(Area Bambini Rossa)* where other families with children with special needs and their school friends come to play in the afternoon. We have our special encounters there, and we go together also to a swimming pool. This served to deepen our relationship and to promote in Dario the idea of continuity.

We all had had a great deal to learn while working on the fine-tuning of supporting each other in our growth and the growth of Dario's sense of identity as he opened to relationships. The reciprocal trust that steadily developed between us made us capable of having less demanding expectations. This was particularly evident at the infant-toddler center in the sense of well-being we all felt. Now at the end of this school year we feel stronger in our solidarity and our hope.

REFERENCES

Gandini, L., & Gambetti, A. (1997). An inclusive system based on cooperation: The schools for young children in Reggio Emilia. *School Leadership.*

Magrini, G. (1997). *Una storia per Davide* [A Story for David]. Unpublished documentation book, Lago Mago Infant-Toddler Center, Pistoia, Italy.

Smith, C. (1998). Children with "special rights" in the preprimary schools and infant-toddler centers of Reggio Emilia. In C. P. Edwards, L. Gandini, & G. Forman (Eds.), *The hundred languages of children: The Reggio Emilia approach—advanced reflections* (2nd ed., pp. 199–214). Stamford, CT: Ablex.

PART IV

REFLECTIONS BY PARTICIPANT-OBSERVERS AND RESEARCH COLLABORATORS

In this final part of the book, researchers from both Italy and the United States offer their conclusions and reflections on the significance of Italian innovations for the United States.

Chapter 13, by Tullia Musatti and Susanna Mayer of the National Research Council in Rome, puts the spotlight on how children's cognitive development unfolds in real time in interaction with the educational environment. Their observations of children's play with objects and materials were conducted in collaboration with the teachers of Pistoia, who were encouraged to join actively in the research process.

Chapter 14, by the editors, focuses on another research partnership in Pistoia and discusses the methods and findings of a 3-year longitudinal study of the growth of close relationships among children, parents, and educators in the infant-toddler center. This research was planned and conducted collaboratively with administrators, teachers, and parents, as a true "colearning partnership." The chapter provides excerpts of observations, letters, and interviews to give the reader a close-up look at the development of relationships.

Chapter 15 is by Rebecca New, a long-time researcher in Italy. Reviewing her different research projects in different parts of the country, she describes how local variation and experimentation with alternative ways of conceptualizing high quality create desirable systems of care and education, and are thus a source of innovation and flexibility.

Finally, in Chapter 16, the editors conclude the volume with a summary of the book's themes and findings, stressing how the success stories of the four Italian cities depend on social and political institutions that treat all participants as developing persons. They highlight how the programs' missions are broad and flexible enough to serve multiple needs of individuals simultaneously. They evolve over time to meet new societal needs, continually placing focus on processes rather than products or outcomes. The chapter ends with a review of Italian guidelines and current debate on the meaning of the social construct "quality" in education and care for young children and their families.

Chapter 13

Knowing and Learning in an Educational Context: A Study in the Infant-Toddler Centers of the City of Pistoia

Tullia Musatti and Susanna Mayer

An educational place for young children should constitute a meaningful context, in both its relational and its cognitive aspects. In Italy, the elements that determine the relational climate in educational settings have been the subject of much study and discussion. These include the relationships between teachers and parents, the need for each child to have a specific teacher as primary caregiver, and the processes of transitioning into the infant-toddler center, and into and out of the center each day. However, we have neglected the topic of how to create a center that is a meaningful context for young children's cognitive development. This discussion is usually directed toward the educational intents and strategies that are adopted in preschools or elementary schools, often focusing only on knowledge content to be transmitted to children. We forget that the ultimate aim of education should be that the child will learn how to learn—that is, that the child will acquire procedures and structures of knowledge. How can the educational intervention support this learning?

Several years ago, Bronfenbrenner (1993) invited us to ask which features of the various environmental systems were "developmentally instigative" for cognitive development. He suggested that at the level of the

---

 ISBN 0-8077-4008-X (paper), ISBN 0-8077-4009-8 (cloth).

microsystem—that is, the immediate setting in which development occurs—one must identify those "particular physical, social and symbolic features that invite, permit, or inhibit engagement in sustained, progressively more complex interaction with and activity in, the immediate environment" (p. 15). We must admit that there are few certain responses to this question about which are the "instigative" characteristics of the educational setting for young children's cognitive development. These responses are difficult because of a few basic reasons. Most important, although we now know many things about children's competences in their first years of life and their acquisition of skills and abilities across ages, we know much less about how children's abilities emerge, develop, and consolidate in real interactions in the environment. In other words, with regard to the cognitive processes of young children, we know many things about their macrogenetic development—that is, about the succession of different abilities along children's development—and little about their microgenetic development—that is, how children's cognitive construction unfolds in real time and interaction with the environment. Yet, from an educational perspective, what is more important to know is precisely the latter: How children grasp, elaborate, and modify the elements of knowledge that their environment offers them.

Inhelder and Cellérier (1992) argued strongly that in the preoperational or preschool developmental period it is particularly necessary to understand the functional changes in children's cognitive interaction, the procedures and modalities by which children check what happens around them, and the goals of their cognitive activity. To understand children's cognitive functioning in this developmental period, we must determine if the children produce goal-directed actions and heuristic procedures, and specifically which ones. From this perspective, the major educational questions are how to bring children to identify problems, construct solving procedures, identify cognitive goals, and organize their activity toward achieving them. Thus, we would argue that an educational environment favors children's cognitive construction to the extent that it

- Allows them to identify their objects of knowledge and to relate those to understandings already mastered
- Supports them in organizing goal-oriented sequences
- Helps them to assign meaning to activities, choose the tools for knowing, and check the adequacy of their procedures to solve an identified problem

In other words, an educational environment supports children on the road of discovery of the world when it both consistently guarantees that children can organize their own knowing activities and offers specific opportunities of knowledge. The relationship between these two poles of educational action—supporting children's cognitive construction and offering specific opportunities of knowledge—is a crucial issue for every pedagogical approach at every age level. In institutions for the youngest children, it is especially so.

QUALITY OF THE EDUCATIONAL CONTEXT

We hypothesize that the context in which the overall, daily experience of children unfolds—the ways the physical space, social space, and rhythm of life are organized in the educational environment—influence children's cognitive construction in at least two interdependent yet distinct ways. First, the microsystem of the infant-toddler center or preschool can sustain children's motivation to know by helping them to identify their objects of knowledge. Second, by helping children maintain their attention around a set of elements continuously, the educational microsystem can consolidate in children a habit of intelligent focus on objects.

The habit of and the motivation to practice knowing are surely the basis for every specific learning acquisition. For this reason, even when our work was aimed just to analyze children's cognitive construction with regard to a fairly specific set of elements, we had to collect our observational data from educational contexts where the general conditions were already in place to encourage children's motivation to knowing and their habit of focusing their attention on a cognitive activity for a relatively long time. That, in particular, explains the collaboration between us as researchers in developmental psychology and the infant-toddler centers and preschools of the City of Pistoia. In Pistoia, it is possible to elicit children to focus on a specific cognitive setting precisely because the children there are more generally and consistently supported to be focused on cognitive activities. As explained by Galardini and Giovannini in Chapter 8, the daily organization, the physical and social space, and the organization of time schedule in Pistoia's educational settings fulfill this function of sustaining children's cognitive construction. We would assert generally that Pistoia centers offer children contexts for meaningful experiences that are varied yet stable. That is, they permit children to repeat and deepen experiences made individually or shared with other children and adults.

These basic conditions in the educational settings of Pistoia allowed us on many occasions to collect observational data. Because of the work already taking place in Pistoia, however, we were able to do this without great methodological disruption to the life of the infant-toddler center or preschool. This was particularly true for the study we will refer to in this chapter.[1] The relative naturalness of the situation allowed us to collect observational data of exceptional quality, including long coherent sequences of goal-oriented activities produced by 2- to 4-year-olds during their exploration of objects. It was also possible to use these data as the basis for an exciting discussion with teachers on how to elicit, sustain, and eventually direct the children's cognitive construction in other educational situations. In this chapter, we will outline the theoretical framework of our study and the most relevant issues raised and will report the educational implications as they emerged from a series of meetings, seminars, and analyses conducted with the teachers who participated in the study.

HOW YOUNG CHILDREN CONSTRUCT THEIR KNOWLEDGE

In the first years of life, children are deeply engaged in the attempt to organize the world that surrounds them. They are engaged in identifying and verifying the relationships of similarity or difference between objects, the spatial relations, and the effects of an action with one object on the placement or identity of another. The phases of this cognitive construction in the developmental period that corresponds more or less to the age span from 2 to 5 years old have not been studied very much. Only a few researchers have undertaken analysis of the processes by which young children accomplish this construction (Inhelder & Cellérier, 1992). Yet, precisely these processes seem to be different from adults' cognitive processes and appear to change during this developmental period.

Above all, what changes progressively is the relationship between the way an action is effectively carried out and what was the intended result. Thus, infants or toddlers proceed in their explorations, consolidating their discoveries step-by-step, for example, by repeating even very simple activities and introducing more or less systematically new elements in substitution or in addition to those already understood. Preschool children, however, organize their activities in a sequence directed at a specific and explicit goal. The developmental path from one type of process to the other is made possible by children's acquisition of representational abilities. These abilities allow children to predict—that is to represent in advance—the result that they want to bring about.

Even these brief considerations are enough to give a glimpse into a more general interest in the study of cognitive processes in this period, when we have more chances to grasp the relationship between children's growing representational abilities and their strategies for identifying and resolving problems. We found that new methodologies for both data collection and analysis were necessary in order to address this study. And it seems important to us to examine the new methodologies in detail because they can have relevant implications for education.

Inhelder and DeCaprona (1992) indicated some elements that define a good observational setting for the study of cognitive processes in young children. We think that the same elements should be considered for designing a good educational setting. The setting must

- Favor the extended interest of children in a way that gives them time to resolve problems proposed
- Solicit cognitive activity and its exercise

- Call on imagination and creativity
- Be meaningful for the children while including problems to solve

Thus, a good observational setting will not be aimed just to verify if the children are more or less able to solve a predefined problem that is presented to them. In this setting, children should be invited to identify cognitive problems and to put into action procedures to solve them. By arranging the setting, researchers can only try to restrain somehow the set of problems that they wish children will identify and solve. Later, when they will analyze the activities produced by children, they will identify the problems that children actually coped with during the sequential process of their activities. Consequently, this analysis must be based on a minute reconstruction of the various elements of the child's activities and on the identification of the relationships between the activities successively produced by her or him or by another child or an adult.

Such a perspective on children's cognitive activity during this developmental period also has educational implications. First and foremost, it calls for a different kind of attention to the activities and materials we present to children. We cannot define abstractly the single learning goal that we want to pursue. We must instead examine more carefully what we propose to children and hypothesize which cognitive activities it may elicit in them. Certainly, the goal cannot be the children's acquisition of a single notion. It is more important to offer a setting that sustains the child's motivation to cognitive activity and makes possible various paths for it. Therefore, in the definition of a proposed activity, we must refine all the elements—physical and social—which, combining in inevitably different ways from one time to the next, can sustain and direct children's cognitive activities. Second, the analysis of how children pursue a particular cognitive goal, connect the result of their activity with other elements in a coherent system, or use it to identify new goals, can allow us to address recurrent educational questions, such as the following:

- How can we sustain the motivation to learn?
- When is the right time to introduce novelty?
- What is the right amount of time and effort to require of children?
- How can we sustain their attention?
- How do we help children develop the habit to learn?

Finally, it is important to offer children the opportunity to exercise their ability to represent, providing them with suitable conditions for it.

IMPORTANT FEATURES OF THE OBSERVATIONAL SETTING

Two features of context seem to be primarily relevant for orienting children's cognitive activity: the number and type of objects immediately available, and the number and type of partners present, children and adults. In recent decades the use of videotaping has made possible the microanalysis of children's activities when confronted with various sets of objects, without an adult's verbal mediation or direction. Objects appear to be mediators of knowledge. The type and quantity of objects presented and the relations that can be identified between and among them orient children's cognitive construction. That is, objects that are offered to children must activate many paths for thinking on various topics and at different levels of complexity—paths that the child can identify and explore easily and autonomously. Our choice of objects is crucial not only with regard to cognitive problems that we want to raise in the children, but also in order to invite interest in exploring those objects (see Figures 13.1 to 13.4).

Past observational studies (Sinclair, Stambak, Lézine, Rayna, & Verba, 1982/1989; Stambak et al., 1983) demonstrated that the presentation of different types of objects to children under 3 years old suggests different responses and orients children's activity in a general way. For example, a set of objects familiar from social life will orient children to pretend play. However, in the presence of a large number of a single type of objects (for example, six boxes, six sticks, or six balls of different sizes), children's activity can be centered on prelogical aspects—the relations of identity, inclusion, or seriation—while objects with physical properties that interact differently as a consequence of the children's actions (for example, objects that are rigid or flexible, open or closed) invite children to analyze those differences.

However, we want to point out that we can see these different focuses of the cognitive activity of children emerge only from analysis of the relationships between successive actions by children. Single actions are actually very simple, such as "put an object into another" or "put it near" or "put it over," and they do not differ greatly from one situation to the next. Fitting four blocks of decreasing size together is realized by "putting into," and the same action of "putting into" is what allows experimentation with the difference between the relative rigidity of a small stick and a string when they are put through the hole into a bead. To sum up, the different cognitive goals of children are determined by the relationships that their actions establish among objects. For this, we must remember that a set of objects does not necessarily orient children's activity toward a single cognitive problem, but rather every setting elicits in children a variety of different questions and activities.

From an educational perspective, these considerations raise interesting new questions:

- How does a specific activity with objects, emerge, maintain, and get to an end?
- Is it possible to identify the particular elements that determine the passage from a specific goal to another with the same set of objects?
- Can we identify which characteristics of the material play different roles in activating toddlers' cognitive processes (Musatti & Mayer,

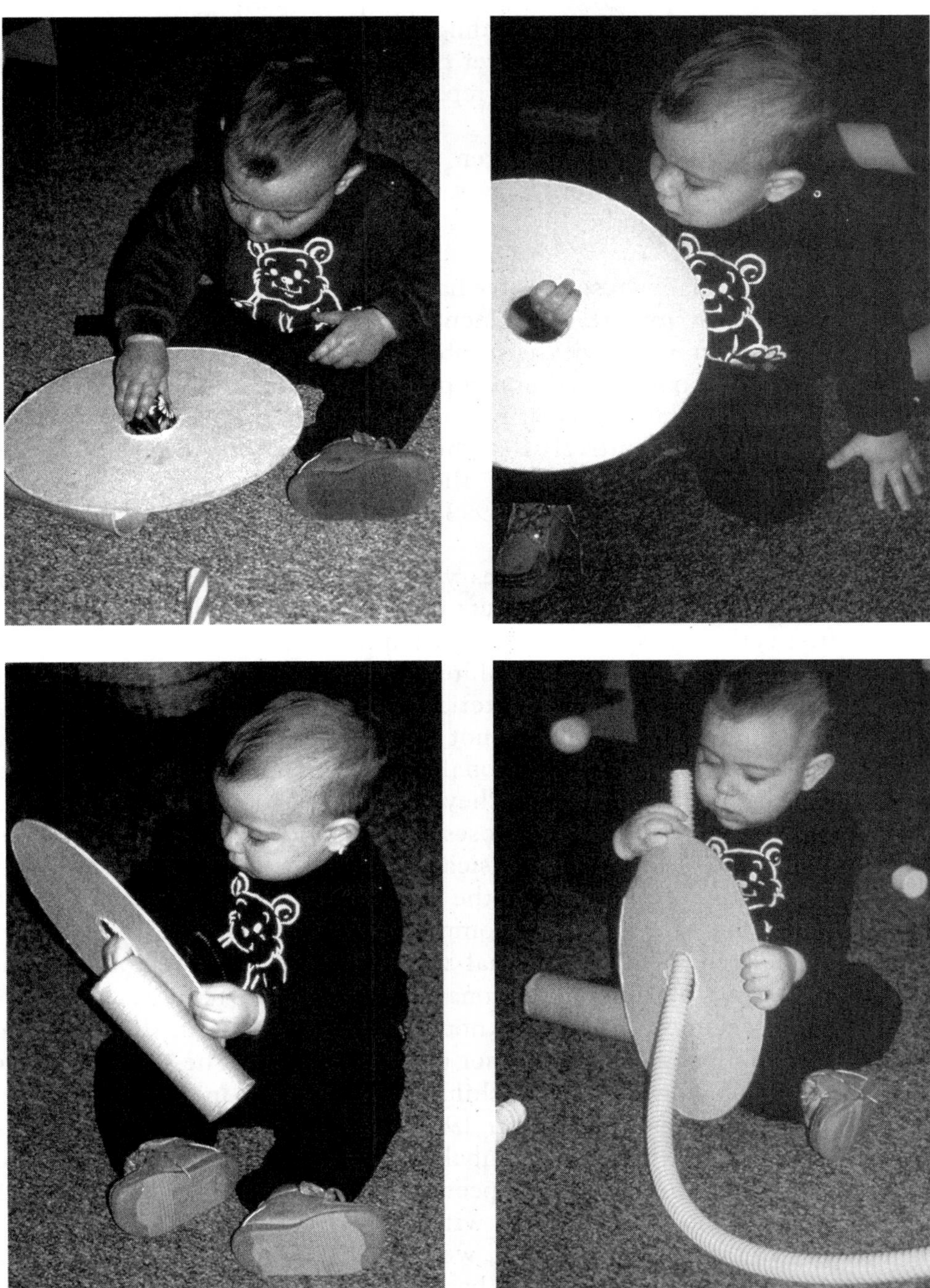

FIGURES 13.1, 13.2, 13.3, and 13.4. Teachers select new objects that encourage familiar activity and, at the same time, possibilities for exploration of more complex questions and combinations. This infant, about one year old, is exploring different ways of putting things through the hole in the cardboard disk. (*Infant-toddler Center Lago Mago, Pistoia*)

1996); for example, in guiding children toward new activities, or in supporting their attention over time on the same activity in order to make possible the discovery of repeated phenomena and the consolidation of heuristic procedures?
- Does the fact that children implement different specific activities by quite similar actions play a role in encouraging the passage from one activity to another?

In previous research, we have observed that the presence of a familiar adult is an important element in a group of young children who are involved in an activity with objects. The adult can help maintain a positive emotional climate and support the motivation of children's activity, even when she or he just responds to children's initiatives. Other studies have shown definitively that the presence of peers influences the cognitive activity of children, even the very youngest ones (Mayer, Musatti, & Verba, 1997; Musatti, 1993; Musatti, Verba, & Mayer, 1994; Verba, 1994).

The prejudice that sees young children as always competing with peers for possession of objects ignores two very important elements. The first is that competition arises when the immediate possession of a particular object is crucial for children in order to go ahead with their activity. Often this is when the materials available in the everyday environment are scarce or when there is not a harmony of social relations that guarantees a generally calm emotional climate for children. If children are accustomed to social harmony, they can foresee that the object, momentarily not available for one's purposes because another child has it, will not disappear into a social and physical chaos and will be available to them later. Thus, objects can become the center of joint, noncompetitive attention rather than the source of competition and struggle. The second element overlooked in the traditional view of toddlers is the source of interest, sometimes absolutely passionate, for the object used by a peer. Often an object seems to be desired not in competition with the other child but precisely because it holds her or his attention: The interest of the other child, for whom the first child feels empathy, indicates that the object must be interesting (Musatti, 1986; Verba & Musatti, 1989). It has also been shown (Musatti, 1993; Stambak et al., 1983; Verba, Stambak, & Sinclair, 1982) that the activity of peers orients young children in identifying a problem and provides them with clues to its solution.

In our study in Pistoia, we proposed a setting of simple and familiar activities for the children, that of manipulating dried beans (in our case, chickpeas) or sand, both offered in a certain quantity to children, along with a certain number of other objects that could be used as either containers or contents and that presented different physical properties, such as rigidity, concaveness, or geometrical forms, such as rectangles, triangles, cylinders, and cubes. Two major considerations guided our choice. On one hand, we noted how children like to play with seeds, grains, and granules. On the other, as we have noted above, the action of "putting an object into another" is already very frequent at the end of the first year of life, and from this action many different activities of different levels of complexity can develop, according to the available objects. These objects were presented to several groups of three same-age children, along with their teachers.[2]

ANALYZING THE CHILDREN'S ACTIVITIES

The setting we devised resulted in long attention spans and the production of long sequences of coordinated activities on behalf of all the children, as expected at different levels of complexity according to their ages (2- to 4-year-olds). We could observe increasingly complex activities of manipulating chickpeas or sand; pouring; constructing clusters of objects; building linear paths with objects in order to move the chickpeas or sand; and finally, combinations of these various activities. In sum, the setting we presented was successful in favoring children's cognitive activities at different levels of complexity (see Figures 13.5 and 13.6).

We would like to call attention to several aspects that seem to us particularly important in terms of their educational implications. The children were capable of exceptionally long sustained engagement with the material presented during which they followed specific cognitive goals or explored successively many different possible uses for the material. This strongly highlights for us the very important role of the basic activities—of simple manipulation of materials and of pouring from one container into another. These activities, which were always inherent in the materials presented, sustained the continued interest of the children, while allowing and even accompanying the physiological alternation between moments of less or greater concentration. They also sustained the children's shifting from one type of activity to another, from a moment of more complex cognitive construction to a simpler one. We must not, however, undervalue the also equally important role of the other objects, that were chosen accurately with reference to the children's possible activities with them. They suggested to the children more and more complex explorations of object properties and relations between them. It seems to us, definitely, that the success of an activity proposed to the children can be sought in this tension between the invitation to a generic acting and the invitation to goal-directed activities.

A deep analysis of children's activities, beyond their apparent diversity and incoherence, showed that even the youngest children could work around a consistent line of thinking over the course of the single observation session or even over the course of several sessions. It seems to us that this finding is an endorsement for educational planning based on the proposal of integrated and coherent (not episodic) activities over time, supporting the continuity of children's cognitive construction.

FIGURES 13.5 and 13.6. The combination of nonstructured materials and semistructured objects encourages this child, 26 months old, to experiment with dropping chickpeas on an inclined plane. (*Infant-toddler Center Arcobaleno, Pistoia*)

We also noticed strong differences, even among children of the same age. There are differences among children in style and in rhythms of action, which, as their teachers noted (Cassaresi & Gelli, 1995), can vary greatly from child to child of the same age and from situation to situation. These differences become more evident during the first approach to the proposed setting. This approach could be immediate or could come after a longer or shorter period of observation by the child. We found also strong individual differences in terms of what activities were undertaken. For example, some children were focused above all on the systematic exploration of objects falling, while others worked primarily to put together and build with the objects. It is important to note that from our detailed analysis children of the same age appeared to be focused on very different problems, even when they were carrying out activities that appeared similar. For example, although three children would pour chickpeas from one container into another during an entire session, one of them appeared to us to be focused on establishing similarities between different couples of containers, while the other ones explored the reversibility of their actions from one container into the other (Musatti & Mayer, 1996). The importance of presenting children with materials that allow such a variety of possible focuses is evident.

In the discussion with the teachers, another important point emerged with regard to the relationship between the children's cognitive competence and the complexity of the activity inherent in the proposed setting (Capecchi, Ventavoli, & Vivona, 1995). It became clear that the children do not always produce activity to the maximum limit of their competence and that often they seem focused on problems that they already know how to resolve. This finding clarifies that there is, and must remain, a great difference between an assessment of the child's competence and an educational intervention aimed at supporting the child's cognitive construction. In other words, we want to point out that the relationship between acquisition of an idea, procedure, or structure; its consolidation; and its application to new sets of problems or in the context of a wider system of knowledge, is still an open question. When a child produces an activity that implies a certain notion, this does not mean necessarily that the child has definite and stable mastery of that notion. Or at least it does not mean that the child does not still need to test the notion constantly, repeating it year after year and in different contexts.

RECOGNIZING THE ROLE OF THE TEACHER

As we noted before, we were able to stimulate the children's cognitive activity on the setting we presented because of the favorable educational conditions that already characterized the infant-toddler centers and preschools in Pistoia. These fundamental conditions are evident through our observations, not only in the children's engagement and interest but also strongly in the atmosphere that permeated the relationships between children and adults. There was evidence of this atmosphere in all the videos we made for our research. We observed groups composed of only three children for exclusively technical motives, not because we considered this situation socially ideal. The children demonstrated their habit of harmonious social relationships with other children by the nurturing gentleness with which they treated one another, as well as the quickness with which they intervened to help a peer who seemed to be having difficulty. This stood out also in negotiation strategies (seldom hostile) that were put into action to resolve the eventual conflicts. We could also see how the child's interest in the peer's activity led to frequent direct or indirect interactions between them about their activities with the objects. Thus, we found episodes when the children collaborated during the same activity or explicitly suggested to a peer a passage from one action to the next, or in other more numerous episodes when an activity by one child stimulated others to use a material in a new way or to carry on a similar activity with other objects.

The adults found that they were in a climate of harmony and cognitive exchange. The observer, by filming right in front of everyone, implied an expectation for the work of children from the world of grown-ups. The teachers who participated with the children in this experience offered themselves to the eye of the video camera with the same naturalness as the children, but with a completely different awareness. We want to stress that the teachers' willingness was predicated on a solid professional knowledge. They were willing to discuss critically their attitudes and behaviors and the role they played in the children's activity precisely because they had already mastered a professional knowledge about boundaries and goals of the adults' intervention into the children's activities (Lippi, Pugliese, & Ravagli, 1995).

In our discussions with the teachers, some fundamental functions that the adult serves and some issues around which to work in the future were identified. First of all, we discussed the function of the adult in supporting and holding the attention of the child, when she or he recognizes the meaning and cognitive goal of the child's activity and knows how to intervene wisely—not directly but creating opportunities for thinking. Crucial questions were raised: Which are the boundaries between an intrusive behavior and a supportive one? When should the adult intervene in the children's activity? We also recognized the importance of the adult's echoing the children's discoveries, that is, her role in making explicit the meaning of the children's activity. In so doing, the teacher supports each child's growing awareness and also favors the cognitive exchanges among the children, bringing discreetly to the attention of the small group the interest and meaning of the individual child's activity. The adult is also the guarantor of a stable emotional climate and sustains harmony, drawing on positive interactions among the children. We examined and discussed the strategies used in cases of conflict over the possession of objects, during which the adult sought to encourage the children to find alternative solutions in order to achieve their goals. In other instances the teachers helped the children participate in their peer's activity, even if only by sharing their surprise and joyful discovery.

The teachers recognized that the positive expectations that they themselves have with regard to the children's ability represent a very important and delicate aspect of their work. Their expectations must not be aimed at soliciting this or that specific activity from the children, who instead may be involved in a completely different cognitive activity, and who must be respected and trusted. The adult's expectations must translate into their great effort to be attentive and available to each child in order to realize a positive relational space within which the children can express themselves according to their personal needs, wishes, and abilities.

NOTES

1. The study was planned and conducted in collaboration with Hermina Sinclair, Université de Genève, Switzerland, and Mina Verba, La Psydée, CNRS-Université de la Sorbonne, Paris, France.

2. Eighty play sessions lasting an average of 45 minutes and involving a total of 54 children and 8 teachers were videotaped. Each group of three children, accompanied by one of their teachers, gathered in a central room where the materials were arranged on a table. To indicate each child's place at the table, there was a large, transparent box containing a bin either half-full of dry sand or with a handful of dried chickpeas inside. At the center of the table all the other objects were placed so that each child could easily reach whatever she or he wanted. Except for the basic materials (bins, sand, little shovels, chickpeas, little balls), there were different numbers of each object, and the objects varied according to the main basic material (sand or chickpeas). In each of the two situations, there were objects that could serve as containers (transparent plastic bottles cut in half, transparent plastic bowls, transparent plastic cones, plastic sacks), objects that could be used to pour (large funnels, cardboard cylinders, little plastic tubes, strainers of different sizes), and objects that could be used for less specific purposes (wooden blocks and wedges, cardboard rectangles, wooden sticks, squares of fabric).

REFERENCES

Bronfenbrenner, U. (1993). The ecology of cognitive development: Models and fugitive findings. In R. H. Wozniak & K. W. Fisher (Eds.), *Development in context: Acting and thinking in specific environments* (pp. 3–44). Hillsdale, NJ: Erlbaum.

Capecchi, A., Ventavoli, L., & Vivona, D. (1995). Problemi e percorsi di reflessione nell'esplorazione [Problems and questions emerging through exploration]. In A. L. Galardini, D. Giovannini, S. Mayer, & T. Musatti (Eds.), Di fronte agli oggetti [In front of objects]. *Bambini, 11*(6, suppl.), 19–22.

Cassaresi, A., & Gelli, S. (1995). Motivazione, ritmo, stile, e impegno dei bambini [Children's motivations, rhythms, styles, and engagement]. In A. L. Galardini, D. Giovannini, S. Mayer, & T. Musatti (Eds.), Di fronte agli oggetti [In front of objects]. *Bambini, 11*(6, suppl.), 13–16.

Inhelder, B., & Cellérier, G. (1992). *Le cheminement des découvertes de l'enfant: Recherches sur les microgenèses cognitives* [The path of infant's discoveries: Research on cognitive microgeneses]. Neuchâtel, Switzerland: Delachaux and Niestlé.

Inhelder, B., & DeCaprona, D. (1992). Vers le constructivisme psychologique: Structures? Procedures? Les deux indissociables. In B. Inhelder & G. Cellérier (Eds.), *Le cheminement des découvertes de l'enfant: Recherches sur les microgenèses cognitives* [The path of infant's discoveries: Research on cognitive microgeneses] (pp. 19–50). Neuchâtel, Switzerland: Delachaux and Niestlé.

Lippi, G., Pugliese, S., & Ravagli, B. (1995). Il ruolo dell'adulto [The adult's role]. In A. L. Galardini, D. Giovannini, S. Mayer, & T. Musatti (Eds.), Di fronte agli oggetti [In front of objects]. *Bambini, 11*(6, suppl.), 25–27.

Mayer, S., Musatti, T., & Verba, M. (1997). Shared cognitive construction and imitative processes. *New Trends in Developmental Psychology: Abstracts of the 8th European Conference on Developmental Psychology* (p. 128). Rennes, France: Presses Universitaires Rennes 2.

Musatti, T. (1986). Early peer relations: The perspectives of Piaget and Vygotsky. In E. Mueller & C. Cooper (Eds.), *Process and outcome in peer relationships* (pp. 35–55). New York: Academic Press.

Musatti, T. (1993). Meaning between peers: The meaning of the peer. *Cognition and Instruction, 2,* 241–250.

Musatti, T., & Mayer, S. (1996, September). *On the road of discovery: The role of play material in young children's constructive process.* Paper presented at the Growing Mind conference, Geneva, Switzerland.

Musatti, T., Verba, M., & Mayer, S. (1994). Peers and the zone of proximal development. *Abstracts Book of the 13th ISSBD International Meeting* (p. 295). Amsterdam: ISSBD.

Sinclair, H., Stambak, M., Lézine, I., Rayna, S., & Verba, M. (1989). *Infants and objects.* San Diego: Academic Press. (Original work published 1982)

Stambak, M., Barriére, M., Bonica, L., Maisonnet, R., Musatti, T., Rayna, S., & Verba, M. (1983). *Les bébés entre eux: inventer, decouvrir et jouer ensemble* [Babies with one another (together): to invent and to play together]. Paris: Presses Universitaires de France.

Verba, M. (1994). The beginnings of collaboration in peer interaction. *Human Development, 37,* 125–139.

Verba, M., & Musatti, T. (1989). Minor phenomena and major processes of interaction with objects and peers in day care centers. *European Journal of Psychology of Education, 4,* 215–227.

Verba, M., Stambak, M., & Sinclair, H. (1982). Physical knowledge and social interaction in children from 18 to 24 months of age. In G. E. Forman (Ed.), *Action and thought* (pp. 267–296). London: Academic Press.

Chapter 14

Research as a Partnership for Learning Together: Studying the Growth of Relationships Inside the *Nido*

Carolyn Pope Edwards and Lella Gandini

Family involvement and participation are a key component of the excellent early childhood systems described in this book. In this chapter we go inside the infant-toddler centers of Pistoia, for a close-up look at how parents, teachers, children, and administrative leadership experience their shared "culture of childhood." This culture (Galardini & Giovannini, Chapter 8, this volume) provides an agreed-upon vision of the needs and rights of young children, including ideas about how the people of the city can collectively nurture them and at the same time be renewed by them.

Our perspective is one of participant-observers and research collaborators who came from outside but joined in and worked alongside the Pistoia professionals in an approach to research that was a colearning partnership. Our findings and data complement the statements of goals and strategies provided by the administrators and teachers of Pistoia in Chapters 8, 11, and 12. The colearning partnership suited the situation very well because it closely resembles the usual way that the early childhood system works in Pistoia and how researchers usually interact with it (see Musatti & Mayer, Chapter 13, this volume). Thus, it was not imposed; it

---

 ISBN 0-8077-4008-X (paper), ISBN 0-8077-4009-8 (cloth).

FIGURE 14.1. Close relationships between children and teachers were observed in Pistoia, and the research project explored how these relationships were first established and how they then unfolded over time. (*Infant-toddler Center Il Sole, Pistoia*)

amplified rather than interfered with the ongoing life in the schools in Pistoia.

On the basis of our data and interpretations, we will describe how the educators working in the public services for infants and toddlers engage in continual professional development and improvement of quality through partnership and information exchange with families and with researchers. At the same time, we will explore how families enter into close and extended relationships with one another and with the educational system as a whole. We will learn something about how parents feel as their children become close to new adults and peers inside the *nido* and then are influenced by those experiences (see Figure 14.1). Through the research, we followed closely a small number of children, their parents, and their teachers, from the time of the small babies' first entry into an *asilo nido* until the end of their third and final years in the program, and documented the unfolding of participation and close relationships among adults and children.

OVERVIEW OF THE RESEARCH PARTNERSHIP

The study actually continued and built upon a fruitful research and training collaboration begun 10 years before between Lella Gandini and the leadership in Pistoia (see Edwards & Gandini, 1989; Edwards, Gandini, &

Giovannini, 1996; Edwards, Gandini, & Nimmo, 1994; Gandini, 1988, 1999). On the basis of these past relationships, in negotiating with the administrators to do the study, we found ourselves seeking a cooperative, nonhierarchical, and interactive model of research partnership, a colearning agreement (Wagner, 1997). The research goals and questions were agreed upon mutually, and the planning and fine-tuning of the research, as well as the preparation of interim reports (given to the parents and educators at the end of each year), were joint efforts. At the end of the study, we had all contributed to understanding the complexity and benefits of supporting relationships among *nido* teachers, parents, and administrators. The practitioners in Pistoia gained insights and learned new strategies for professional development as well as for providing services for families. The researchers have drawn upon their insights and data for use in consultation, teacher training, and professional development activities in other places as well as Pistoia, such as the United States.

In going over the research agenda in October 1995, and considering that the fundamental aim was to study the development of relationships with families, formal goal statements were made. Annalia Galardini, as system director, stated that her purpose was to promote the professional development of teachers involved in the study, to make them more aware of what goes on in the classroom and how to observe, collect, and organize data about it. In a larger sense, she also wanted to help the system better understand how the *nido* serves families and to go beyond the limits of current conceptions and perceptions. Donatella Giovannini, as pedagogical coordinator, added that the research would help administrators and teachers better understand how families understand their experience—indeed how families coming from different social backgrounds and with different previous contacts with the early childhood system enter into relationships with the *nido*. Lella Gandini, as lead researcher, stated that her goal was to see how research on the teacher-parent relationship could be used to promote teacher preparation and motivate educators to grow by making what happens more visible to them. Carolyn Edwards hoped the research would demonstrate how research can immediately and directly translate into something useful to schools and centers, not only in Pistoia but also cross-culturally in the United States. Both Carolyn and Lella wanted to explore the subjective side of the usual 2- or 3-year teacher-child continuity on children's well-being and parents' participation. We wanted to uncover the conflicts and discrepancies experienced by parents, gaps in continuity, and such consequences as any disappointments or frustrations left in their wake. We wanted to explore, with the parents and teachers, how relationships unfold over time in the *nido*, what happens in the second year that is different than the first and in the third year that is deeper and richer than the second. Taken all together, the goals of the research are summarized in Figure 14.2.

The study sample for the research included 12 children and their families, as shown in Figure 14.3. Six infants and families were followed for a

1. How do parent/teacher/child relationships unfold and change through the first, second, and third years of participation in the infant-toddler center?
2. How does the nature of parent participation in the municipal early childhood system evolve over the years?
3. What disconnects and discontinuities occur in parental or child experience, and with what effects?
4. Does participation in the research study promote teacher professional development and/or system quality improvement, and if so, in what ways?

FIGURE 14.2. The Study Questions

3-year period, and six for a 2-year period. The sample evolved over time. The initial nine children, aged 5–10 months old, were enrolled in two full-day infant-toddler centers selected because the teachers there had not participated in other research studies and were eager to do so. The families were blue-collar, white-collar, and professional in background, and all but one had two parents living with the child. One family had recently arrived from Eastern Europe and was receiving assistance from social services. All children were healthy and without disabilities, though the centers included children with a full range of abilities. During the first year, two children dropped out of the study (including the family from Eastern Europe who left Pistoia). Also, another child who moved to a different toddler program in the system remained part of the research since one of the study teachers moved there too. Five new children were added to the study, all beginning the *nido* experience. During the third year, three boys moved to a newly opened full-day center, now also added to the study. By the end of the third year of research, in June 1998, the 11 children were aged 38- to 40-months-old, in four infant-toddler programs.

6 infants (3 male, 3 female) were followed for 3 years.
6 infants (3 male, 3 female) were followed for 2 years.

Year 1 began with 9 infants (5 male, 4 female), aged 5-10 months, newly enrolled in 2 infant-toddler programs.
Year 2 began with 12 infants (6 male, 6 female; 7 originals, 5 new) aged 14-17 months, in 3 programs.
Year 3 began with 11 infants (6 male, 5 female; 6 originals, 5 continuing from year 2), aged 26-28 months, in 4 programs.

FIGURE 14.3. The Study Sample

Besides children and families, in the study we also followed teachers. The group of teachers who were closest to the study children were part of the research in order to find out how the long-term relationships between children, parents, and teachers would unfold and be experienced.

There was more teacher change and turnover than anticipated during the research period, and this offered an unexpected opportunity: the chance to look at the contrasting experiences of both continuity and discontinuity. We began the research focusing on the five teachers assigned to work with the youngest infants in the two centers. All were experienced, long-time teachers who had not participated in prior intensive research projects. A good deal of change in teacher personnel then occurred in our study and the Pistoia system as a whole, resulting from legislation that made it possible for *nido* educators to advance to a higher salary by moving to a preschool. Many experienced *nido* educators took advantage of this opportunity, resulting in a good deal of musical chairs all over the system. By the end of the study, only two of our original five teachers

1. Interviews with parent(s) of each child were conducted once a year by teachers and twice a year by researchers. Particularly important were tape-recorded interviews at the beginning of the study, and videotaped interviews looking at the "diary" at the end of the study.
2. Videotaped group discussions with parents, including short lecture followed by open discussion, were conducted once a year. These usually involved viewing and discussing videotapes of the children in the classroom.
3. Videotaped or audiotaped group discussions with teachers were conducted either as one whole group or two subgroups four times a year. These sometimes involved viewing and discussing segment of classroom videotapes.
4. Collective letters were sent by teachers to parents twice a year. Individual letters, from teachers to researchers, were collected during the second year.
5. Videotaped observations of children (with teachers and/or peers and/or parents also present) were collected 4 times a year by research team or the study teachers. Particularly important were the *inserimento* and *re-inserimento* videos collected near the beginning of each school year.
6. Attachment Q-Sorts, focused on each child's relationship with mother and with primary teacher, were collected once a year.
7. Documentation of many sorts was gathered: monthly calendars on each child; observations on each child; photographs and notes about the center environments on each research visit; anecdotal records; photograph records of some of the "diaries"; and research booklets summarizing each year's work presented as gifts to the parents each June.

FIGURE 14.4. Research Methods and Instruments

remained at their same center. Therefore, we added several new teachers to our study pool at both years 2 and 3.

The final upshot was that, in terms of continuity experienced, six study children (three at each of the original two centers) had one teacher who remained with them across all 3 years. The other study children experienced less continuity, but all but one remained close to one or more teachers for at least a 2-year period.

Data were collected by a variety of strategies, including interviews, observations, group discussions, and questionnaires focusing on children, parents, and teachers, as summarized in Figure 14.4. Based on all of these methods, the research provided a rich opportunity to learn about and share different perspectives on the unfolding relationships among the key protagonists—parents, children, teachers, administrators, and of course, ourselves, the researchers. We are just beginning to synthesize and interpret the corpus of observations, interviews, and questionnaires, but certain key findings have emerged about continuity and discontinuity. In the remainder of this chapter, we will present highlights of these findings but shall not attempt a systematic account of all the data and findings.

THE FIRST YEAR AS A DELICATE TIME FOR BEGINNINGS

In their first interview (June 1995), the administrative leadership recounted the sequence of events that prepared the families and children to enter the infant-toddler centers and the research study. Their answers made evident that the first responsibility of the city administration was to communicate an image of the system and programs that would immediately reassure parents and make them feel welcome in the infant-toddler centers.

In fact, this positive message coming from the city administration has been constructed over time and takes the form of all sorts of documentation, including booklets, posters, and notices widely distributed throughout the town. These sources of information are backed up by the special celebrations and lectures put on by the system and open to the town as a whole, as well as the informal reports and grapevine communications of families who have used the programs. For the new families, each contact, from the first trip to the Office of Public Instruction for registering, to the first visit to an infant-toddler center, to the encounter with the teachers to plan the child's transition into the center, has to be carefully and thoughtfully prepared and executed.

Galardini and Giovannini discussed how they planned, designed, and shared with the study teachers a sequence of strategies and set of instruments that we had discussed together. For example, the teachers had carefully prepared special record books and devices for communicating with parents (see Figure 14.5). The teachers next held their usual dialogues with the families newly admitted to the youngest infant room. On this occasion, as part of the *inserimento* or "process of transition," the teachers

FIGURE 14.5. The teachers in each center developed special times and means for communicating with parents, such as these transparent envelopes used for exchanging notes. (*Infant-toddler Center Il Grillo, Pistoia*)

explained to the parents about the research project, how it would directly involve them, and asked if they would like to participate. Most of the parents who were approached agreed enthusiastically. The teachers then began the data collection by videotaping portions of each child's period of transition, resulting in a set of tapes about 15 minutes long for each child, capturing moments from about four occasions during the child's first week in the *nido*.

In these videos, the heightened emotion of participants is easy to see. The video revealing the most ambivalence involved the family from Eastern Europe. In their interview, the parent (mother) displays body language suggesting distance from her child, and the teacher has difficulty establishing rapport with her. In all the other interviews, the parents clearly entered the new situation with expectations of pleasure, and the children looked at their parents' faces to read their parents' emotional reactions (social referencing). The teacher receiving the new family (mother, baby, sometimes also father, in one case also grandparent) showed them around. She introduced them to the attractive booklets or folders prepared for communicating and exchanging information and then took them into a prepared place, cozy and friendly, containing baskets of toys.

For example, one tape shows a teacher, Franca, warmly greeting a mother and her baby, Carla (fictive name), 10 months old, at the door.

Together the three came into the center, and the teacher, holding the willing baby at the mother's invitation, said to Carla, "Let's show your mother your room." Thus, the teacher talked to the mother "as if" through the baby: the baby became the focal point and bridge for the communication. Sometimes she spoke "for" the baby to her mother, "Here I will put my clothes," and so on like that.

They went around to look at different areas and Franca said, more to the mother now, "Here there will be notebooks compiled by both parents and educators—a notebook to go back and forth. You can write what you see, and we will respond with what we see." Thus, Franca began to introduce the mother and baby to a special "language of the *nido,*" for describing and engaging in the life there. Then she said to the baby, "Why don't we sit down, and your mother will tell me everything about Carla." As they sat, teacher and mother in turn offered toys to Carla, which she happily accepted. The interview questions included: "What does Carla like to eat? How did you decide to bring your child to the *nido?* What do you expect from the *nido?*" Carla's mother said that she did not want her baby to be one of those little girls "who are so shy that she won't talk to anyone; maybe coming to the *nido,* she will become an outgoing girl."

Carla was very interested in all of the toys. Franca introduced her to the plastic farm animals, "Hello, cow, hello, pig," as if to help her make friends with the environment. Just then, Carla's attention was attracted by the sight of a little boy slightly older than herself and coming around the corner into her area. This little boy was already adjusted to the program. Franca picked up immediately on Carla's attention and drew a connection to the mother's previously expressed desires for Carla. She told the mother, "Carla is very interested in other children." The mother nodded, "Yes, yes."

Franca gently carried Carla close to the small boy and introduced the two, in the affectionate, respectful, slightly formal style an Italian mother might use in introducing any two children. Thus, (in our interpretation) she used the "language of the home" to establish rapport. She talked to the boy about Carla's clothes, how elegant they were, and told the boy that Carla was beautiful. Carla seemed to key into this three-way interaction. She reached out to put her hand softly onto the boy's head, as Franca said that he was "*bello*" (handsome). Now Carla did something remarkable. She turned for the first time to look directly and fully into the face of her new teacher, as if to take in who she was. Then Carla glanced over toward her mother, an act of social referencing to reassure herself. Her

> mother was gazing with a warmly smiling face, signaling to Carla that she approved of Carla's interest in these new people.

This beginning of participation by parents was the aspect on which we focused with great attention in the first year. Lella Gandini met with each set of parents, shortly after their child's and their own transition into the center was completed, to have a conversation about their experience and thoughts. In three cases, mother and father came together, in one case the father came alone, and in the rest, the mother came alone.

For instance, Lella met with the mother of one girl named Alma (fictive name). Lella began the interview by asking how much the mother had known about the program before applying and why she had chosen to bring their child to this *nido.* The mother explained that she was friendly with two "splendid" teachers, and also that she had seen the very positive *nido* experience of her nephew, now aged 4. She recounted how her nephew had become very sociable and able to play and share with other children, in contrast to another little boy they knew, at home with his nanny, who only "wants to impose himself on others and does not accept suggestions from adults, even his parents."

Lella next asked about the *inserimento,* which the mother said had gone very well. She went on to tell a story to show how attached her child now is to her *nido.*

> When we leave the house in the morning, we usually drive first to the *nido.* But yesterday I first had to go to the post office. So when she entered the post office, she looked around and not recognizing the *nido,* looked me straight in the face and went, "Oh?" She is 11 months old, but I could see how disappointed she was. Then, when we finally got to the *nido,* she was screaming with happiness.

Further questions asked about what changes the mother had seen in her child since entering the *nido,* and whether she would recommend the program to others. Like other parents interviewed, she revealed her satisfaction with the center and its teachers, her approval of the child's budding sociability and autonomy (in feeding herself), and her awareness of the names and identities of the child's new playmates. As she put it, *"Viva, nido!"*

THE SECOND YEAR: LEARNING AND PLAY, CONTINUITY TAKEN FOR GRANTED

At the beginning of the second year, children's readjustment periods (*re-inserimento*) went even more smoothly and easily than in the first year. Most children were glad to see former playmates and quickly took up old play patterns and familiar toys. One girl, Beatrice (fictive name), cried with her usual dramatic distress at any transition, but her young, cheerful mother minimized her tragedy and quickly helped her reenter her group and reestablish her place in it. The focus of the children seemed to be on learning and play, and the videotapes of their play with toys and materials show complex patterns of exploration, strong interest and curiosity, and little conflict. Many of the children resumed their relationships with preferred play partners (children they knew well), but also played well with all of their peers. They moved throughout the spaces with careful awareness of one another, going around each other's bodies so as not to disrupt them, and often they either offered one another toys or else seemed not to mind if others took their toys, seeming to expect that the toys would "come back" (which they did). Our observations included many instances of toys and materials circling through the small group, and of cycles of imitation and of positive action. Their ease with the space and with one another was evident when compared to newly arrived children, who were usually able to enter a group and to briefly exchange looks and materials with peers but not yet ready to engage in the longer cycles of turn-taking.

In one observation, a boy, Daniele (fictive name), offered Beatrice mouthful after mouthful of cake at lunch, carefully holding the fork up to her mouth and waiting for her to open it before putting in the bite. Daniele checked with his teacher to see if it was okay to offer his cake, and as he fed Beatrice, he opened wide his own mouth at each bite, the way adults do when spoonfeeding their babies (see Figure 14.6).

Of course, conflicts occurred as well, and these the teachers handled calmly, playing them down and modeling and guiding children to touch gently, move calmly, look and speak politely. In fact, so serene was the children's (and parents') adjustment that discontinuities in their teachers were not disruptive to them, in a way that was a little surprising to us, the observers.

During this second year, due to the system changes discussed previously, many teachers were changing their place of work. We immediately began to track and try to understand the impact of these disruptions of continuity. We had several group meetings with teachers in order to discuss collectively the changes and found the teachers to be rather reserved about what must have been rather significant changes for them. Therefore, looking for another strategy, we decided to write a letter to the teachers asking them to write to us about their personal reflections about the changes. Although throughout the study, all of us involved (researchers, administrators, teachers, and parents) often communicated through written messages, on this occasion, the letters turned out to have a particularly personal and reflective tone. We include here one of those letters, from January 1998:

> Dear Lella and Carolyn,
>
> We are Marzia and Manuela and we answer with great

FIGURE 14.6. As children became good friends with the others in their group, they showed how much they liked each other's company and trusted their intentions. (*Infant-toddler Center Il Grillo, Pistoia*)

pleasure together because we work with the same group of children. We have also lived through together the changes that have taken place inside our infant-toddler center, and together we discuss them. First of all, we missed very much Cristina [teacher], who went to work in a preschool. We miss her both at the level of personal affection and at the level of work as a colleague.

Marzia and I have talked a great deal about what we were feeling and were missing, losing our colleagues. Speaking freely, we confided to each other our anxieties and fears and what was pressing us inside. So we became closer, and this has given us a push to overcome the disorientation that we felt and to return to work with trust and serenity.

The parents have appreciated very much our engagement and have often offered to help us in many kinds of work at the *nido,* or at least every day they showed us that they appreciated the work we do with children. The children in turn come with pleasure to the *nido.* As the transition of the adults has taken time, the three older children who already knew us well

> built a strong friendship among one another and began to make friends with the little ones. Unfortunately, there has been a temporary substitute who stayed only a short period of time. Now we wait with trust for the arrival of our new [permanent] colleague who will be with us as a teacher.

In general, in the letters there was description about the great solidarity on the part of parents, who seemed less concerned than the teachers about the changes (apart from one mother who was herself also an infant-toddler teacher). Another recurring observation made with specific reference to the particular children who participated in the research, was the tendency on the part of the children to get closer to the remaining friends from the previous year. One phrase that teachers often used to describe the reemergent sense of belonging among children (for example, speaking about those children who transferred to the new infant-toddler center), was that after a while they became again "owners of the space."

THE THIRD YEAR: A TIME OF CONSOLIDATION, CELEBRATION, AND PREPARATIONS TO MOVE ON

During the third year, the children reminded us of college students during senior year. They moved around their classrooms with confidence, seeming to know everyone and how to use the toys and materials just in the way they wanted. Their language had taken great strides, of course, and they spoke a great deal to one another and to the adults. The teachers made a symbolic event out of their *re-inserimento* by setting aside a day for each child on which he or she would formally "present" to the others the plastic box full of treasures collected with the help of parents over the summer. These presentations took place with a sense of ceremony. The teachers showed animation and affection for each child as he or she revealed the treasures, and the other children looked and listened with attention, seeking to touch and examine each item in turn. Then, at lunch, that child had the further honor of being the one to help the adults serve the meal and set the table. They did this with an evident sense of belonging, making sure every child around the table got everything needed.

By the end of spring, the time for parting was coming close. Many moments of celebration and closure were provided for the children and their families. One especially important event was the giving of the *diario* (diary). In the month of June, when the children were now about 3 years old, the teachers surprised the parents with a special parting gift. This was a sturdy notebook or album, a special journal compiled from documentary materials accumulated during the 2- or 3-year life in the center of each child. The teachers prepared these precious collections with obvious care and delivered them to the parents at the infant-toddler centers, at the end of the school year, during a special celebration, charged with joy and longing (see Giovannini, Chapter 11, this volume).

We asked the teachers if it were possible, at the end of the third year of research, to be present when the study parents were receiving the diary of their child. We wanted to capture and record the parents' fresh responses to the diaries and hear their reflections about their sense of their child's experiences at the infant-toddler center, as the concluding moment of their participation in the research. Contrary to our initial predictions, we detected no verbal or nonverbal differences between parents whose children had experienced greater teacher-child continuity and parents whose children had experienced more discontinuity. Therefore, on the basis of the interviews, we concluded that the parents felt smooth relations in all cases, with particular individual teachers but also with the infant-toddler system as a whole. Within their close relationship to that whole system, changes for their child in teachers or setting were not experienced as major disruptions.

Here follows an excerpt of the dialogue with the mother and father of Daniele, as they opened up their diary and reminisced about the past three years (see Figures 14.7 and 14.8). Daniele's parents were an exceptional case because they participated as a couple in every meeting and interview and had a team approach to their parenting role.

> The parents opened the diary, placed it on the table, and expressed admiration and surprise. Daniele was with them and started right away to point to his own pictures and the ones of the other children, saying their names and what they all were doing together at the time. They conversed intensely with him, moving slowly through the pages. After a few minutes Daniele ran away to play with the children in the other room.

Lella: Are you surprised?

Father: You know, we were expecting it but this is beyond any expectation. I do at times [for my own work], help with a designing a newspaper, or at least I prepare flyers. But this is such a beautiful design! Very professional in all its details! It is a very positive result to see this big book. This document shows that the teachers have respect for the children, also through the graphic design. Excellent in all its details! It is not even part of their job description! Therefore, I want to give public thanks to the teachers that have done it. It shows how much thought they put into this work. It is an excellent memory of all Daniele's steps of growth.

Lella: A teacher yesterday told us the story of an encounter with a 22-year-old girl who is now at the university. She recognized the teacher and reminded her that she had been in the infant-toddler

FIGURE 14.7. One of the first interviews with Daniele's parents during his first year at the infant-toddler center, a time still vividly recalled two years later.

FIGURE 14.8. Daniele and his parents look over for the first time the diary recording his 3-year experience in the infant-toddler center.

center with her. She added that she still loves to look through her *nido* diary.

Mother: I believe that this can become more and more precious with time. It is important also because all the children are in there in one picture or another.

Lella: Yes, it is a way to keep that group connected. What are your memories and impressions of the *inserimento?* You are a truly special team, we have met one time all the fathers, but we see above all the mothers. You have been present always together. Your point of view about your son's experiences is of particular interest to us.

Mother: Because of the way our work-life is organized, we work together and we share everything together.

Lella: I see a particular strength in your following your child's experience outside the home together.

Father: I think that at some level it is a deliberate choice on my part. He has already his particular identity as a person, and I do not want to miss out. I already think that he will grow up and go away.

Mother: Hum. Too early. But that he grows too quickly, yes, that is true!

Father: I do not want to invade his life, but I want to live the life of my child.

Lella: What do you think about the first transition into the infant-toddler center?

Mother: He has never created problems for us. None in the beginning, none in the changes that have taken place with the teachers. He seems to have adapted well to each new situation. So it has not been difficult for us. Not difficult for him and not difficult for us. Through time he seems to have accepted all of what the infant-toddler center was offering him, the presence of the adults and of the children. We have to recognize that the initial group of children remained solid all through the three years, even though other children came into their room after the first year. It is also understandable that some mornings the children might be in a bad mood, but if it has happened it has been just for a few minutes.

Lella: Among the pictures in the diary, are there some that remind you of a particular high point?

Father: Many. But I would like to point out this one that shows Daniele who has fallen asleep with his head on the table next to his lunch. For me, the fact that his teachers have included this picture shows that they really have understood him and captured a characteristic of his way of being and his personal rhythms. He is not too interested in food, but he eats, and when he is through he needs to sleep right away, no matter what. And we think it is nice.

Lella: Your impression is then that the teachers really understand the personality of your child?

Mother: Yes, yes. The relationship with the teachers has been very strong.

Lella (referring to the photos Carolyn took of Daniele feeding the cake to Beatrice in the second year): We observed that he collaborates with children in play.

Mother: Certainly the relationship with the children in his group is notable. I did not think it would be possible with children so young.

Lella: What have been the high points of your three years of experience?

Father: It is our first experience as parents, and we have been surprised and have marveled at the quality and quantity of work that these children have done. During these three years I have observed at times without being seen, or I have had lunch with the children and I have been surprised many times by their experiences with manipulating materials or with visual materials. These children have received stimuli of all kinds: with clay, with colors, with symbols and numbers. Although I know this is a formal aspect of education, I think it is important. He knows how to count to 10, and he is only 3! He is not a genius; all the children in that group are at the same level!

Lella: It is important that you know also what the other children know and do.

Mother: Those children are all at the same level, they learn together!

Father: We did not know that there would be so much learning. It is good to realize that he absorbs like a sponge but also to realize how much the teachers offer.

Mother: Daniele has been a little slower than the other children in doing things and speaking, but now [we are surprised] he speaks a lot and knows how to tell all the details of things that happened in a complex way. But I think that this is common to children.

Lella: Perhaps it would not be so where children do not receive this attention in their relationship with the teachers.

Father: We are convinced of this because we have seen it happen.

Mother: What I meant is that it is common of all the children of this group.

Lella: What do you think about the group breaking up next year in different preschools?

Mother: Pistoia is a small town. I think the children might be together in part or they will see each other. Perhaps it could be an advantage for Daniele to make friends also with other children.

Father: It is amazing how this group of parents who participated in the research have established a good relationship with each other. They are committed to their children's education and to maintain the friendships. They also help each other. In fact, we want to thank you and we want you to keep in touch and send us what you write about this study and our child. [*This interview continued for 10 more minutes, in total half an hour, and ended with long, collective farewells.*]

A SYSTEM BASED ON EMPATHY AND CONCERN FOR INDIVIDUAL GROWTH

The better we got to know the system in Pistoia, the clearer it became that its particular nature and brand of effectiveness derived from the ethical values and character of its leaders, and their deeply felt commitment to their community and the people within it. Annalia Galardini, in a spontaneous interview at the end of the research, selected the term *empathy* to summarize her moral ideal of leadership. Donatella Giovannini and the teachers present readily agreed that this quality does characterize her way of being and style of leadership, indeed, the ideal way in which all protagonists within the system should regard one another, all the way down to relations among children.

Teachers described to us how the lead administrators of the early childhood system had complementary talents that enabled them to depend on one another utterly and to work together well and support each other. All the leaders were unified in a strong attitude of trust in the teachers and staff within the system. This trust and respect provided for substantial autonomy to be given to each center and preschool, so that teachers, staff, and families there together worked out and developed over time their own particular style of teamwork and way of carrying out the system's mission and goals. Teachers said they trusted the leadership to decide upon and communicate to them the important overall long-term goals for the system, and then they felt trusted, in turn, to execute those goals in their own way in their daily collective work in close-knit teams.

The professional culture of teacher development in Pistoia clearly contained room for frank discussion, shared decision making, satisfaction and dissatisfaction, individual and group risk taking, mistakes as well as successes, and problem solving that moved the system continually forward. Teachers said that their administration showed "consideration for each educator and staff person as individuals," which allowed flexibility in assessing each person's situation. For example, teachers with family difficulties had been allowed special time off to deal with them. Teachers with extraordinary talents (for example, in storytelling, making soft toys, creating a lending library for children and parents, theater skills, or designing documentation) were called upon by others and became known throughout the system for their unique contributions.

The system looked for and depended upon the growth potential of individual members, leading to positive improvement of the system as a whole over time. It was this desire to foster growth that had inspired Galardini and Giovannini to join us in the research partnership, and which they had talked of in stating their original goals for the research agenda.

Therefore, at the end of the research, we interviewed Donatella Giovannini about what effects, if any, she thought participation in the research had on the study teachers. She saw several types of benefits:

- Teachers became part of a working group with colleagues from other infant-toddler centers. Because of the duration and continuity of the research, the relationships among the teachers (within and between the different centers) became more consolidated.
- Teachers became more aware of and articulate about the strategies for building relationships with families. They had used these before but now found them to be more apparent and meaningful.
- Teachers were able to consolidate their close relationships with particular children and parents. They became more aware of these developing relationships through the reflective processes involved in the research methods.
- Teachers became more aware of and more competent with regard to strategies of documentation. The requirements and deadlines built into systematic data collection increased their capacity for a certain kind of responsibility.
- Teachers gained confidence from seeing their administrative leaders (and the researchers) investing time, attention, energy, and ideas in them.

In sum, the colearning partnership that was the formal model for the research study, also stood as the model and ideal of everyday work and life in the infant-toddler centers. It represented the appropriate way for teachers, parents, and children to relate to one another. Empathy, respect, pleasure in learning, and generosity of attitude (Galardini & Giovannini, Chapter 8, this volume) colored everyday interactions in a visible way that was easily learned by children, reinforced by the images in the documentation covering their center walls, and reiterated in the preferred style that administrators used in interaction with their staff, the public, and outside visitors, and in turn by teachers with their colleagues and families. The system benefited from being small enough that its leadership could allow a personalized rather than bureaucratic mode of operation. Stable over time and coherent in its principles, the system still strives to be open to change and dynamic in its forward movement.

REFERENCES

Edwards, C. P., & Gandini, L. (1989). Teachers' expectations about the timing of developmental skills: A cross-cultural study. *Young Children, 44*(4), 15–19.

Edwards, C. P., Gandini, L., & Giovannini, D. (1996). The contrasting developmental timetables of parents and preschool teachers in two cultural communities. In S. Harkness & C. Super (Eds.), *Parents' cultural belief systems* (pp. 270–288). New York: Guilford.

Edwards, C. P., Gandini, L., & Nimmo, J. (1994). Promoting collaborative learning in the early childhood classroom: Teachers' contrasting conceptualizations in two communities. In L. G. Katz & B. Cesarone (Eds.), *Reflections on the Reggio Emilia approach* (pp. 81–104). Urbana, IL: ERIC.

Gandini, L. (1988). *Children and parents at bedtime: Physical closeness during the rituals of separation.* Unpublished doctoral dissertation, University of Massachusetts at Amherst. (University Microfilms No. 8906282)

Gandini, L. (1999). With children, for children. In A. Galardini, D. Giovannini, & S. Iozelli (Eds.), *L'immaginario bambino: The educational experiences of Pistoia city council in the drawings and graphics of Andrea Rauch* (pp. 112–119). Bergamo, Italy: Edizioni Junior.

Wagner, J. (1997). The unavoidable intervention of educational research: A framework for reconsidering research-practitioner cooperation. *Educational Researcher, 26*(7), 13–22.

Chapter 15

Quando c'e' figli (When There Are Children): Observations on Italian Early Childhood

Rebecca S. New

In her classic ethnography of an Italian hill town, Sydel Silverman (1975) observed the vital role that children serve as links through which adults in a community come together. In subsequent decades, analyses of Italian social policy confirm the extent to which the care and education of young Italian children is a social responsibility that extends beyond the family to include the larger society (Moss, 1988; New, 1993). The purpose of this chapter is to explore the implications of this powerful image of the Italian child as a catalyst for and beneficiary of adult conversation, collaboration, and political commitment. The basis for this discussion spans more than three decades of personal and professional experiences within the Italian culture, many of them involving the care of infants and toddlers.

My first introduction to Italy took place in the fall of 1967, when I traveled to Florence to live and study for a year. It was a rich and intoxicating experience for a young woman raised in a loving but conservative southern family, and I learned a great deal about alternative perspectives on food, pleasure, family, and friends. A second visit in 1971 firmly established my resolve to make Italy my second home. It was not until I lived in Italy with my own children, however, that I began to grasp the significance of that culture's role in adult decisions on behalf of children, particularly those decisions that reflect broader political agenda.

Since those first experiences in Italy and the start of my own career as an early childhood educator in the United States, I have been drawn to the challenge of trying to disentangle cultural sources of influence on young children's development as they appear in the forms of professional knowledge, political positions, and personal realities. Italy has served as a provocative catalyst for these efforts and for my own understandings of what it means to be a parent, an educator, a citizen, and a contributor to cultural change. In the pages to follow, I will describe three Italian adventures that have contributed much to my current understandings regarding the care and education of very young children. I use the term *adventure* because in each case I entered Italy with a strong sense of enthusiasm and anticipation, fully aware that I would be unable to predict all that I would encounter and be challenged to comprehend.

ADVENTURE 1: ANTHROPOLOGIST WITH CHILD IN CENTRAL ITALY

In 1980, I returned to Italy for another extended stay, this time deeply involved in a five-culture research effort[1] motivated by the aim of exploring the relationship between cultural values, parental goals, and strategies of caring for young children (LeVine, 1974). In retrospect, much of my current way of thinking about the dialectical tensions among community norms, parental ideologies, and infant care practices grew out of that year-long experience in anthropological fieldwork. Many of these understandings came about not only because of my research focus—I was, after all, conducting an ethnographic study complete with periodic home observations, questionnaires, and interviews on a sample of 20 families with infants—but because of my personal circumstances. I was in Italy with my infant son and his father. At 7 months, our child was the same age as half of my sample. I now understand that numerous other researchers, particularly women utilizing anthropological methods, have struggled with issues of personal identity and professional roles when they are "in the field" (Golde, 1986). At the time, however, I was unprepared for the multiple conflicts, including professional and personal dilemmas, that would result from my (interpretation of *my*) responsibilities as a researcher.

Officially, I was in Italy to study and understand those aspects of parental behavior that might be particular to the local and cultural contexts. Unofficially, our family of three was also a subject of study (and amusement) as we struggled with the demands of a very public family life. We lived in the working-class town of Civita Fantera (a pseudonym), one hour's drive north of Rome. My experiences within that small community helped me to understand the subcultural differences linked to Italy's regionalism, as the working-class traditions of central Italy occasionally contrasted with those imported from Italy's impoverished south, where approximately half of my sample originated. The daily challenges of living in that small community also contributed to a gradual awareness of myself—as an anxious, well-educated, middle-class North American mother—and of the assets and liabilities that accompanied my own push for independence even in my very young son. For example, we were routinely chastised for allowing our baby boy to freely crawl both in the home and out; we were also the recipients of countless offers of assistance and support in what might have otherwise been an isolated year of first-time parenting. As we devised ways to maintain some sense of autonomy and privacy in our adult lives, our son and his new cadre of friends showed us another style of living. Over the many months that we lived in the community, we watched our son become increasingly comfortable in dense social settings, responding with glee to the numerous opportunities to be played with and held by others. These understandings gave heft to my growing appreciation of the powerful role of cultural values and subcultural contexts on adult behavior and children's learning and development; and of the varied interpretations possible of a "good" child, or a "competent" parent (see Figure 15.1).

At the time, I believed that the most significant findings of this fieldwork would result from what I was studying, not what I was experiencing. One of my earliest impressions was that there were many rules to which mothers had to comply in the care of their young infants, most of them seemingly self-imposed. Fathers seemed to have only one rule—to stay out of the mother's way (New & Benigni, 1987). For the most part, the primary concern expressed by the 20 mothers in the sample was in regard to the quantity and quality of food that their young infants consumed. Mothers were seen as the only ones who could understand the cries of the child, particularly those related to hunger and nutritional needs. Mealtime was thus the mother's responsibility and prerogative, and it was a rare household where an infant was allowed to feed himself or herself. Even less likely was a father or other male figure to be found feeding an infant. Because our own parenting was contrary to these local norms, it was thus a source of community fascination tinged with dismay as we were observed allowing our child to feed himself. Teenagers, elderly men, shopkeepers, and especially grandmothers were similarly disapproving to see us offer him empty *gelato* cones; or to learn that his father prepared some of his meals and that we served him uncooked green peppers, day-old eggs, and cold beverages. On the bases of these experiences (handily couched under the "participant-observer" method of data collection), I regarded these Italian mothers' infant care priorities as custodial, with concerns about the child's developing psychological needs secondary to those regarding his or her physical health. In turn, we were regarded as careless American parents—but no worse than what might be expected, as one informant kindly explained.

It is interesting to note that much of what I initially *thought* I had learned from this first study was influenced by what I expected to see—or at least what I had been trained to identify as important. This training, I

FIGURE 15.1. The observer and the observed: Anthropologist with child "in the field."

should add, emphasized the use of anthropological research paradigms as an effective means of addressing contemporary issues in developmental psychology. I was particularly influenced by recent studies on mother-child interaction, which simultaneously utilized minute units of analysis in terms of mother-child interaction even as environmental features such as the presence or absence of other figures of stimulation were taken into account (Clarke-Stewart, 1973). In the Italian setting, therefore, I took note of the presence and participation of nonmaternal and nonfamilial "others" even as I faithfully recorded the sequencing of approximately 100 criterion-referenced infant and caregiver behaviors. I returned to the United States with hundreds of hours of observational data and dozens of interviews collected over the 12-month period of the field study.

When I turned to the challenges of analyzing my data, I again drew upon anthropological findings and the rare child development study on the significance of adult social networks (Cochran & Brassard, 1979) as sources of influence on the quantity and quality of children's experiences. I was further aided in my interpretations by the growing body of research on the social life of children and the critical importance of "significant others" in early childhood (Borman, 1982). At the same time as my theoretical understandings of social relations were expanding to include the multiple-partner and simultaneous interactions of my observational data, I relied upon newly developed methods of analysis of observational data (Lamb, Suomi, & Stephenson, 1979)—most of which were developed for and tested on dyadic exchanges. I also struggled to align my observations with LeVine's (1974) parental goals model, in which concern for infant health and survival assumes priority over an emphasis on other aspects of development. I ultimately challenged this hierarchical model to the extent that it fails to acknowledge the complexity of traditional cultural values as they are manifest within a changing cultural context (New, 1988). It took me much longer, however, to redress some of my own assumptions regarding the bases and benefits of Italian mothers' strategies of care.

As I reread my first ethnographic account of Italian infants and their social lives (New, 1984), I am struck by the number of ethnocentric observations that I made through the narrow lenses that I brought with me, colored by points of view provided by other social scientists. My current understandings of Italian infant care reflect a gradual convergence of insights garnered from this ethnographic study of parenting beliefs and behaviors (my own and others') and similarly challenging experiences in the decades and journeys to follow.

ADVENTURE 2: REGGIO EMILIA, LORIS MALAGUZZI, AND DAP

Subsequent Italian challenges to my own sense of efficacy and the meanings of diverse approaches to the care of young children were less personal but no less keenly felt. It was in the mid-1980s that I first traveled from Rome to the region of Emilia Romagna to see the beautiful infant-toddler centers of Parma, Modena, and Reggio Emilia. It was also at that time that I met Loris Malaguzzi, and heard him indignantly proclaim that in Italy, traditional out-of-home care "makes children stupid." This notion of nonmaternal child care as a risk factor in children's lives was not a new one to me. As a well-educated American mother in the 1980s, I was quite aware of burgeoning theoretical hypotheses and statistically significant findings on the risks of nonmaternal infant care (Belsky & Steinberg, 1978). What *was* new was Malaguzzi's notion that this risk factor was not due to the presence of nonmaternal others in children's daily lives; rather, it was the general lack of collaboration, imagination, and hard work that went into the provision of these services as traditionally imagined and implemented.

My initial visit to the region of Emilia Romagna was brief, and yet it was readily apparent to me that there was much to be learned from the region's industrious and innovative cities and their educational leaders. In the years to follow I brought small groups of American preservice teachers, most of whom were too young and inexperienced to fully appreciate what was being shared, to visit Parma, Modena, and Reggio Emilia. These visits took place in the days before large delegations forced tighter restrictions on the number and type and length of visits during the Reggio Emilia centers' regularly scheduled hours. I now understand how precious that opportunity was, as we were invited in to closely observe teachers working together and with infants, toddlers, and preschoolers. Ultimately, in spite of my admiration for the infant-toddler programs that I visited in Modena and Parma—and surely in part because I knew of *no* such counterparts in the United States to make use of their example—subsequent visits focused on Reggio Emilia. I was fascinated with Malaguzzi's emphasis on children's creative and intellectual potentials and the concept of children's multiple symbolic languages. The city's comprehensive system for children from birth to 6 years was unique and intriguing. In hindsight, I suspect that I was also drawn to the challenge of trying to understand what made this particular community so special. It was soon obvious that this city and my professional relationship with its members would serve as a critical testing ground for my own scholarly endeavors, with challenges that were distinct from those that I first experienced in Italy.

My first experiences in Reggio Emilia served as both a remarkable contrast and complement to my experiences in Civita Fantera. In each case, I was overwhelmed with the centrality of children within the life of the community. In the wealthy northern community of Reggio Emilia, much as was the case in the working-class central Italian town, private lives were public as neighbors discussed each other's problems and shared a sense of pride in their children's accomplishments. In each setting, adults presented themselves and young children at their best when they were in the public eye, and no expense was spared—or at least so it seemed—to purchase fine shoes and clothing. On the bases of these and other features of community life, I was confident that even Reggio Emilia's highly sophisticated approach to the care and education of young children had its roots in centuries of Italian traditions (New, 1993). In many respects, Reggio Emilia confirmed what I was learning about what it means to be *Italian.*

At the same time, Reggio Emilia presented me with a somewhat different and competing set of insights, understandings, and options. While my earlier ethnographic study of Italian infant care had contributed substantially to my conceptual understandings of culturally distinct patterns and goals of parenting, I felt no urge to recommend these infant care practices to others. In contrast, as I came to appreciate Reggio Emilia's response to early childhood, it was difficult *not* to share the specifics of my observations with others. In particular, I was struck by the citywide investment to the period of early childhood, a commitment that I soon learned is shared, to varying degrees, by numerous other communities in northern and central Italy. The remarkable results of Reggio Emilia's commitment to children provided me with a powerful example for use in my own advocacy for high-quality and affordable child care in the United States. The program's emphasis on the role of the environment, children's multiple symbolic languages, and its complex approach to curriculum in the form of long-term and open-ended projects *(progettazione)* all served as useful challenges to contemporary U.S. interpretations of children and the early childhood curriculum (New, 1992). It was not long before American educators clamored for more information on Reggio Emilia's approach to early childhood education (see Figure 15.2).

Besides learning more about Reggio Emilia, my early experiences in that city also helped me to understand that some of my more literal interpretations of the cultural values as expressed in Civita Fantera were often naive and sometimes quite off the mark. For example, my prior impression of the predominant role of women in the care of their children—they did, after all, tell me that "*nessuno* [no one] helps them" with child care—seemed increasingly inadequate. I began to rethink my earlier interpretations of the sample mothers' expressed attitudes and caregiving practices. I recalled that even as they proclaimed the critical nature of the maternal role, they also created numerous occasions—including awaking an infant from a nap—so that the baby could enjoy the company of other children and adults. I was finally beginning to comprehend Italians' firm belief in *both* the essential nature of maternal care within a familial context *and* multiple and extrafamilial social relationships in early childhood. This understanding was further strengthened when Sergio Spaggiari, the Director of Reggio Emilia's educational services, responded to my inquiry about parental support for out-of-home care for infants and toddlers by explaining that parents understand that children need more than the family; it is through interactions with others—being a part of a group—that one gains a sense of self, of personal identity. It took some time, however, before I fully understood the subcultural variability that exists with respect to this general premise, the processes through which adults might come to such an understanding, and the extent to which the child's earliest social relations might be a collective experience.

Throughout the 1980s, however, few in the United States were aware of Reggio Emilia's work with young children. It was not until the arrival of its traveling exhibition, The Hundred Languages of Children, and the additional notice garnered through conference presentations and publications (Edwards, Gandini, & Forman, 1993; Gandini, 1984; New, 1990) that American educators were challenged to reconsider some contemporary early childhood issues in a new light. As noted previously, my own increasing familiarity with Reggio Emilia's work with young children coincided with a growing controversy in the United States among scholars as well as the general public regarding out-of-home care for infants and toddlers (Phillips, McCartney, Scarr, & Howes, 1987). The social density of the Italian child's early childhood provided me with a compelling counterexample to the mother-child dyad that was represented as the American norm. Of greater influence were those features of Reggio Emilia's municipal early childhood program that served as challenges to the dominant interpretation of "developmentally appropriate practice" in early childhood settings (Bredekamp, 1987).

Reggio Emilia's example provided compelling support for the arguments that (1) there are cultural differences in how adults structure and interpret children's development, (2) there is more than one effective and

FIGURE 15.2. Reggio Emilia teachers influence the quality of children's play through the provision of such provocations as this projected image of an Italian city as a backdrop for children's constructive play with blocks.

sensitive way to respond to children's developing interests in the social and physical world, and (3) teachers need support and opportunities to study the children they teach rather than assumptions drawn solely from textbooks to sufficiently guide them in their work (New, 1994). Ultimately, more widely shared knowledge of Reggio Emilia's work coupled with growing understandings of both cultural and developmental diversity contributed to the revised position statement on developmentally appropriate practices (Bredekamp & Copple, 1997; Mallory & New, 1994). For U.S. educators, Reggio Emilia's elaborate interpretation of curriculum as *progettazione* (Rinaldi, 1998) has served as a particularly useful means to address children's diversity and curriculum goals simultaneously. A reconceptualization of the very concept of DAP draws heavily on Reggio Emilia's examples of teacher *documentation* and *advocacy* coupled with family and citizen *participation* as the best way to provide children with the educational experiences that are appropriate for them in particular sociocultural contexts (New, 1997).

From both Reggio Emilia and Civita Fantera, I had learned that children seem to fare well when adults pay attention to their needs, even when those needs are conceptualized somewhat differently. I was also beginning to understand that one of the primary characteristics of an Italian early childhood, in contrast to that in the United States, is that adults routinely collaborate on children's behalf.

ADVENTURE 3: NEW UNDERSTANDINGS OF SOCIALLY CONSTRUCTED COMMUNITIES

In the fall of 1996, I embarked on my most challenging Italian adventure to date, in the form of a collaborative research partnership that had been in the making since I first arrived in the region of Emilia Romagna. I had long wished for a better understanding of the extent to which Reggio Emilia is like, and different from, the rest of Italy. I also hoped to study Reggio Emilia's efforts and accomplishments in a way that would better contribute to educational practices and also expand upon contemporary theories of culture and human development. These goals ultimately resulted in a five-city project that now involves colleagues in the United States and Italy, most notably Reggio Emilia and collaborators in the municipalities of Milan, Trento, San Miniato, and Parma.[2]

By the time this research initiative began, a great deal had been learned about parents' cultural belief systems, including the significance of their expressions and their consequences (Harkness & Super, 1996). Parental priorities regarding such routine child care issues as sleeping and eating schedules were increasingly understood to correspond to larger and more fundamental views about children and their relationships to family and community (New & Richman, 1996). There was also increased attention to early education policies (Saraceno, 1984) and programs (Tobin, Wu, & Davidson, 1987) in diverse cultural and national contexts as they reflect and support different views of children, families, and societies. And yet relatively little effort had gone into the study of the ways in which parents and teachers in diverse cultural contexts make sense of their respective roles and relationships within educational settings. Nor had many attempted to examine the interface between cultural values, national policies, and the early childhood services that make such policies visible (Cochran, 1993; Kamerman, 1991). Even less was understood about the role of subcultural diversity in reflecting and contributing to cultural values and community norms regarding the occasions of early childhood (New, 1993).

This study, which continues at the time of this writing, represents a convergence of these issues. Utilizing a multimethod approach to data collection, the conceptual framework draws upon a cultural model of child care that, itself, grew out of a study on parental behavior in a cultural context (LeVine et al., 1994). This Italian study is thus focused on the relationships among national policies ("the moral direction"), local programs ("pragmatic design"), and personal behavior ("scripts for action") as they characterize Italian responses to home-school relations in the period of early childhood. As a means of focusing research questions and methodologies, local interpretations of two national guidelines are highlighted: that involving the process of *inserimento* (first-time entry into child care) and the practices of *gestione sociale* (social management) of child care services.

Through the processes of participating in this study, I have learned a great deal about the Italian cultural setting as a backdrop for contemporary policies and programs in early childhood. My collaborators and I have a vastly improved appreciation of the potentials and challenges of effective home-school relationships as manifest in infant-toddler and preprimary programs in five Italian cities. We also have begun to reconceptualize the concept of collaborative action research as yet another form of cultural expression and socially constructed knowledge. The experience of participating in this study also supports and expands upon my earlier Italian experiences, particularly as they contribute to my understandings of the critical importance of adult relations to children's well-being. Two preliminary findings warrant brief mention as they illustrate the potential of (1) educational strategies aimed at adults and (2) multiple and diverse interpretations of appropriate programs and places for young children.

Not-for-Children-Only

The national guidelines assigning priority to the careful management of the first out-of-home caregiving experience have been translated into a variety of strategies designed to ease the child's transition into an early childhood setting. And yet the strategies for *inserimento* observed and documented in this study were clearly not for children only. As is the case in many other parts of Italy (see Bove, Chapter 9, this volume), teachers, parents, and administrators repeatedly emphasized the critical importance of adult comfort and satisfaction with the child's transition to the *nido* or *scuola dell'infanzia* (New, 1999). In observing teachers and parents negotiate the practical details of a child's first feeding in the *nido* or confer on the best time and way for the parent to leave the child for the first time, I gained much-needed insights into the possibilities of a *pedagogia del benessere* [pedagogy of well-being] (Mantovani, 1997) for its contributions to adult mental health as well as to infant development. Similar values were expressed with respect to the *gestione sociale* as a structure for adult social relations. While the benefits to young children were always presented as the primary rationale for high levels of engagement in this parental advisory capacity, the personal gain for mothers, fathers, and teachers *as adults* was mentioned repeatedly. Repeatedly, parents who described their own degree of involvement and satisfaction in this component of the home-school relationship assigned significance to the opportunity for adult solidarity, companionship, and support in their roles as mothers and fathers. As one mother from Reggio Emilia explained, "At first I came for my child. Now I come for myself" (see Figure 15.3).

Diversity in Quality, Quality in Diversity

Equally salient in terms of first impressions generated in the research process is the diversity of interpretations of child care and the associated

FIGURE 15.3. Parents and other visitors to San Miniato's mixed-age *asilo nido* are invited to linger, to look at the photographs, and to read the messages and other forms of documentation that the teachers have so carefully and strategically displayed.

adult relations—and the strategies by which to achieve them—that were expressed and/or observed in the various subcultural contexts. Data analyses thus far support both the common ground and the extent to which such knowledge constructions draw upon local and individual processes of meaning making (Caronia, 1997). Indeed, the image of the child that has been so well articulated in Reggio Emilia is but one of many images of childhood (Hwang, Lamb, & Sigel, 1996) that have been portrayed by Italian educators. Different interpretations of children's needs and capabilities, in turn, are linked with different ways of conceptualizing adult relations and the appropriate educational responses. Thus Milan has developed its system of part-time family-child centers (*Tempo per le famiglie*) to respond to the needs and characteristics of single parents, immigrant families, and others lacking in the traditional neighborhood and family supports of the Italian family (see Mantovani, Chapter 6, this volume). The tiny town of San Miniato, in response to its small size as well as the decline in the Italian birth rate, has created a mixed-age 0–3 *nido* setting where children and parents can learn from the experiences of being with more- and less-experienced peers. Pistoia's services for children and their families are linked with a citywide emphasis on the cultural life of this Tuscany town, while Reggio Emilia's citizens define their civic identity through their high level of *partecipazione* in the municipal early childhood program (see Bondavalli, Chapter 5; Galardini & Giovannini, Chapter 8, this volume). In each case, adults work collaboratively and purposefully to construct what could be called highly particularized cultural contexts for children's development (Goodnow, Miller, & Kessel, 1995).

CONCLUSION

Each of the three experiences described above has furthered my attachment to and fascination with the culture of Italy and her people. These experiences have also helped me to make sense of the theoretical premise of cultural "situatedness"—or belonging to a particular time and place—of adult beliefs and decisions regarding children's care and education. More important, however, both for my own understandings and use of this theoretical construct, is the increasing recognition that it is not culture per se that contributes to children's development, but rather the individuals and institutions that make up the cultural milieu. I began this chapter by observing the essential role of the Italian child as a catalyst for adult conversation, collaboration, and political commitment. For the many Italians whom I have come to know and respect over the past three decades, the care of young children reflects much more than a culturally constructed image of the child. That is, while the decision making—both routine and formal—that takes place surely reveals some of what adults think about children, such deliberations also represent the moral principles that bind any cultural group together (Shweder, 1997).

And yet, the notion of a singular Italian orientation to children, family, and what LeVine (1974) calls the "presumptive tasks" of early childhood has also been challenged through these experiences. Within our research project, we now regard the varying interpretations of high-quality early childhood programs and effective home-school relations as a metaphor for locally varying interpretations of community, participation, and social responsibility.[3] There is no question that all of the Italian adults with whom I have spoken over the past three decades support the generally shared cultural belief in the importance of social relations to human development, beginning in early infancy. At the same time, experiences in the cities coinvolved in the research and elsewhere have also made clear that this general cultural belief system has diverse forms of interpretation. Such differences are marked at both the regional and local levels. This diversity in interpretations of quality has lead me to hypothesize that the care of young Italian children might well be likened to Italy's other outstanding reputation—for high-quality cuisine. Few coming to Italy from outside its borders have failed to notice the intensity of interest and pleasure associated with an Italian repast, nearly always composed of a good wine, pasta, and cheese among other delights. But to anticipate that similar offerings would appear on tables and menus across the country denies the Italian sensibility regarding the social significance of local cuisine. As noted in a recent history of Italian cuisine, *"L'Italia delle cento città e dei mille campanili è anche l'Italia delle cento cucine e delle mille ricette"* [The Italy of 100 cities and 1000 bell towers is also the Italy of 100 kitchens and 1000 recipes] (Capatti & Montanari, 1999, p. vii). This variety of traditional Italian cooking endeavors is not randomly distributed, however. Rather, it serves as a *"specchio di un'esperienza storica segnata dal particolarismo e dalla divisione politica"* [mirror of a historic experience marked by particularism and political divisions] (p. vii). The widespread appreciation of various ways to do something especially well is clearly—although it was not initially so easily understood—more than a preference for diversity. Each of these interpretations—whether of a good cheese, a good wine, or the proper way to make a certain pasta dish—is associated with a particular place and its people, with both the benefits and the burdens of responsibility shared by the stakeholders. These diverse interpretations, in turn, draw upon and contribute to the cultural values and quality of life to which Italians aspire—some shared, others particular to time and place.

It seems quite likely that these features of the Italian culture—a commitment to high standards, a multiplicity of interpretations, and a sense of shared responsibility—can be applied to the design and implementation of high-quality services for young children. If so, then one of those quality indicators for early care and education would be the purposeful nurturing—through diverse and locally determined strategies—of respectful and collaborative adult relations such as those we have observed in each of the cities involved in this research project. These adult relations have a direct bearing on the usefulness of the collective discourse and the "developmental appropriateness" of the solutions generated with regard to the challenges of caring and educating Italy's youngest citizens. As has been noted by others (e.g., Woodhead, 1999), a "greater openness to cultural possibilities" (p. 16) in supporting children's development has the potential to encourage the construction of new interpretations of early childhood.

The notion of early childhood as a "forum for civil society, with possibilities for many and varied projects" is now playing a major part in postmodern discussions of early education (Dahlberg, Moss, & Pence, 1999, p. 186). The examples set forth by the many who have hosted me over the past three decades suggest that Italy, a country whose collective history is as old as the story of Western Civilization, has much to contribute to this "new" postmodern perspective. Among other things, these Italian experiences convince me of the importance of protecting the local dialects in such conversations, not only as a means of enhancing the authenticity of what is identified as "developmentally appropriate" for children, but also for insuring that parents and other citizens join in the conversation. And perhaps it is this lesson for which I am most grateful to the Italian culture. I understand now what Loris Malaguzzi tried to explain to me over 15 years ago: "If you take good care of the children, the rest will follow." When adults work together to take good care of young children, not only do they foster children's development, they also enhance their own lives and contribute to the vitality of their community. This premise may well be the not-so-hidden secret to the high-quality child care that is described in this chapter (and throughout this volume). It also may well be a clue to the indomitable spirit of the Italian culture.

NOTES

1. The Comparative Human Infancy Project (C.H.I.P.), under principal investigator Robert A. LeVine, was a five-culture comparative study of infant care among the Gusii of Kenya as well as sample families in the United States, Sweden, Italy, and the Yucatan.

2. "The Sociocultural Construction of Home-School Relations: The Case of Reggio Emilia and Contemporary Italy," Rebecca New and Bruce Mallory, coprincipal investigators. 1996–1998. Funding provided by the Spencer Foundation.

3. And thus the title of a second phase of this research project, "Concepts of Community, Civic Participation, and Social Responsibility: Childcare as Metaphor," Rebecca New and Susanna Mantovani, coprincipal investigators. 1998–2000. Funding provided by the Spencer Foundation.

REFERENCES

Belsky, J., & Steinberg, L. D. (1978). The effects of day care: A critical review. *Child Development, 49*, 929–949.

Borman, K. (Ed.). (1982). *The social life of children in a changing society*. Hillsdale, NJ: Erlbaum.

Bredekamp, S. (Ed.). (1987). *Developmentally appropriate practice in early childhood programs serving children from birth through age 8*. Washington, DC: National Association for the Education of Young Children.

Bredekamp, S., & Copple, C. (Eds.). (1997). *Developmentally appropriate practice in early childhood programs* (Rev. ed.). Washington, DC: National Association for the Education of Young Children.

Capatti, A., & Montanari, M. (1999). *La cucina italiana: Storia di una cultura* [The Italian kitchen: The history of a culture]. Rome: Editori Laterza.

Caronia, L. (1997). *Costruire la conoscenza* [To construct knowledge]. Florence, Italy: La Nuova Italia.

Clarke-Stewart, K. A. (1973). Interactions between mothers and their young children: Characteristics and consequences. *Monographs of the Society for Research in Child Development, 38*(6–7, Serial No. 153).

Cochran, M. (1993). *International handbook of child care policies and programs*. Westport, CT: Greenwood.

Cochran, M., & Brassard, J. (1979). Child development and personal social networks. *Child Development, 50*(3), 601–616.

Dahlberg, G., Moss, P., & Pence, A. (1999). *Beyond quality in early childhood education and care: Postmodern perspectives*. Philadelphia: Falmer Press.

Edwards, C. P., Gandini, L., & Forman, G. (1993). *The hundred languages of children: The Reggio Emilia approach to early childhood education*. Norwood, NJ: Ablex.

Gandini, L. (1984, Summer). Not just anywhere: Making child care centers into "particular" places. *Beginnings*, pp. 17–20.

Golde, P. (1986). *Women in the field: Anthropological experiences* (2nd ed.). Berkeley: University of California Press.

Goodnow, J. J., Miller, P. J., & Kessel, F. (Eds.). (1995). *Cultural practices as contexts for development* (New Directions for Child Development No. 67). San Francisco: Jossey-Bass.

Harkness, S., & Super, C. (1996). *Parents' cultural belief systems: Their origins, expressions, and consequences*. New York: Guilford.

Hwang, C. P., Lamb, M. E., & Sigel, I. E. (Eds.). (1996). *Images of childhood*. Mahwah, NJ: Erlbaum.

Kamerman, S. (1991). Childcare policies and programs: An international overview. *Journal of Social Issues, 47*, 179–196.

Lamb, M., Suomi, S., & Stephenson, G. (Eds.). (1979). *Social interaction analysis: Methodological issues*. Madison: University of Wisconsin Press.

LeVine, R. A. (1974). Parental goals: A cross-cultural view. *Teacher's College Record, 76*(2), 226–239.

LeVine, R. A., Dixon, S., LeVine, S., Richman, A., Leiderman, P., Keefer, C., & Brazelton, T. (1994). *Child care and culture: Lessons from Africa*. Cambridge, U.K.: Cambridge University Press.

Mallory, B., & New, R. (Eds.). (1994). *Diversity and developmentally appropriate practices: Challenges for early childhood education*. New York: Teachers College Press.

Mantovani, Susanna (1997). Ruolo e funzione dell'educatore: Una pedagogia del benessere [The role and function of caregivers: A pedagogy of well-being]. In

N. Terzi, L. Cantarelli, G. Berziga, & B. Battaglioli (Eds.), *Il Nido compie 20 anni: La qualita della relazioni* (pp. 49–54). Bergamo, Italy: Edizioni Junior.

Moss, P. (1988). *Childcare and equality of opportunity: Consolidated report to the European commission*. London: London University.

New, R. (1984). *Italian mothers and infants: Patterns of care and social development*. Unpublished doctoral dissertation, Harvard University.

New, R. (1988). Parental goals and Italian infant care. In R. A. LeVine, P. M. Miller, & M. M. West (Eds.), *Parental behavior in diverse societies* (pp. 51–64). (New Directions for Child Development No. 40). San Francisco: Jossey-Bass.

New, R. (1990). Excellent education: A city in Italy has it. *Young Children, 45,* 4–10.

New, R. (1992). New interpretations of an integrated curriculum. In C. Seefeldt (Ed.), *Review of research in early childhood curriculum* (pp. 286–322). New York: Teachers College Press.

New, R. (1993). Italy. In M. Cochran (Ed.), *International handbook of child care policies and programs* (pp. 291–311). Westport, CT. Greenwood Press.

New, R. (1994). Culture, child development, and developmentally appropriate practices. An expanded role of teachers as collaborative researchers. In B. Mallory & R. New (Eds.), *Diversity and developmentally appropriate practices: Challenges for early childhood education* (pp. 65–83). New York: Teachers College Press.

New, R. (1997). Reggio Emilia's commitment to children and community: A reconceptualization of quality and DAP. *Canadian Children, 1,* 7–11.

New, R. (1999). Here, we call it "drop off and pick up": Transition to child care, American-style. *Young Children, 54*(2), 34–35.

New, R., & Benigni, L. (1987). Italian fathers and infants: Cultural constraints on paternal behavior. In M. Lamb (Ed.), *The father's role: Cross-cultural perspectives* (pp. 139–167). New York: Lawrence Erlbaum.

New, R., & Richman, A. (1996). Maternal beliefs and infant care practices in Italy and the United States. In S. Harkness & C. Super (Eds.), *Parents' cultural belief systems: Their origins, expressions, and consequences* (pp. 385–404). New York: Guilford.

Phillips, D., McCartney, K., Scarr, S., & Howes, C. (1987). Selective review of infant day care research: A cause for concern! *Zero to three, 7,* 18–81.

Rinaldi, C. (1998). Projected curriculum constructed through documentation—*Progettazione:* An interview with Lella Gandini. In C. P. Edwards, L. Gandini, & G. Forman (Eds.), *The hundred languages of children: The Reggio Emilia approach—advanced reflections* (2nd ed., pp. 113–125). Stamford, CT: Ablex.

Saraceno, C. (1984). The social construction of childhood: Childcare and education policies in Italy and the United States. *Social Problems, 31*(3), 351–363.

Shweder, R. (1997/October). *Cultural psychology—What is it?* Paper presented at Society for Psychological Anthropology Fifth Biennial Meeting, San Diego, CA.

Silverman, S. (1975). *Three bells of civilization: The life on an Italian hill town.* New York: Columbia University Press.

Tobin, J., Wu, D., & Davidson, D. (1987). *Preschool in three cultures: Japan, China, and the United States.* New Haven, CT: Yale University Press.

Woodhead, M. (1999). Reconstructing developmental psychology—Some first steps. *Children and Society, 13,* 3–19.

Chapter 16

Conclusions for Now, Questions and Directions for the Future

Carolyn Pope Edwards and Lella Gandini

In this book, we have heard many narratives, interpretations, speculations, and evaluative accounts about the family-centered systems of care and education for infants and toddlers in Italy. As with any set of stories, the levels of meaning are many; and the stories can be read from multiple points of view. Many of the authors begin with principles and then bridge theory into practice, delineating strategies or guidelines; many authors also lay out their approaches to political action and advocacy. What lessons and implications can be drawn lie not only in the direct messages intended by each author. They also arise from how the chapters add together and resonate in relation to one another, like the paintings in a gallery, where the messages of each piece emerge from the whole arrangement and movement of the show.

Educational change is a dynamic, nonlinear, and unpredictable process. Certainly, we cannot predict how successfully this book will bridge between English- and Italian-speaking professionals, or how helpful it will be. Instead, we must trust to future events to inform us as to how useful and influential the Italian experiences and insights can be as they travel to North America. Because issues in education are complex and multifaceted, dialogue across cultural and linguistic boundaries requires an effort by both sides to go beyond superficial first impressions and overcome any barriers to appreciative understanding. What we can say for sure is that the contributors to this volume have spoken loudly and clearly in answer to many of the questions that are most frequently asked by Americans about the infant-toddler centers of Italy. The contributors have declared themselves in favor of certain strong beliefs and conclusions, even if they cannot address every issue. Indeed, we hope this summary and conclusion chapter raises new, deeper questions, opens up new areas for debate and discussion, and points readers in new directions as they go about their own work with children.

EVERYONE CONNECTED: A BASIC WAY OF SEEING AND WORKING

The first set of answers set forth by the contributors concerns the basic *whats* and *hows* of the programs. What are the goals of the best-known Italian programs, and how are they implemented? How do the programs serve and involve parents? How do teachers provide safe, stimulating, nurturing environments that promote healthy well-being and development? How do teachers and administrators work together to improve processes of professional development and system improvement? On the most general level, how does each city respond to all its constituencies and create programs that balance the multiple and sometimes competing needs of children, parents, professionals, and the public, in a fair, coherent, and integrated way?

This last question, about balancing needs, has no simple answer. Rather, our Italian experts suggest that balance and cohesion are approached through institutions that treat all groups of participants as developing persons, with broad needs inclusive of others' needs, too. That is to say, the best way to balance the needs of parents, children, educators, and the public is to take a long view that brings people into extended relationship and discussion (including debate and conflict) with one another, as members of a community. After all, parents are highly identified with the developmental needs of their children, in addition to their status as adults who need to get to work and as members of the taxpaying public. Children are young now but will soon grow up to be adult citizens (and possibly parents themselves, or even teachers!). Teachers are members of the public and often are parents, too; they may have their own young children served by the same system for which they work. Many adult citizens of the public in an Italian city grew up there, and may even have once attended the public preschools. Thus, our contributors have worked against any narrow vision of needs to be served, or any strict prioritization. Instead, they want to open the door and listen to all voices and perspectives. Furthermore, this way of opening the door seems to be a major part of the Italian answer to all of the other practical questions as well.

Thus, the preceding chapters have made clear that the Italian approach to infant-toddler services differs from (in fact, opposes or goes beyond) "compensatory education," "special education," and "gifted education." It cannot be captured by any term available, such as "child care," "infant stimulation," "early intervention," or "family support," because it combines all of them. It is ideally *inclusionary* of all the categories of service and all the participants. The infant-toddler setting is intended to be a place for living, where life together harmonizes with the pace and rhythm of children's existence and supports each individual's development, including that of the adults. It should be a place where relationships and interactions among adults are respectful of the *particular* people involved. These are the individual participants, who together create a context for emotional, affective, cognitive, and social development, as well as identity formation for children. The program is the site of a complex set of relationships, and the concerns, actions, and attitudes of the adults involved are as important and significant as are those of the children. The programs are not simply "child-centered," not simply "family-focused," and certainly not "teacher-centered," but instead "relationship-focused." Each program is an ecology with a particular organization of space, time (Musatti, 1992), and resources selected to balance and interconnect people with their multiple and changing wants and needs. It is a small community nested within and supported by the larger community.

Within this overall way of looking at things, more specific generalizations readily emerge about the excellent infant-toddler programs described in this book. All place a focus on *process* rather than *product* or *outcomes*:

- System and program goals are decided upon as works-in-progress. Philosophical issues enter into the cycle of improvement at all points, and go in different paths in different localities. Participants at all levels of the system take some part in reflection, critical observation, and discussion of basic values and guidelines as ongoing activities, not steps in a sequence. Statements of philosophy are not background but foreground, kept vital through ongoing discussion and debate, not contracts or starting points.
- Professional development and teacher education, likewise, are ongoing processes based on activities of observation and reflection. In-service education has been the primary vehicle for bootstrapping system change and improvement (though in the future, standards for preservice preparation may rise). Work requirements for teachers are demanding yet flexible and personalized, and strong emotional and organizational supports are provided to make it possible for teachers to function with high professional expectations.
- Families are brought in and involved in multiple ways, particular to the city and region, the specific kind of program, and the times. Families are regarded as partners, not "consumers" provided with a fixed product, nor "clients" treated by experts; and they are expected to grow and change through the process of moving through the infant-toddler center experience with their child.

• Group life is the focus of the infant-toddler center experience for children. The group experience, considered as the child's first entry into civil society, is a good thing, a source of enjoyment, pleasure, and lasting friendship.

• Strategies which have received particular study and discussion in Italy, such as *inserimento* (delicate period of transition), documentation, inclusion, and the *diario* (memory book) are useful precisely because they enable parents, teachers, and children to extend and focus on process rather than performance.

Now, these are not proposals that shock or turn off most U.S. early childhood educators. Instead, quite the opposite is true! The forms of inclusionary and democratic participation we have described resonate with a strong stream of American social thought, for example, the writings of John Dewey (1916), founding philosopher of progressive education in the United States (Greenberg, 1992). Furthermore, as J. Ronald Lally describes in Chapter 1, the United States is gradually (if unevenly) moving toward more holistic and relationship-centered models of early care, education, intervention, and family support. The federal performance standards for Early Head Start require that programs consider the establishment and development of secure and trusting relationships between infants and caregivers as the starting point of quality infant care and as the base for healthy development. Primary caregiver models and continuity of care are methods of choice. In promoting this perspective, the National Center for Infants, Toddlers, and Families, publisher of the bulletin, *Zero to Three,* has done more than any other national organization in the United States to lay out and promote approaches to early intervention and parent education based on the latest research and theorizing about the child's first relationships and attachments. The National Association for the Education of Young Children (NAEYC) also stands for a unified approach to early care and education for children from birth through the primary grades, as evidenced in the Standards for Developmentally Appropriate Practice (Bredekamp & Copple, 1997), Criteria for High-Quality Early Childhood Programs (NAEYC, 1998), and Guidelines for Preparation of Early Childhood Professionals (NAEYC, 1996).

DECENTRALIZED CONTROL AND LOCAL EXPERIMENTATION

Italy (population 57 million people, area 116,000 square miles) is certainly a more compact and culturally and linguistically homogeneous nation than is the United States. Nevertheless, as in the United States, regional differences are a treasured source of cultural pride, and progress in early childhood education has depended on what New (Chapter 15, this volume) aptly calls "diversity in quality, quality in diversity."

Broad national discussion, accompanied by regional and local experimentation, has been the great source of vitality and innovation in the early childhood field in Italy. Our contributors have made clear that variation and decentralization are an important part of their answers to questions that go beyond the *hows* and *whats,* and ask *why* their systems are so good. That is to say, without the possibility of local experimentation and flexibility, things would have turned out differently. The major forces and long-term trends in Italian society, culture, and politics would never have come together to make the Italian nation and its cities into such vital sites for creative experimentation and innovation in early education and care. The early childhood systems of Reggio Emilia, Pistoia, Milan, Parma, Modena, San Miniato, Trento, and other Italian cities vary not in level of quality (which is better?) but rather in kind (what is distinctively good about each?). The differences in kind result from particular, localized visions about what is good for children, families, and community—visions that underlie and motivate choices and directions. Thus, it seems that the Italian national system of public early care and education displays the strengths of flexibility and decentralization, without suffering from the extreme fragmentation and unevenness evident in the United States. Indeed, the United States does not yet have national standards or a national system of public early care and education, apart from Head Start and Early Head Start.

An interesting feature of the current Italian scene, related to flexibility and decentralization, concerns the contemporary trend to expand services through adding private and nonprofit solutions to the mix of public programs. This move reflects the influence of economic constraints on the evolving system of early care and education. The decade of the 1970s marked the time when the new infant-toddler programs were first created and defined, while the 1980s and 1990s witnessed times of consolidation and advocacy to preserve (and extend) programs in the face of both increasing public demand and budgetary constraints. The demand for infant-toddler services was continually rising, especially in those places in Italy where the systems developed particularly well, because parents were coming to see them as a quality benefit for children, not merely a service to working families. Meanwhile, conflict over financial resources was mounting. Although Italian economic growth forged ahead during this time period (and Italy has now the third largest European economy behind Germany and France), nevertheless budget crises have been recurrent. In recent years, pressure for public funds has continued to be tightened by Italy's membership in the European Union and the monetary controls imposed as part of the process of establishing a unified European currency. The upshot of all these conflicting pressures on government has been a move in Italy to expand the national system of infant-toddler care and education, but financed through a variety of public and private, nonprofit solutions. Ghedini (see Chapter 3, this volume) describes the proposed national law, first put forward in the middle 1990s, to provide infant-toddler care and education for all children through a public and private mix. Thus, Italy seems to be moving toward a more comprehensive and diversified system. At the same time, Italian society itself is becoming more diverse (ethnically and racially); large numbers of workers from West and North Africa and central Europe are immigrating on a permanent or semi-permanent basis into all of its cities. The principle of "diversity in quality, quality in diversity," we conclude, faces a tough test in future years as Italy comes to terms with rapidly changing economic and social conditions. Certainly, however, this principle provides more promise and allows more leeway for innovation and experimentation than would a heavily standardized, bureaucratic, and centralized national system.

RECENT AND CURRENT DEBATES: WHAT IS *QUALITY*?

By the late 1980s and into the 1990s, the climate of discussion among Italian administrators, educators, and researchers took a new turn as they entered into discourse with their European colleagues. Italian educators discussed their work in a wide forum including intellectuals and leaders from other parts of western and northern Europe. They joined discussions comparing operational aspects of their respective systems as well as asking far-reaching questions about philosophical assumptions and psychological theories sustaining their respective approaches (David, 1993; Ghedini, 1995; Moss & Pence, 1994; Oberhuemmer & Ulich, 1997; Penn, 1997). One major topic that moved to the forefront concerned the basic issue of "what is good" with respect to early care and education; that is, how to define and/or measure *relative quality.* Can a valid definition of "quality" be formulated, and if so, how? How should recommendations or guidelines for practice be laid down? Is it legitimate or appropriate to consider evaluation of the quality of programs?

Out of these discussions with their European colleagues, Italian educators arrived during the 1990s at the following three main criteria for defining quality in early care and education in their programs: child well-being; family satisfaction; and professional dignity and work conditions. From these three basic criteria, more specific guidelines or sets of "quality indicators" were derived. Many such guidelines were published in Italy (e.g., Balageur, Mestres, & Penn, 1992; Barberi, Bondioli, Galardini, Mantovani, & Perini, 1998; Bordigoni et al., 1993; Centro Nazionale, 1998; U.O.C. Infanzia ed Adolescenza, 1998). They have been used in many different ways, most often as a springboard for collegial discussion and professional development, although a few handbooks for program evaluation have been published. The guidelines have different emphases, breakdowns, and wordings, and yet seem to agree on basic substance. We chose to make the following compendium that bears a close resemblance to many conclusions put forth by the contributors to this volume.

Definitions of Quality for Infant and Toddler Care: A Summary View

• *Image of the system and accessibility to families.* Families should be informed about what programs and services are available, and so they should find these to be transparent in their organization, open for visiting in advance of registration, and flexible to different needs and varieties of families.

• *Environment and space as a stimulus and a resource.* The physical setting should be safe and healthy for children and adults. It should promote children's daily life, feelings of well-being in aesthetic surroundings, and learning experiences. It must provide a good climate and space for adult work, moments of rest, and sociality.

• *Activities, objects, and materials for children.* Children should have opportunities for exchanges with peers and familiar adults in personalized, affective ways. Teachers should offer a generous variety of learning activities for individual and small group play. Materials should be safe, age-appropriate, noncommercial, and inviting to children for exploration and interaction.

• *A system of relationships.* Close attention should be paid to the formation of a complex set of relationships for each child and family entering a program. The welcoming process should lead to trust and rapport and not be overwhelmed by bureaucratic transactions. It should be attentive to parental requests, informative, and accepting of parents' complex and sometimes ambivalent feelings.

• *Educational work: collegiality, professionalism, and pedagogical support.* Work organization and conditions should support teachers and caregivers and provide them with satisfaction and a sense of value for their delicate and demanding work. It should promote cooperation, opportunities for professional growth, and technical support from consulting supervisors (pedagogical coordinators).

• *Documentation as communication and assessment.* Teachers need to document their educational work in order to reflect upon their own actions and initiatives and to avoid casual improvisation. Good documentation communicates to children the value of what they do and promotes their self-confidence and awareness of what others do. It helps parents and the public to become aware of their children's experiences at the center and to acquire a stronger image of childhood.

• *Relationship with parents and family participation.* Programs for children should communicate to parents the primary contribution they make to their children's development and provide space, time, and opportunities for occasions that help parents feel and become competent participants in the life of the center.

• *Continuity, connection with other services, and inclusion of diversity.* Starting from the premise that each child develops in a unique way, educators must focus attention on individual growth and development.

They should share responsibility with families and the community to support full inclusion of all children, representative of the full range of abilities and circumstances. They should foster a dialogue that supports continuity of experience for children from birth through 6 years of age. They should contribute to a process of creating coherence and shared objectives among different kinds of programs and services for young children, as well as among choices of policy at the national and local levels.

- *Balance between costs and benefits.* Programs must stand up to scrutiny from an economic perspective and provide good value. This includes not only direct and indirect costs and benefits, the complex set of economic effects of programs, but also the holistic benefits the programs produce.

A Second Stream to the Debate: Critique of Quality, Indicators, and Outcomes

At the same time that many educators in Italy and abroad were attempting to improve early education and care by defining quality and its indicators, certain among them were raising basic questions about whether it is worthwhile or even possible to do so. This second stream to the discussion about quality is particularly alive at present. Leaders in the European discussion include Gunilla Dahlberg of Sweden, Peter Moss of the United Kingdom, and Alan Pence of Canada. In their 1999 book, they analyzed the difficulties associated with finding a universally valid definition of quality, its indicators, and outcomes. They brought attention to the fact that the language of quality carries the dangerous assumption that "both indicators and outcomes are universal and objective, identifiable to application of expert knowledge and reducible to accurate measurements given the right techniques" (p. 5). The search for quality inclines educators to prefer strategies and methods that ensure standardization, predictability, and control in early education and care (Cremaschi, 1995). Quality becomes a technical challenge, something to be "achieved," rather than a problem, something to be "questioned." Instead, they say, educators should be engaging in critical inquiry with one another about what is good in education and debating such subjects as the purposes of early childhood institutions in contemporary times and how to understand development, knowledge, and learning. They propose leaving aside the search for quality and instead engage in "meaning making," that is, in the shared construction of values and beliefs to use as the basis for action and decision making. For example, stakeholder groups and professional associations engage in a worthwhile alternative to a discussion of standards and outcomes, when they seek to understand and build consensus around such fundamental issues as how to promote children's well-being, how to make good pedagogical judgments and choices, and how to draw wisely on personal experience in teaching. An essential tool for meaning making is pedagogical documentation that assists educators in thinking critically and reflexively, entering and understanding the perspective of a young child in a particular context, and basing classroom and program evaluation on these very processes of meaning making (Dahlberg, Moss, & Pence, 1999, Chapters 5 and 7).

CLOSING THOUGHTS

This book has ushered us into a "forum" where the style and substance of the discussion have followed the customary rules that our Italian friends and colleagues use when discussing educational issues. Our contributors passionately desire to speak to colleagues overseas and to share their success stories as well as their quandaries and doubts. We hope that readers have appreciated the value of coming close to hear about the assumptions, theories, and practices of a society very different from their own, as well as the opportunity of being present at a dialogue where cultural insiders and outsiders have taken turns at analyzing and interpreting certain Italian ways of educating and caring for the youngest children. The intensity and variety of the discussions and the questions raised by the contributors give a clear indication of the continuing vitality of the international field of early childhood education. We believe they point toward a fruitful period ahead in which debates about early care and education will continue to be widened by contact not only with the questions and best answers of people in other countries, but also with their intimate debates and dialogues. The best use of this material may be to help readers step outside and see their own situation through new eyes, ask different questions, and engage with their colleagues, students, or school communities in more far-reaching professional development and system improvement activities. The Italian-inspired language of "relationship," "participation," "documentation," "culture of childhood," "generosity of attitude," "strong image of the child," "favorable" or "amiable spaces," "delicate period of transition," and "memory book" may find a useful role in such discussions and lead readers down unexpected and rewarding paths. By accepting the invitation of our contributors to join their ongoing conversations and then take away to remake for ourselves any strategies or proposals, all of us gain the chance to participate and contribute to their history of ideas as well as our own.

REFERENCES

Balageur, I., Mestres, J., & Penn, H. (1992). *Qualitè des services pour les jeunes enfants: Un document de reflexion* [Quality in services for young children: A document for discussion]. Brussels: Commission of the European Community. (Italian version published in *Bambini,* June 1995).

Barberi, P., Bondioli, A., Galardini, A., Mantovani, S., & Perini, F. (1998). *Linee guida per la qualità del servizio asilo nido nella provincia di Trento* [Guidelines about quality of infant-toddler services of the province of Trento]. Assessorato all'istruzione e formazione professionale, Trento, Italy.

Bordigoni, F., Casini, L., Catarsi, G., Faenzi, G., Fortunati, A., Galardini A., Maffei, S., Musatti, T., Profeti, R., & Saitta, L. (1993). *Gli indicatori di qualità per l'asilo nido* [Quality criteria for infant-toddler centers]. Regione Toscana & Istituto degli Innocenti.

Bredekamp, S., & Copple, C. (Eds.). (1997). *Developmentally appropriate practice in early childhood programs* (Rev. ed.). Washington, DC: National Association for the Education of Young Children.

Centro Nazionale di Documentazione ed Analisi sull'Infanzia e l'Adolescenza [National Center for Documentation on Infancy and Adolescence]. (1998). *Infanzia e adolescenza: Diritti e opportunitá* [Childhood and adolescence: Rights and opportunities]. Florence, Italy: Istituto degli Innocenti di Firenze.

Cremaschi, F. (1995). Come valutare la qualità: Intervista a Peter Moss [How to assess quality: An interview with Peter Moss]. *Bambini, 11*(6), 10–13.

Dahlberg, G., Moss, P., & Pence, A. (1999). *Beyond quality in early childhood education and care: Postmodern perspectives.* Philadelphia: Falmer Press.

David, T. (1993). *Educational provision for our youngest children: European perspectives.* London: Paul Chapman.

Dewey, J. (1916). *Democracy and education.* New York: Macmillan.

Ghedini, P. O. (1995). La qualità come strategia [Quality as strategy]. *Bambini, 11*(6), 14–20.

Greenberg, P. (1992, March). Why not academic preschool? (Part 2) Autocracy or democracy in the classroom? *Young Children,* pp. 54–64.

Moss, P., & Pence, A. (1994). *Valuing quality in early childhood services: New approaches to defining quality.* New York: Teachers College Press.

Musatti, T. (1992). *La giornata del mio bambino: Madri, lavoro e cura dei più piccoli nella vita quotidiana* [My child's day: Mothers, work and care for the youngest children in daily life]. Bologna, Italy: Il Mulino.

National Association for the Education of Young Children (NAEYC). (1996). *Guidelines for preparation of early childhood professionals.* Washington, DC: Author.

National Association for the Education of Young Children (NAEYC). (1998). *Accreditation criteria and procedures.* Washington, DC: Author.

Oberhuemer, P., & Ulich, M. (1997). *Working with young children in Europe: Provision and staff training.* London: Paul Chapman.

Penn, H. (1997). *Comparing nurseries: Staff and children in Italy, Spain, and the UK.* London: Paul Chapman.

U.O.C. Infanzia ed Adolescenza, Istituto degli Innocenti (Ed.). (1998). *Manuale per la valutazione della qualità degli asili nido nella regione Toscana* [Handbook for assessment of quality of the infant-toddler centers in the region of Tuscany]. Bergamo, Italy: Edizioni Junior.

About the Editors and the Contributors

Lella Gandini is Adjunct Professor of Education at the University of Massachusetts at Amherst and Lesley College (Cambridge, Mass.). She earned her Ed.D. from the University of Massachusetts and master's degree in child study from Smith College. She serves as liaison on behalf of Reggio Children for dissemination in the United States and as correspondent for the Italian educational magazine, *Bambini*. She conducts research, lectures, consults, and writes in Italian and English on many issues around early childhood teaching, parenting, children's fears, nursery rhymes, bedtime rituals, and parent-teacher-child relationships. She coedited and contributed to *The Hundred Languages of Children: The Reggio Emilia Approach to Early Childhood Education* (with Carolyn Edwards and George Forman; second edition published in 1998).

Carolyn Pope Edwards is Professor of Psychology and Family and Consumer Sciences at the University of Nebraska at Lincoln. She earned her doctorate and bachelor's degree from Harvard University and has been an invited fellow at the Norwegian Centre for Advanced Study in Oslo and visiting professor at the National Research Council (CNR) in Rome. Besides *The Hundred Languages of Children,* her works include *Promoting Social and Moral Development of Young Children* (1986), *Children of Different Worlds: The Formation of Social Behavior* (1988), and articles about early childhood education and social and moral development. She and Lella Gandini have worked together on several research projects in Italy and the United States; and she is currently studying parental values and serving on projects focused on teacher preparation.

Cristina Bondavalli has been a teacher since 1983 and part of the early childhood educational system of Reggio Emilia, Italy, since 1991. She taught for several years at the Peter Pan infant-toddler center and for two years at La Villetta preschool; she works now at the Documentation and Research Center of the municipal department of education. Fluent in English, Cristina has visited the United States on two occasions and assists Reggio Children in consulting and coleading professional development sessions for foreign teachers on study tours.

Chiara Bove is a graduate of the Institute of Pedagogy at the University of Milan. She consults with infant-toddler and preschool programs in several north Italian cities and is currently working as a teaching assistant at the University of Milan,

Facoltà di Scienze della Formazione Primaria, in the Department of Educational Psychology. She was awarded a national research fellowship to study attachment relations associated with the first transition to child care in the United States and Italy; she also participates in the collaborative research project of New, Mantovani, and Mallory. She is coauthor with Susanna Mantovani and Laura Saitta of *Attachment and Inserimento in the Nido: Relational Styles and Stories* (2000).

Marialuisa Cantarelli is pedagogical coordinator for the infant-toddler centers of the city of Parma, Italy. She has a degree *(Laurea)* in philosophy and psychology from the University of Bologna and a further specialization in clinical psychology. She has been intensely involved in the professional development of infant-toddler educators in Parma, as well as other cities, and has given particular attention to group dynamics. She has published several articles in the teachers' magazine, *Bambini,* and has coedited with Nice Terzi and contributed a chapter to the 1996 book, *Il Nido Compie Vent'Anni* [The Nido turns Twenty].

Annalia Galardini has been a founding leader (since 1972) of early childhood services in Pistoia, Italy, and is now Director of Education, Social Services, and Cultural Affairs in the city administration. She holds a degree *(Laurea)* in education from the University of Florence. Prominent at the national level, she has organized in-service work in several Italian cities and has had a long-standing relationship with the National Research Council (CNR) in Rome. She has published articles and chapters about the organization and goals of services for young children. She is on the board of directors of the National Group of Work and Study on Infant-Toddler Centers and of *Bambini* magazine and is a member of the European Institute for the Development of Potential of All Children (IEDPE).

Patrizia Ghedini is the director of childhood services for the regional government of Emilia Romagna, Italy, and the Italian representative of the European Community's Committee for the Childhood Network. She participates in the work of national commissions connected with early childhood education and has been instrumental in writing the (pending) new national law on infant and toddler care and the parallel (approved) regional law for Emilia Romagna. She is on the board of directors of the National Group of Work and Study on Infant-Toddler Centers. She is a regular contributor to the teachers' magazine, *Bambini,* and has published several articles and many book chapters.

Donatella Giovannini is the pedagogical coordinator for infant-toddler services of Pistoia, Italy, and has been instrumental in supporting the professional development of infant-toddler educators in Pistoia and its sister city, Palermo. She has a degree *(Laurea)* in philosophy from the University of Florence. She provides in-service training for teachers throughout Italy and is involved in research carried out by the Psychology Institute of the National Research Council (CNR) in Rome. She has published several book chapters and articles in the educational magazine *Bambini* and in journals concerning children's literature.

Jeanne Goldhaber is Associate Professor in the Early Childhood Pre-K–3 Teacher Preparation Program at the University of Vermont (UVM). She received her Ed.D. from the University of Massachusetts at Amherst. She and her colleagues at the UVM Children's Center have been investigating the role of documentation in teacher professional development, inquiry, and collaboration, with publications appearing in journals such as *Young Children, Childhood Education, Science and Children, Early Care and Education, Journal of Early Childhood Teacher Education, Early Childhood Education Journal,* and in the book edited by Joanne Hendrick, *First Steps Toward Teaching the Reggio Way.*

J. Ronald Lally is the director of the Center for Child and Family Studies at WestEd Laboratory in San Francisco. He received his doctorate from the University of Florida and was for many years Professor and Chair of the Department of Child and Family Studies at Syracuse University. His interests center on policies and programs for young children and their families and on methods for supporting teacher development. He writes and speaks widely and serves on many national boards; he is a founding member of Zero to Three: National Center for Infants, Toddlers and Families. Much of his research deals with social emotional development in infancy and the impact of early intervention on adult functioning.

Gabri Magrini, a teacher who has also acquired a diploma in special education, has been working in the municipal system of early childhood education of Pistoia, Italy, for 10 years and has conducted with particular interest research on activities with children from 4 months to 3 years of age. Her particular training has also involved her in research on strategies to facilitate the transition *(inserimento)* into the infant-toddler centers of infants and toddlers with special needs, and to support their parents.

Susanna Mantovani is Professor of Educational Psychology *(Psicopedagogia)* at the University of Milan-Bicocca. During the past 20 years, her work and numerous influential publications have dealt with early childhood education and early childhood policies in Italy as interpreted from both national and international perspectives. She founded the project, *Tempo delle Famiglie* [Time for Families], in Milan, and is current president of the National Group of Work and Study on Infant-Toddler Centers. She is a coprincipal investigator with New and Mallory in a study of home-school relations in Reggio Emilia, Milan, Parma, Trento, and San Miniato.

Susanna Mayer is Researcher in the Institute of Psychology at the National Research Council (CNR) in Rome. Her primary research interests concern communicative and cognitive development in early childhood, with particular focus on pretend play. Her publications include "Towards the use of symbols: Play with objects and communication with adult and peers in the second year," *Infant Behavior and Development* (1992), with Tullia Musatti, and "Contributions of language to early pretend play," in *Cahiers de Psychologie Cognitive* [Current Psychology of Cognition] (1998), with Musatti and E. Veneziano. She is currently participating in a European collaborative research project with Musatti on the role and functions of pedagogical coordinators of educational centers in Italy.

Tullia Musatti is Senior Researcher in the Institute of Psychology at the National Research Council (CNR) in Rome. Her major research interests focus on cognitive and socialization processes in early childhood. She has published extensively on early peer interaction and cognitive processes, including "Meaning Between Peers: The Meaning of the Peer," (in *Cognition and Instruction,* 1993). She also led a national study on the daily routines of young children (*La Giornata del Mio Bambino* [My Child's Day], 1992). A long-time consultant to the infant-toddler system in Pistoia, she currently directs an action research project promoting innovations in parent-child and child care centers in Rome.

Rebecca S. New is Associate Professor of Child Development and Director of Teacher Education at the Eliot-Pearson Department of Child Development, Tufts University. She received her Ed.D. from Harvard University. Her primary research interests and numerous publications focus on social and educational environments as sites for the production and manifestation of larger cultural values. She is participating in a 12-nation review of early care and educational policies by the Organization for Economic Cooperation and Development (OECD) and serves as the rapporteur for the Italian review. She is also a coprincipal investigator with Mallory and Mantovani in collaborative research in Reggio Emilia and four other Italian communities studying home-school relations, and a consultant to Early Head Start programs in New Hampshire.

Carlina Rinaldi is Executive Consultant to Reggio Children, the international institution devoted to research and dissemination of the Reggio Emilia approach. She was for many years a pedagogical coordinator before becoming the director of Early Childhood Education in Reggio Emilia, Italy, a position from which she retired in 2000. She has a degree *(Laurea)* in education and child development from the University of Bologna. She was the first pedagogical coordinator to work with Loris Malaguzzi in developing the preschools and infant-toddler centers of Reggio Emilia, and is a prominent speaker and writer about those experiences, including contributions to *The Hundred Languages of Children* and *Innovations in Early Education: The International Reggio Exchange.*

Nice Terzi is the director of infant-toddler education and care for the city of Parma, Italy. She holds a degree *(Laurea)* in education from the University of Parma and a degree in psychology from the University of Padova. She acts as consulting psychologist and leader for professional development of infant-toddler personnel in Parma and the surrounding region, Emilia Romagna. She has published several articles for the educational magazine, *Bambini,* and with Marialuisa Cantarelli for *Il Nido Compie Vent'Anni* [The Nido Turns Twenty] (1996). She is on the board of directors of the National Group of Work and Study on Infant-Toddler Centers.

INDEX

NAMES

SUBJECTS